Getting to Heaven by Going Through Hell

Scot Hodkiewicz

# DEDICATION

There are a lot of people who are the reason I wrote this story. Certainly those most important in my life are my wife, Mona, and my three kids, Alexa, Victoria, and Chase. They are the inspiration for everything I do and this book is no different. We, as the story will demonstrate, have been through great pain, fear and doubt. But those same experiences have brought us great joy and strength. To them, I dedicate this book. I really wrote it to tell *our* story, not mine.

Yet, there are many others to whom I owe a great debt. Many of them I either never met or never knew by their names. They are the "angels" that I mention throughout the story; the men and women who stepped forward when they were needed to do what was good and right. Whether it was Dr. Lang, who was so pivotal in the events of my life, or the unknown people who seemingly appeared, did what God had put them in place to do, and then just as quickly vanished, never to be seen again. These were all angels in our lives and it is to them that I also dedicate this book; the people who took action, who refused to sit by and do nothing, the ones who needed no recognition, no glory. In fact, many likely never got anything for their services other than the joy of knowing they made a difference; that one day, they were in the right spot and at the right time and jumped in to help someone else. These are the angels in our lives that I now strive to emulate. These people, placed so carefully in our lives at just the right time and in just the right circumstance, I will never be able to repay. It is to the angels here on Earth that I dedicate this book.

But in keeping with this effort to repay what is owed, a portion of all proceeds from this book will go to various charities whose sole purpose is to be an angel to others in need.

# CONTENTS

Scot Hodkiewicz

## ACKNOWLEDGMENT

There were two people who were instrumental in getting this story told. The first was Monica Martin. Monica is an author, client, and friend. She writes a series of children's books detailing the adventures of a dog named "Cheech Mageech" who travels to different states teaching kids about each one. Her excitement for my story was the final push I needed to get my book out there. She was an angel placed in my office at just the right time having "just heard about" my second angel, Daria DiGiovanni.

Daria was yet another angel who became my editor and collaborator. The founder of the Writestream Radio Network, she was invaluable in putting my story into a form where it could be told. Her editing and publishing expertise took this book from a rough draft sitting stagnant on my computer for the last few years and, in just a few months, got it ready to be shared with others. I hope there are readers out there who can see themselves in my book and take some comfort in its pages. This would only be possible because Monica came into my office on that particular day, and because of Daria's hard work and dedication.

# Chapter 1

## ∞ My Great Plan ∞

I thought I had a great plan.

I had always done well in school. I was valedictorian at my high school graduation, and ranked second in my undergraduate class in college, although I never received my undergraduate degree. Because I'd been accepted into veterinary school, I left a year early to fulfill my dream of working in medicine. Why veterinary school? In spite of my academic accomplishments, I was shy as an adolescent, with a bit of an inferiority complex; being a top-notch physician taking on the responsibility of treating people seemed too much for me to handle. When you're lacking in confidence, putting another human being's life in your hands is way too risky. So instead, I became a veterinarian.

Of course, I still have to cope with a great deal of pressure as a vet because my patients are often regarded as members of the family. Yet it pales in comparison to what human physicians face every day. Even now, losing someone's beloved pet rattles me, but losing someone's child or spouse would haunt me forever. During my training, I discovered that veterinary medicine fit my personality perfectly; I absolutely *loved* it. I enjoyed the challenge of medicine and the freedom that working with animals affords. Because I was in my element, I developed confidence, lost my shyness, and blossomed. This type of career just made sense to me; I had found my calling. Four years later, I graduated at the top of my veterinary class with job offers everywhere I applied.

My great plan.

Step One: Become a vet. Step Two: Get a good job. Step Three: Get married and start a family.

Right out of vet school I married Mona – a beautiful, intelligent woman from the veterinary class behind me. Since she had her pick of guys, I felt incredibly lucky to have won her over. Mona and I began working at a mixed animal practice where we treated dogs and cats as well as farm animals. Here, I perfected my craft and honed my skills by developing a specialty in surgery. I became especially adept at orthopedics – fixing broken bones.

Soon after, we started our family. With the birth of our first child Alexa, we took yet another step on my carefully laid-out plan.

The last step? Open our own veterinary hospital.

Five years after graduation, Mona and I got our chance and moved to a beautiful area in Lake Geneva, Wisconsin. Home to about ten-thousand residents, this Midwestern town boasts a gorgeous lake and constant activity, in addition to safe neighborhoods and great schools – the perfect place for us to raise our family. We spent the next eight years building a successful veterinary practice and expanding our family to include another daughter, Victoria, and a son, Chase.

Life was good. I truly believed the hard part was over – the 60-hour work weeks spent building a new business and the constant reading and studying to sharpen my skills in surgery and medicine. All of this was winding down and life was getting progressively easier. We'd survived the baby stages and the *terrible two's*, having changed countless diapers and dealt with constantly interrupted sleep, courtesy of either crying kids or emergency calls. These experiences probably scarred me for life since I rarely sleep through the night now and often awaken at three in the morning to complete some project I couldn't finish during the day.

The rest of my plan was simple. We'd already put in the hard work building a practice and raising the kids so we could coast by the time they grew into teenagers. At that time, we'd hire more staff, work fewer hours, and play more. With our eyes on retirement at sixty, we'd practice veterinary medicine for another twenty years, then sell the business for a bunch of money. Thereafter, we would travel. Yes, sir. We had it all figured out. By sticking to our great plan, we were now in complete control of our lives as successful business-owners, parents, and pet owners (even our dogs listened well). Not only were we were making good money, we were the toast of the town – regular invitees to the best parties and events hosted by the wealthiest people in Lake Geneva – most of whom were also our clients.

*Was it any wonder Mona and I were absolutely convinced we could handle anything life threw at us?*

We'd built it all ourselves without any help from anyone else. I figured now I could sit down and write a self-help book about my great plan, in which I'd tell others how to build the perfect life. People would rush to read all about it. It would be a best-seller and elevate me to a whole new level of success, with Oprah and Dr. Phil calling to interview the young veterinarian who'd achieved it all by his late 30s.

Yeah, great plan.

Then came that fateful October. We were returning home to Lake Geneva from our cabin in northern Wisconsin following our "get ready for winter" weekend. The boat needed to be winterized and the local dealer up north had offered a special deal: *"Saturday only, winterization for $65."* Since the winterization down where I lived often cost over $200, this was a bargain I couldn't resist (boy was I smart!). Of course, the cabin required some maintenance too: the gutters were full of pine needles and a few windows were in desperate need of caulking. Soon snow would be piling up two-feet high on the roof (and in the driveway, on the roads and everywhere else). Although there were also some dead trees around the property in need of cutting, I figured that task could wait until next time we were up. *No rush, plenty of time.*

The weekend had been productive but still fun. Our cabin has no TV – just the way we like it – so we'd spend most of our time outside fishing (or at least *trying* since we've never had much luck on the lake) and hiking with our two dogs (a Golden Retriever named Annabelle and a little Yorkie-poo named Olivia). We'd make "pudgie pies," a family tradition of meat, spaghetti sauce, and cheese cooked in a sandwich iron over a fire. We'd talk and eat s'mores around the bonfire until either the weather or the mosquitoes chased us inside, where we would then play *Clue* and *Battleship*. Often the night ended with blackjack, which is a pretty easy game to understand for three little kids. In fact, at the last parent-teacher conference prior to this October weekend, Chase's teacher had commented on my son's remarkable addition abilities as a pre-K student. When I replied that Chase was really good at adding to 21, I got the "bad parent" look and a kick from Mona under the table. At the ripe-old age of four, he was already becoming quite a little card-shark!

I loved fall in Wisconsin. Actually, I enjoy all four seasons here: hot summers, cold winters, and beautiful springs, but fall is by far my favorite. Wisconsin is known for long, frigid winters; Packer games at Lambeau Field; and brats on the grill. When most people think of Wisconsin, they automatically start to shiver. To me, there is nothing better than being in a warm sweatshirt next to a hot fire with a book in hand when the leaves are changing colors. During that October weekend, the temperature had ranged from high 50s during the day to low 40s at night. This is the season when fishing picks up and we toss footballs in the driveway. The time of year when being at the cabin is all about campfires in the cool nights; countless twinkling stars; a crackling fireplace; and a thick, warm comforter. The best part? No bugs. In Wisconsin, our state bird is the mosquito and our state mascot is the tick, but come October, both are thankfully gone and we can put away the bug spray until spring.

By Sunday we'd completed our chores and playtime at the cabin; it was time to head home. To avoid traffic, we'd left early. There are typically a lot of cars heading back from northern Wisconsin on Sunday nights, so we got on the road around Noon. Naturally, I timed the three-hour trip so I could listen to the Packers game on the way, having been a die-hard fan since I was a kid. My dad was at the famous *Ice Bowl* of 1963 (game time temperature of -13 degrees), when the Packers beat the Cowboys on a last-second quarterback sneak by Bart Starr. Of course, half of Wisconsin claims to have been there along with him!

Because Mona does not share my enthusiasm for the *Green-and-Gold*, she sleeps when we drive so I can listen to the game. Our minivan was also equipped with a DVD for the kids, who sat with their headphones on, watching a Scooby-Doo cartoon. Mona and the dogs, exhausted from the activity of the previous 48 hours, drifted off to sleep. As per her habit, Mona doesn't even try to stay awake and is usually asleep within a mile or two of leaving, feet propped up on the dash and seat set as far back as possible.

This was every dad/husband's definition of peace and tranquility: mom asleep, the kids watching a video, and a football game playing on the radio. It was definitely *my* idea of heaven. The leaves were changing and the temperature was a pleasant 55 degrees. The Packers were having a good season, with a high probability of making the playoffs. All was right in my world.

Yes indeed, my plan had come together perfectly. *What could possibly go wrong?*

Although an avid fan, I was not really listening to the game that day because I was too busy using the time to figure out ways to make the veterinary clinic more successful, i.e. more *profitable*.

What if I learned to do a different surgery or added another piece of equipment? How much money would that bring in? Could I raise my prices or cut back on staff? The business was now booming and my focus had shifted. When I started, I wanted nothing to do with the business side; I just wanted to work on my patients. Now I'd set my sights on how much money I could make, doing what Americans naturally do – pursue happiness through the accumulation of wealth. And why not? Our earnings were already paying for our cabin in the woods; what was wrong with wanting more?

Truth be told, I was losing my way by chasing other people's definition of the American Dream. Although I did have some misgivings about my relatively new and nearly exclusive focus on income versus the care and healing of animals, I'd usually brush them off. After all, I was making good money, running with the wealthy in town, enjoying the respect of my community, and buying anything I wanted. And still, I wanted even more.

Oh yes, I had it all figured out. Life was perfect. We would miss church again this Sunday but who cared? We hadn't really been going much anyway because we were just too busy living the dream. At some later point, we'd start to attend more regularly. *Plenty of time for that.*

I don't remember the impact.

I heard and felt nothing. The only thing I know is what witnesses have told me. The other car was a 2005 Jeep, purchased from a dealer the day before by a drunk driver with a record of seven DUI's and a suspended driver's license (legal in Wisconsin). Today would be his eighth offense. The driver, a man about my age named Mike Jacobs (not his real name), had spent the morning driving around with a case of Miller High Life in the car. He had stopped by his mother's house that morning already drunk but had driven away (she had not even tried to stop him) and continued guzzling beer. He had already spent seven years in prison, three after his sixth DUI, and four after his seventh. As soon as he'd get out, he'd start drinking all over again.

Jacobs was out on parole the day of the accident, but like every other time prior to that it mattered little to him. He'd violated the conditions of his parole numerous times since his last stint in prison. The pattern would go like this: his mother would call his parole officer to report he was drinking again; the parole officer would stop by his house, see beer in the fridge and empty cans all over the place (a condition of parole was that no alcohol could be on the premises); give him a warning; and leave. *Nothing* had been done. Jacobs had been caught driving drunk a month earlier in a hotel parking lot and once again let off with only a warning. In Wisconsin, DUI can only be charged if you are on a public road. On that particular day, he had been in violation of his parole since he wasn't supposed to drink in the first place. He was forbidden to be in possession of car keys – much less *drive* a car – after consuming alcohol. Although Jacobs could have been sent back to serve more prison time, instead he was given another meaningless warning. These warnings and threats of punishment carried no weight and he knew it. By one o'clock on this particular Sunday afternoon, he was over half way through another case of beer.

Our decision to leave early that day to avoid the worst traffic put us directly in his path. He was going to change everything I knew; everything that was so right in my perfect world and my perfect plan. Good thing I hadn't written my self-help book yet.

About halfway home, just outside of Madison Wisconsin, the crash happened. Jacobs was heading north down Interstate 94; we were heading south. The median at that point was only about 15 feet across and there was no guardrail – only a shallow ditch to separate the northbound and southbound lanes. I was probably going about 70 miles per hour, as was he. Though I don't remember anything about the collision, Mona does. She had drifted off to sleep but was awakened by my voice. I can't say I muttered anything too intelligent or profound as I realized there was a Jeep about to hit us. My words of wisdom after being the class valedictorian and becoming a doctor were, *"Oh shit!"*

That is about all I had time to say and it pretty much summed up what was about to happen: our lives were about to change forever and we all were going to go through a lot of "shit."

In retrospect, it is humbling to consider the force such a crash can generate. It spun a 1500-pound vehicle one-and-a-half times, moved the front end and engine by a foot-and-a-half, and *still* had enough energy to smash bones and mangle bodies. The impact was simply incredible.

I always figured that in a crash I could "just hold on" and ride it out. I was in pretty good shape at 38 years-old and had never had any serious injury. My job as a veterinarian kept me on my feet for eight hours straight and required lifting dogs weighing over 100 pounds (the 150-pounders I no longer lifted by myself like I used to). At the start of my veterinary career, I had done 50 percent dairy work which meant dealing with very large and often stubborn animals, so I was in decent shape. I had kept my weight fairly well in check at about 175 pounds on a five-foot, ten-inch frame. Not bad for a guy pushing 40, but still no match for the pounding I was about to take from a half-ton vehicle hitting us at a combined closing speed of 140 miles per hour.

The half-second I had to react gave me no time and no good options. They were basically limited to turn right, turn left, stop, or speed up. Actually, stopping was never an option since I was going way too fast. I instinctively hit the brakes but had no way of avoiding a collision. Plus, Jacobs was drunk or passed out and not trying to stop anyway. Speeding up isn't an option either when a car is careening toward you in your lane while you're driving a mini-van that's not exactly known for its great acceleration. Turning left would have turned us into the Jeep coming across the median from the other direction; that didn't seem like a very smart choice. Turning right would have put Jacobs's front end into my door or, worse yet, into my son Chase's door (he was strapped into his car seat right behind me). That would have put three inches of door in between us and the front of Jacobs's car as it sped right into us. There were no good choices: the crash was going to happen and it was going to hurt. All that could save us was the car's engineering and God's help. As for me, the only thing I could do was hit the brakes and hold on for dear life.

*"Oh shit!"*

The front corner of Jacobs' Jeep hit the front driver's side corner of our van. The engine was instantly pushed back, forcing the front driver's compartment back into my legs. The van spun, coming to a rest on the guardrail three lanes over facing the opposite direction. The impact smashed my body with such force that multiple bones shattered instantly. Bones in my arms, legs, pelvis and nose were all simultaneously broken. In spite of the airbag and seatbelt, the impact to my chest and abdomen ruptured vessels, causing massive internal bleeding. Mona was thrown forward and to the right, her head impacting the car door, knocking her unconscious. The kids were whipped violently forward and sideways. For us to just survive this amount of impact would be a miracle.

There was nothing I could do. And in the end, I didn't do much. I simply hit the brakes. I didn't even swerve because it happened too fast. I just braked and braced for impact, knowing our lives were about to change in a very bad way. The crash was completely out of my control. And it was definitely NOT a part of my perfect plan.

Scot Hodkiewicz

Scot Hodkiewicz

# Chapter 2

## ∞ Is This How It Ends? ∞

Some things went right. Because they'd been fastened correctly, the car seats and seat belts for the kids did their jobs. While not a huge car, the minivan had some mass to it. A small, fuel-efficient car may be great when you fill up the tank, but not when you have to survive a head-on crash with a Jeep at 70 miles per hour. Here, size mattered.

Airbags cushioned the blow for Mona and me but an impact was inevitable. There is no airbag in the world that can protect a body from this kind of hit. The injuries were going to be severe and the pain was going to be intense – there was just no way around it.

Luckily nobody else was hit as our cars were spinning to a stop, which was unbelievable since the interstate was packed with traffic. The impact was head-on but mostly on my side. Although the driver's side was completely smashed in, since it was his front corner to my front corner, our car was able to spin off, thereby dissipating a ton of energy that would have otherwise been transferred to us.

I had done what is natural during a crash; I locked my arms against the wheel, pushed both feet to the floor, and braced for impact. Though I don't think you can consciously change this kind of reaction, it is ultimately the worst thing to do because it results in what the doctors later told me were "aviator injuries." These are the injuries typically seen in pilots after plane crashes where you lock your elbows to hold the steering wheel, push one foot onto the brake and the other against the floor, while wedging your pelvis against the seat and locking your knees. Then on impact, your body continues forward at whatever speed you were traveling. The seatbelt holds your body back but the steering wheel, dash and floorboards are now hurtling at you with your hands and feet pushed against them. With my elbows and knees locked like that, the bones had to give. The force was just too overwhelming.

When the cars collided, my heels were both firmly anchored against the floorboards, which now began moving instantly at 70 miles per hour right back at me. Tantamount to getting hit with a baseball bat, the result was two smashed heels and a broken ankle. These were the first of my "aviator injuries."

Higher up, the steering wheel pushed into my now straightened arms and locked elbows. The elbows bent backward, shattering the bones – an injury I could have avoided if I'd only bent my arms even slightly. Had I done that, the elbows would have simply bent normally and remained intact. Instead, they bent backwards and shattered. A complex joint comprised of the upper arm bone and two lower arm bones, the elbow joint is designed to move through a range of motion until fully straightened. In that position, two of the bones contact each other, preventing further movement. On impact, the elbows bent well beyond the point where the bones normally came together and they simply had to break. With bones no longer held in place and elbows dislocated, my hands fell to the side, the joint grotesquely bent beyond anything that could be normal. More "aviator injuries."

But broken elbows were just the start. Because of their locked position on impact, the force continued up my left arm. The bone broke just below the shoulder while simultaneously forcing the shoulder out of joint. I was left with the ball of the shoulder sitting behind my back and my arm twisted over ninety degrees past where it would normally go. If I could have looked, I would have seen the back of my elbow.

Though I hit the airbag and was seat-belted in, my upper body did not escape unharmed. Safety advances notwithstanding, your chest still hits the seatbelt and airbag at 70 miles per hour, much like doing a belly flop off a three-story building onto a 10-inch pillow. The impact tore vessels in my lungs, liver and spleen, initiating a gusher of blood. Bleeding in the lungs fills them up like a sponge absorbing water; as the blood saturates the little air sacs, it interferes with their ability to transfer oxygen. Once too much blood consumed the air sacs I would suffocate to death. Worse yet, there is no way to stop bleeding in the lungs once it starts. Even if someone got there in time, they could not apply pressure or a tourniquet. Either the bleeding stopped on its own or I would die. As I struggled to take in air, every breath became a bit shallower, a bit more difficult as the blood invaded my lungs.

In my abdomen, the impact tore my spleen. The spleen is a highly vascular organ that sits just below the ribcage on the left side – which was where Jacobs slammed into us. It is particularly susceptible to tearing after automobile crashes because it is not covered fully by the ribs and is very near the surface. Because the spleen is also highly mobile, it tends to move around on impact, tearing its attachments. Its large blood supply practically guarantees it will bleed profusely when ruptured. Upon impact, my spleen tore in half and its three large arteries began pumping blood into my abdomen.

Weighing in at about three pounds, the liver is the largest organ in the body. Like the spleen, it is also very vascular because its job is to filter blood. On impact with the seat belt and airbag my liver – a three-pound sack of potatoes – went from 70 miles per hour to zero. Its forward progress had only been stopped by my ribs, which had already been arrested by the airbag. Luckily, the tough outer capsule that encloses the liver did not tear through, which helped contain the bleeding. In essence, it served as its own pressure bandage. A large clot would inevitably develop but a tear in the capsule would have been catastrophic, creating even more blood loss. By the way, that capsule is less than a sixteenth of an inch thick. My survival – my entire life – hung on something that thin.

To stand a chance, I needed all these injuries to clot and the bleeding to stop – or at the very least – slow down until I could get to the hospital. Large clots started to form as my body fought desperately to stem the flow. In addition to the torn major vessels, thousands of smaller vessels tore also. Each one would have to clot. Their success in clotting would determine whether I lived or died.

It never occurred to me that someday my life would be saved by some nameless, faceless engineers in Detroit, but the van design had helped to lessen the blow. It had been engineered with "crumple zones" in the front that allow certain areas of the front end to accordion in, or "crumple" while the areas around the passengers remained intact. The bending of the frame and metal exterior used up much of the energy without transferring it to the passenger compartment. The more solid areas resist crumpling while redirecting the big, heavy engine away from the "vital" areas. It moved toward us but in a downward direction, which saved Mona and I from enduring a thousand pounds of hot metal being pushed back into our laps, burning and crushing our chests and abdomens. This would have almost certainly been fatal for both of us.

Unfortunately, my legs were not in that vital area and were going to be crushed – the price that must be paid in order to protect the organs higher up in the body. While the Detroit engineers were good, an impact like this is simply too much for any engineering to absorb;

it is just impossible to protect everything from this amount of force. The crush of metal and plastic had missed my chest and abdomen giving my heart a place to beat and my lungs to expand but nowhere for my legs to go. On impact, the dash was pushed back and down, thus pinning my left knee against the front edge of the seat, while the rest of my body above the knee was still moving forward. Something had to give. Although the thighbone, the femur, is the biggest bone in the body, it had no chance of resisting this kind of force. It snapped instantly shattering into multiple pieces. The jagged end was driven like a spear, cutting through the thick quad muscle on the outside of the thigh, the shards of bone exploding through the skin like shrapnel.

Even though I was seat-belted in, the impact traveling through my legs from the floor broke my pelvis. The pelvis is a "box of bone," – multiple bones all fused together to make a solid "box." Any solid box must break in at least two spots (take a box and try it) and my pelvis was no exception to the rule. Add two more fractured bones to the list.

We didn't know it then, but this break in my thigh would nearly kill me more than once. The thighbone is the biggest, strongest bone in the human body. It takes an awful lot of trauma to break a thighbone and mine had shattered just above the knee. As the upper thighbone bone blew out the side, the lower part of the fractured bone cut in to the inside where the femoral artery and vein are located. Because the artery and vein are each about the size of an index finger, a tear in either will kill you very quickly. And since they run right next to each other, there is almost always damage to both in a case like this. A tear in the vein will result in a gusher of blood fast enough to cause death in five minutes; a tear in the artery two minutes, and a tear in both just one minute. My vein was sliced in half by a three-inch thick piece of jagged bone but somehow it missed the artery entirely. Another bit of luck that would at least give me a chance to survive.

We collided head-on, driver's side- to- driver's side, which meant the car had spun furiously, throwing all of us laterally against the interior. The impact broke my nose and bent it flat against my face as I hit the airbag. However, Mona got it the worst. First, her head hit the airbag before smashing against the side window. Then it impacted the door at whatever speed we were spinning in, while her brain hit the inside of her skull at the same velocity. Being pretty tough, the skull withstood the impact, but since the brain is soft and "floats" inside the skull in a very thin layer of fluid, it does not handle impact well. Consequently, we were both knocked unconscious.

On impact, the nerve impulses went haywire. There are literally billions of connections between the nerves in the brain; millions of them are firing off at any one time. All were shaken with such violent force that the signals – so very well organized a second ago – were now a jumbled mess. Like a computer with a frazzled hard drive, our brains shut down to protect themselves. Luckily, the basic but essential functions like heartbeat and breathing continued working because they are controlled in the brainstem – the lower parts of the brain – buried deeply away from the skull. However, the more complex functions of conscious thought, information-processing, logic, speech, and memory abruptly ceased. Mona and I had been completely knocked out until our brains could reboot – if they ever did.

As Mona spun, she was forced against the door. Attached to the seat by the seatbelt, her butt moved with the car to the left but her top half did not. The force of the twisting overwhelmed the three bones in the middle of her back, breaking them instantly. Exactly how they had fractured and whether they'd hit the vital spinal cord running through the middle of them would determine if she would ever feel her legs again. In that horrific moment there was no way to tell: she was out cold.

The van came to stop now facing the other way. Debris was thrown all over the road and the engine boiled steam. I sat pinned in with a torn femoral vein, ruptured spleen, and multiple other sources of bleeding, with the nearest ambulance 15 minutes away and the nearest hospital another 20 minutes beyond that. All signs pointed to me being a dead man: I would survive the crash but die in the next few minutes as the blood drained from all these torn vessels and organs. Since nothing had perforated the skin, the bleeding in my abdomen would be contained, creating at least a chance for clots to form. But the torn femoral vein in my leg would pour blood onto the floorboard until it was all gone and my heart stopped. As I sat there unconscious, there was nothing I could do about it; I could not even *try* to stop the bleeding myself. Compounding the matter, I also had two broken arms. In the movies, they wrap a tourniquet around the leg or "stick a finger in the hole" to stop the bleeding but even I hadn't been knocked unconscious, I wouldn't have been able to do anything about it. All I could do was bleed to death.

However, I would be gifted with a few vital minutes. Thankfully, the shattered bone tore the vein and *not* the artery. This was a stroke of luck because the artery is under so much pressure that stopping the bleeding is like trying to hold off a garden hose. Pressure may slow it down but it is almost impossible to stop. A tourniquet is usually needed for a torn artery and I did not have one handy. The vein is under much less pressure so bleeding is slower and can more easily be controlled. Unfortunately, nobody was in any condition to apply any pressure. Mona was barely conscious, the kids were in shock and still buckled in. My oldest was only ten.

What saved me? A wild stroke of luck and those crumple zones. The front end of the van crumpled in while the dashboard moved back and down, pinning my leg between the two. It crushed the muscle and locked me to the seat, but applied enough pressure to hold off the torn vein and limit the blood loss until the paramedics arrived. In fact, there was surprisingly little blood in the car when I was removed. Pictures of the car afterward showed the left front of the driver's seat was bent down to almost vertical from where my leg was trapped, but hardly any blood on the seat. By the time the helicopter and paramedics arrived, 20 minutes had passed; I should have bled to death. However, the crushing weight of the car simultaneously smashed the leg *and* held off the bleeding long enough for help to arrive. Another twist of fate that would give me a chance to survive.

Obviously, the impact and spin would have killed us all had we not been securely buckled. Wisconsin, like most states, has a mandatory seatbelt law for adults and all kids must be in child seat or boosters until seven years of age. I remember when the law passed I was completely against this invasion of my freedom because it was my choice whether or not to wear a seatbelt. The government had no right to interfere in my life. Furthermore, I had grown up long before this law was passed and NEVER used seatbelts. Turned out, this invasion of privacy by the ever-intrusive government would ultimately save our lives. I had been wrong; thank God they had been smart enough to enact this the law. While I still believe our government should get out of our lives, I'll concede this is one thing they got right.

The kids were buckled in the back and since we hit head-on they were mostly protected – at least physically. Chase, our four year-old, was in a car seat with a five-point harness but his little body was deeply bruised by the belts. Flying glass cut his face, chest, and hands. Today he will proudly show you the scars that signify his bravery, but at the time he just hurt all over. The glass sliced into his shirt so badly it looked like moths had eaten it.

Victoria, our seven year-old, was in the far back and buckled with a shoulder strap and a booster seat. Although she was at an age when she'd soon be out of boosters, luckily she was in one today. While severely shaken up and bruised by the straps, she was otherwise alright.

Alexa, our oldest, was in a seatbelt but did not have a shoulder strap so she was thrown around harder, especially during the spin. We had been traveling with an antique chicken coop Mona and the kids had found at a flea market that weekend. The kids had started raising chickens in the backyard and were a bit crazy about them. Alexa was excited to have found this coop and couldn't wait to bring it back for her birds – a place for them to roost every night as the temperature began to drop on the way to another cold winter. As the car spiraled out of control, the chicken coop smashed against her left arm breaking it near the shoulder. As for the coop, it was so badly damaged it had to be thrown out. Even the chickens were going to have a tough few months.

The only ones not buckled in – our family dogs – were tossed around like rag dolls. Having been sitting on Chase's lap when Jacobs slammed into our van, our little eight-pound Yorkie Olivia endured the worst, having been ejected through the side window. Her head hit it with enough force to shatter the glass and hurl her body right out of the car. Though the skull is a very hard bone, she was an eight-pound dog breaking quarter-inch thick tempered glass. Like Mona's concussion, the dog's brain bounced off the inside of her skull as it hit the window. Olivia fractured her skull and immediately began to have a seizure as she landed outside of the van. Ultimately, the state patrol would cover her with a blanket expecting her to die.

Olivia was Alexa's dog. She'd arrived as an eight week-old puppy on Christmas day a few years earlier, and Alexa had raised her. Ironically, Olivia was a second choice after our breeder called us two days before Christmas to announce she was keeping the puppy we'd already agreed to buy from her. Yes, really. *Two days* before Christmas, and the woman blindsides us with the news that she is no longer selling the pup we'd already planned to give our young daughter. Mona had spent the entire next day searching the internet and making frantic calls looking for another puppy to give her in time for Christmas. We settled on Olivia because we didn't have much of a choice but she ended up being a great dog for our family. Now she lay seizing on the side of the road, having been thrown through the window of a smashed minivan.

Annabelle, the Golden Retriever, was thrown against the vehicle door, bruised and terrified. As soon as she could get out she fled, disappearing into the surrounding countryside. More concerned for the human family injured in the terrible accident than their dog, everyone let her go. Our beloved pet was on her own, beaten up, terrified, and lost in a cornfield 50 miles from home.

Within a few seconds, we had gone from a normal, healthy family traveling with hundreds of other cars down the highway to a mangled mess of broken and battered bodies. Mona and I were dying in our seats. The kids were in shock and terrified. All were bruised and battered, and Alexa had a broken arm. One dog was seizuring on the side of the road; the other had run away injured into an unfamiliar area with the temperature dropping to freezing in a matter of hours. Our perfect plan was not to be; another plan was starting to unfold, one over which we had no control. The one that Mona and I had worked so hard to achieve was gone forever and life would never be the same. While it was very clear that our original plan was no longer relevant, I didn't know at that time just how much our lives were about to change. We hadn't even considered or anticipated this unwelcome fork in the road. And where the road now led, nobody could predict. We had *no* plan now; we just were hoping to take another breath.

# Chapter 3

## ∞ Angels Appear ∞

In the aftermath of the accident people stopped immediately and rushed to the van. They had no choice *but* to stop since there was debris all over the road and two cars now blocking three lanes of traffic.

They hurried to open the doors in the hopes of freeing us but the van was locked. Since Mona and I were both unconscious and all three kids were in shock, we were oblivious to     pounding fists on the windows. Some of these folks ran to get gloves to pull out the smashed glass and get inside. Steam billowed from the ruptured radiator while the smell of burning rubber permeated the air. The threat of fire was foremost on everyone's mind. With the doors locked, kids buckled in, and two unconscious people in the front, the flames would consume us all very quickly as the horrified crowd stood by, helplessly watching and listening to us burn to death. They had to get the doors open.

It was Alexa, our 10 year-old, who finally stepped up. She was belted in the back and unable to reach any door, broken left arm lying limply by her side. So she did the only thing she could: she yelled to her mother, "Mom, wake up, *wake up*! The doors are locked. *Mom, you need to unlock the doors!*" It took a minute of constant yelling for a seriously dazed Mona to comprehend the instructions but Alexa didn't give up until she was heard. That's when Victoria and Chase began to cry while our would-be rescuers kept pounding on the glass.

Alexa looked at the people trying to get in and noticed one in particular, a man in his 30s with a small beard and mustache. He had blood running down his face from a cut on his nose. As she gazed at him, he gazed back at her before abruptly turning to leave. She would only lay eyes on him again sometime later in the newspaper: it was Mike Jacobs, the man who had just nearly killed us.

Mona started to come around and felt for the button to unlock the doors. She didn't know if the electric locks would work and wasn't aware enough to even realize what she was doing. She just obeyed Alexa's urgent commands to open the door locks. After trying every button, Mona finally hit the right one. She drifted back to unconsciousness while our good Samaritans yanked open the doors and flooded in to help us.

Neither one of us was in any shape to move; luckily, no one attempted to make us even try. Mona had a broken back and I was prevented from bleeding out to certain death by a collapsed dashboard pressing down on my leg. By now, the kids were more awake and able to get out of the crushed minivan. If the vehicle caught on fire, at least the kids would be safely out of harm's way. Although Mona had the potential to be pulled out of the van, my trapped leg guaranteed I would burn to death. Onlookers dialed 911 from their cellphones and the interstate came to a complete stop, creating a traffic jam that would eventually stretch for 20 miles.

Within minutes of opening the doors, the kids were taken off to the side guardrail as people wrapped them in blankets taken from their own vehicles. It was about 50 degrees outside and none of them were wearing coats. Three women appearing like angels held them close, comforting them without knowing if their parents would survive. One held Victoria in a blanket and gently her rocked back and forth while she sang a hymn. I never did find out the names of these earth angels that appeared seemingly out of nowhere and took care of my children. They had been placed there at the right time to do what they could: hold each child in a warm embrace and comfort them with their words or hymns until the police and paramedics could take them to the hospital. The one thing they were powerless to do was tell them that their parents would be OK. I was still unconscious and starting to cough up blood. Mona was slowly coming around but had obviously taken a major impact to the head. Nobody could predict if I would make it out of this ordeal alive, or if Mona would ever be the mom our kids knew and loved. It certainly did not look good. Then more angels started to appear.

Mona's angel was a large, bearded man who looked like he carried boulders for a living. He had yanked her door open and stayed with her, trying to calm her as her brain began to process what had happened. He held her in her seat and told her to not move, to wait for the ambulance and to keep talking to him. Mona kept repeating that her back hurt. He would repeat in response, "Don't move. Let the paramedics check you out. They are almost here, just don't move." Mona kept complaining about her back pain and started to unfasten her seatbelt in an effort to free herself from the van. Once again, this man stopped her. He soon realized she was oblivious to anything he said; she just kept repeating herself, unaware that she had just said the same thing ten seconds earlier. Most people would have become frustrated with this strange, crazy woman who refused to follow the simple instructions to sit still and wait.

Notwithstanding our horrific crash and a serious back injury, Mona kept fighting her way out. But this burly angel patiently talked to her, keeping her still and in place by holding one hand on her shoulder. The large man with the strong hands never once lost his cool or raised his voice. While Mona might have been able to push past a smaller person, or one that was not so determined to keep her still, she could not prevail against this unyielding angel. Even with a scrambled brain, she eventually understood that trying to overcome him would be futile. By the grace of God, he'd been the first to arrive at Mona's side just when she needed a person with the calm understanding and the pure brute strength to keep her in place – an angel with muscle.

A man rushed to my aid also. It was obvious I'd sustained severe injuries: blood was streaming down my face through my broken nose while I simultaneously coughed it up from my lungs. My rescuer could hear the gurgling as I struggled to take each successive breath with more and more blood in my throat. I was drifting in and out of consciousness with my right arm lying down by my side – bent backward and twisted, obviously broken. My twisted left arm was limp by my other side and the palm was turned 30 degrees beyond where I could have placed it normally. It was not only broken in three places but dislocated in two, with the elbow smashed and the ball of the shoulder joint now sitting four inches past where it should have been. All this man could say was "The kids are OK and you are going to be alright."

A well-meaning lie. The kids were anything *but* OK; they were terrified and hurt. Anyone who witnessed my twisted limbs, blood-soaked body and bloody regurgitations could easily deduce that I was likely to die any minute. I looked far from "alright."

I couldn't see the kids since the airbag was blocking a large part of my view and I could not turn to look behind. My angel knew I didn't need a rundown of just how dire our circumstances were. He simply did what most of us would do under similar circumstances; he told a small lie rather than a terrible truth. The gurgling of blood worsened with every breath.

Sirens could now be heard in the distance.

The state patrol arrived first. I never thought I'd feel this way but their sirens and lights were soothing; this modern-day bugle cry signaled that our cavalry was here and that the paramedics would soon take over. Our angels at the scene were there to comfort us but we needed much more than comfort; we needed serious medical help because our bodies were broken. If we didn't get medical attention soon, Mona would likely be paralyzed and I would either bleed to death or suffocate as my lungs inflated with blood.

The highway patrol took over the scene and ordered the paramedics to hurry. After one look at me they called for a helicopter; I would obviously need flight for life. Although we were only about 10 miles from the University of Wisconsin teaching hospital – a Class-A trauma hospital – an ambulance would have been too slow. Located on the opposite side of town on the other side of a lake, the hospital's 20-minute distance guaranteed certain death. A helicopter was my only hope.

The patrolmen could only give basic first-aid, so they allowed the angels to stay by our side while they concentrated on preventing the car from catching on fire. Fire extinguishers were preemptively sprayed on the engines to douse any potential flames. By now, the paramedics were arriving to deal with the injuries and the fire department was in charge of getting me out. The police started interviewing witnesses to determine what had happened. They soon discovered that we had been heading south and the Jeep had been heading north when it jumped across the median, bounced across a shallow ditch between the north and southbound lanes, and flown up and into our lane, colliding head-on with our van. The Jeep was now resting on the side of the highway but its driver was long gone. No one had seen him leave and none could not describe him with any more detail other than the fact that he was a white man sporting a goatee. While the witnesses had concentrated on helping us, the other driver had just slipped away, leaving his vehicle at the scene. The police immediately called in the license plate to track down the owner. It came back registered to Mike Jacobs.

All things considered, it was a miracle that the kids were pretty well intact with no life- threatening injuries; the down side was that they remember it all. Oddly, the thing Alexa remembers most was the smell – the stench of burning rubber permeated us all and even a week later, she could still smell it in her hair and on her skin. It just refused to wash off; a constant reminder that her life was now completely changed. Aside from this offensive odor, they also remember the noises – tires screeching, glass shattering, and metal bending.

Worst were the voices: mine yelling out and Mona's screaming. Then the unforgettable sounds of wailing police cars and fire truck sirens, Mona's shrieks of pain, police converging upon the scene. After my initial "Oh shit!" I was quiet, save for the gurgling sounds I made as I struggled to breathe past the blood.

Victoria was the most shaken. She had been farthest in the back and the most protected during the crash, enabling her to hear and see it all. Now she was on the outside sitting with her angels on the guardrail as the paramedics began to extricate me from the van just a few feet away. One of the paramedics hung a blanket between me and the open side door, blocking the kids' view but not muffling his voice. Another paramedic asked why he was doing this since the blanket was not really going to protect me or keep me warm as they pulled me out. His answer was simple, "I don't want the kids to see their dad die." Although he tried to speak quietly, he was just loud enough for Victoria to hear. She is a stoic child – our thinker – but now it started to sink in: Mom and Dad were really hurt badly. For the first time in her young life she began to contemplate life without parents. *Would she and her siblings be orphans?*

Her mind raced to the movie *Annie* and the orphanage. Would they be sent there to live with the mean lady who ran the place? Or would they be shipped off to live in another town with their aunt or grandparents? At best, they would no longer have a dad – and Mom was going to be on her own. The shock started to fade and the reality began to sink in. She was only seven, bruised and beaten by the impact, but she now saw the possible consequences of what had just happened: she could lose her parents today, an event that had never occurred to her before. Fear paralyzed her; she was too scared to even cry.

Paramedics were beginning the long process of extricating us from the car. Since Mona's side of the vehicle was not crumpled like mine, getting to her was relatively easy; her back was the problem. They did not ask her if she could move her feet or arms since it would make no difference to their work; they would treat her as a possible spinal fracture and let the doctors determine the extent of the damage. While they noticed she was moving her arms but not her legs, they remained quiet, fully aware that a crash victim tends to panic and lose the will to fight once they realize they can't feel their lower extremities. Quietly watching for any signs of motion, they removed her from the van, each saying a silent prayer.

Next came the backboard and stretcher. A brace was carefully placed around her neck to prevent any movement, then multiple paramedics and policemen jockeyed into position to slide her carefully out of the van and onto the board. Because spinal fractures are inherently unstable, the major concern was Mona's transition from sitting in the van to lying on the board. The vertebrae of the spinal column form a tunnel called the spinal canal, within which runs the spinal cord. About an inch thick, the cord is comprised of all the nerves that carry messages from your brain to various body parts. The messages that control the body start in the brain, run down the cord, and exit via the holes between the vertebrae. Spinal fractures can move bone into the canal or onto the nerves as they exit, resulting in severe damage. Any damage to the nerves will stop the messages from getting through, which leads to numbness and paralysis from the site of the injury on down.

To further complicate things, spinal fractures can tear the blood vessels that feed the cord, while also causing bleeding in the canal. The blood flow into the small space between the cord and the vertebrae creates a vicious cycle: the bleeding only quits when it fills the space and creates enough pressure to make it stop; then this pressure causes further damage to the cord – which may not be apparent for up to 24 hours after the trauma even though it is just as devastating. Any pressure on the cord leads to the same result – nerves that no longer work and damage that is usually permanent. It can result in anything from numbness in the feet and legs to shooting and devastating pain to complete paralysis. Paralysis may not be a consequence of the actual crash but from the movement of an injured body afterward, when an unstable fragment of bone moves or a blood vessel tears. Paramedics are trained to be extremely careful when transporting anyone with a back or neck injury. Victims are slowly and carefully strapped down to a board as they are extricated to prevent further movement that may inflict even more damage.

With the backboard in place and multiple hands around her, Mona was lifted out of the car and onto a stretcher. As they slid her into the ambulance, she continued to repeat her complaints of a sore back and requests for a pillow. The paramedics ignored her ramblings in favor of driving her immediately to the hospital. By this time, her burly angel had disappeared. We never knew his name and would never see him again. He appeared when he was needed most and disappeared just as quickly.

The kids were now crying again as they watched their mother – tied flat to a board – being carted away, unable to signal them that she was alright. They'd seen paralysis before. We have a family friend who has been paralyzed for the last eighteen years, ironically, after also being hit by a drunk driver. Staring at their immobile mother, the tears flowed quickly while the angels who continued to hold them close could not promise that their mom would walk again; they could only say they were praying for her. It was in God's hands now.

The paramedics came and loaded the kids into a second ambulance to get them to the hospital while their comforting angels vanished without a word and returned to their lives. I would meet one of these angels later on; she lived only one town over and knew us as the local veterinarians. She'd been two cars behind us when the Jeep crashed into our van. Another 50 yards – a second or two – and she would have been hit. Instead, her role that day was to be an earth angel placed at the scene to comfort a child she didn't even know.

With Mona and the kids off to the hospital, the paramedics focused on me. First, the door and roof had to be cut away. They covered me with a blanket to protect me from glass and metal and keep me warm as the car was disassembled. The roof was cut off and peeled back. The windshield, shattered but designed to stay in one piece and minimize flying glass, was pulled away. Now they could see that my left leg, broken and bent just above the knee, was crushed between the seat and the dash. The dash would have to be lifted to get my leg out. The jaws-of-life were brought in but it was difficult to find a good spot to place them. My leg had moved to the left during the crash so it was now on the left edge of the seat. Unfortunately, the seat did not have a solid place to put the bottom jaw to enable them to lift the dash. The fireman tried again and again but the jaws kept slipping out. Finally, they managed to wedge it between the dash and the van's frame, which was bent in from the impact. By this time the helicopter had arrived, waiting to transport me to the hospital. The order was given, "Lift the dash and get him out!"

The diesel engine powering the Jaws-of-Life roared while thick smoke belched forth. Although the diesel fuel had a terrible odor, for me it was smell of salvation. The fireman gunned the engine and the dash started to rise. My leg was freed.

Paramedics rushed in to get me out, unable to see that my leg, now relieved from the crush of the dash, had started to bleed profusely. Up to this point, the dash had applied pressure to the torn leg vessels while the seatbelt had applied pressure to my ruptured spleen and liver – giving me precious time. Now both had been removed, igniting a gusher of blood from the vein and internal organs. The clock had started ticking when the cars collided; now it had an endpoint. With this rate of blood loss, I would have only minutes to live. The bleeding from my leg was increasing as the clots that had been formed by the pressure of the dash now succumbed to the incredibly large volume of blood rushing out from the torn femoral vein. My team moved fast but if they couldn't stop – or at least *slow* the bleeding – my fight would be over quickly.

But these angels among us knew what they were doing, having seen plenty of these crashes before. They did not pry up the dash and extricate me from the van until the helicopter had landed and the gurney transporting me to it had been set in place. This was critical since (as the paramedics suspected I was still alive), the crush of the car was holding back some of the bleeding. They had looked in the van and had not seen much blood in the car. Of course, the airbag was bloody from my broken nose but this loss was not life-threatening. Given all indications, my leg should've been bloodier than it appeared. That's why pulling the dash off my leg and removing me from the van before the helicopter was ready would only extend the time between the pressure being lifted and me getting to the hospital. My angel paramedics wanted the dash lifted *only* when everything else was in place. Now, the helicopter had landed and was ready to take off as soon as I was in.

After they got me out, it was obvious that my left leg was crushed just above the knee. As they placed me gently onto the gurney, they noticed the sheets turning red. The leg flopped lazily from side to side, an obvious indication that the bone was completely broken. The helicopter was about 50 yards away on the highway. It had landed on the asphalt just south of the crash site. Once securely transported into the helicopter, I met my next angel – the flight nurse named Robert.

Scot Hodkiewicz

# Chapter 4

## ∞ Lessons from a Warzone ∞

Robert was in his early 30s and just what you would expect from a guy working on a rescue helicopter. He was lean and muscular, having been trained as a search-and-rescue medic in the U.S. Army. He'd spent two tours in Afghanistan pulling wounded soldiers out of shitholes and patching up injuries much worse than mine; he'd also been a star athlete in high school. As a result, he was extremely competitive and hated to lose. This was now his battle – Robert versus death – and he wasn't going to let death win.

When he laid his eyes on me, his adrenaline started pumping. He knew I was brutally injured and it was his job to get me to the hospital. As a paramedic, it always became a very personal fight to save his victim. Even though he had no idea who I was or anything about my background, it didn't matter because he simply hated to lose. Yes, he was well aware that he could not save them all but he would fight like hell to keep them alive. Robert viewed each lost victim as his own personal failure – no matter how badly they'd been torn up he considered it *his* fault if they died en route. And he wasn't about to let that happen today.

He spoke loudly over the noise of the helicopter, hurrying the paramedics to get me inside, wanting me transferred to his care ASAP because he thought of himself as the best at what he did. Once they'd placed me securely in the chopper he took over. Robert had an attitude that all of the great ones display – he believed that only *he* could save me; he just needed them to get out of his way and let him work. After the paramedics loaded me into the helicopter they quickly retreated, allowing the transport to throttle up and begin to lift off. I was in Robert's care now. He was in charge.

Afghanistan had been his hell but it had trained him well for this role. By now he was  very good at dealing with trauma and could anticipate the extent of the injuries based on how they had happened. Per his military training and experience, Robert had carefully surveyed the crash site as the helicopter converged on the scene. He surmised from the damage to the two vehicles that this had been a head-on crash; he'd also figured I was most likely the driver of the minivan, due to the fact that most males like to drive. Since the driver's side had been completely demolished, it seemed to him a logical conclusion. Further, since this was an interstate, Robert deduced that the crash had occurred at high speed. I was still alive, so I must have had a seatbelt on but nevertheless sustained terrible injuries. As the one behind the wheel of the minivan in a high-speed crash, I would have chest injuries from the seatbelt and from impacting an airbag; I would be bleeding into my lungs as well as probably leaking air into my chest cavity from a punctured lung. I would have ruptured my spleen and suffered multiple broken bones, including a femur fracture of my left leg (fractures of the thighbone right above the knee are common in drivers of minivans involved in head-on crashes). Robert had seen it a hundred times before and figured one of us had been driving drunk.

His job now was to stabilize me and get me to the hospital. In order to accomplish this, he went through the ABC's of trauma:

**A – Airway**: I was spitting blood but had started to talk in spite of my injuries. Even though he couldn't hear what I was saying he didn't really care; my talking told him my airway was clear enough – at least for now.

**B – Breathing**: I was breathing. He checked my lips and saw they were red, not blue. If the lips turn blue, it means there is not enough oxygen getting into the blood. Mine were still red but he made sure to watch me breathe; he'd seen enough soldiers wounded by roadside bombs to know what an impact to the chest can do. Witnessing my fast and shallow breathing confirmed his suspicions even though the roar of the helicopter made it impossible to listen with a stethoscope. My labored breaths and bloody mouth told him all he needed to know; I had bruised and possibly punctured lungs.

Though the airbag and the seatbelt prevented my body from impacting the steering wheel, my lungs – tucked away inside the ribcage – were still going 70 miles per hour when the rest of me stopped. Thus the moving lungs and heart impacted the ribcage, tearing things apart. Even worse? Because I saw it coming, my reflex was to suck in a breath and hold it during impact – my *"Oh shit!"* response, which shut off the only escape mechanism for the air when the lungs are violently compressed. The impact pressed on the now fully inflated lungs like hands squeezing a balloon and just like a balloon they popped, shredding the tissue and blood vessels. Consequently, air leaked out into my chest while blood seeped into the airways. Both created a deadly scenario.

A tear in the side of the lung allows air to escape into the chest cavity, a pneumothorax, literally air (pneumo) in the chest (thorax). Breathing happens with the diaphragm moving down and sucking the lungs along with it since there are no attachments from the diaphragm to the lungs. The downward movement of the diaphragm simply creates a vacuum that pulls the lungs open as they suck in air.

With air leaking into the chest cavity, the vacuum is lost. Now, as my diaphragm moved down to expand my lungs, air was pulled out of my ruptured lungs and into the chest cavity. Worse yet, the tear opened more as the lungs expanded on inhalation and closed down as my lungs were pushed smaller on expiration. This allowed air to flow out into the chest on inhalation only to remain trapped there on expiration, similar to an air pump that moves air in only one direction – the classic "tension pneumothorax" or "sucking chest wound." Each breath filled the chest with more air and further compressed the lungs, making breathing more difficult and less effective. My lungs were progressively collapsing with each successive breath due to the "tension" or pressure of the air being pumped into the chest cavity. Eventually they would not expand anymore, making breathing impossible. My breaths were becoming shallower and faster as my body tried to make up for the decreasing lung volume. If I could not move enough air, Robert would have to stick a needle in my chest and suck the air out. In anticipation of this likely event, he set out a large needle and syringe that he would insert between my ribs.

But that would only be a last resort. Blindly sticking a sharp needle into the chest in a moving helicopter can easily rupture a lung and create yet another tear along with another leak. Robert knew he could unintentionally make things worse so for now he monitored. He had done it before and was ready. At that moment, in spite of my shallow breathing I wasn't blue, which meant I was moving a sufficient amount of air. He would have to watch it closely as the helicopter lumbered toward the hospital.

Aside from the air leak, the lungs themselves were bleeding as a result of the impact, which tore hundreds of small vessels contained within. Blood was filling the tiny pockets where oxygen is absorbed into the blood. Even if I could continue to move air, I was getting less and less clear lung tissue to allow the oxygen to pass into my bloodstream. If the bleeding didn't stop, the lungs would be soon be engorged with blood. Artificial respiration and oxygen only help if there is a way for the oxygen to pass into the bloodstream. If all the sponge-like little spaces in the lungs that transfer oxygen are filled with blood, even these measures won't work. Blood cannot be drained from the lungs; attempting to do so is like trying to get fluid out of a sponge with a soda straw. It simply doesn't work. If my lungs continued to absorb all of this blood, I was surely going to die.

Robert kept an eye on this, knowing exactly what was happening. He had placed an oxygen monitor on my finger and noticed that my levels were starting to drop. Notwithstanding the oxygen mask he placed over my mouth, the levels continued to decrease; I had started at 90 percent oxygen and was now at 85 percent. He needed to start an IV but had to monitor the oxygen levels. Alarms would go off on the monitor if I fell below 80 percent – and I was perilously close.

**C – Circulation**: Now he checked the circulation. Seeing the blood pooling under my leg, he cut my jeans to better determine the source. As the jeans were cut away, the extent of the injury became apparent: blood was welling up through a gaping hole in the outside muscle of my thigh, just above my knee. A jagged piece of bone protruded through the torn skin, surrounded by a huge blood clot. Purple-red muscle pushed out from the hole like raw hamburger. The muscle normally oozed blood but it was flowing out of the hole at a rapid rate that indicated a major blood vessel had been torn somewhere within all that mess. Robert grabbed some gauze and pressed it into the hole. I moaned from the pain. After a few seconds, he pulled the gauze out again and watched for the wound to refill with blood. At this point, the goal was not to stop the bleeding but to ascertain how quickly the wound refilled. Because the blood returned instantly to fill the hole, Robert surmised that the femoral vessel – the main supply of blood running down my leg – must've been torn in the accident. These were the only vessels in that area big enough to cause this much bleeding. Since the blood wasn't spurting, it was most likely the vein and *not* the artery. He should be able to stop it with a pressure bandage.

Robert had missed this once before and had long ago vowed, *never again*. In Afghanistan, he'd been deployed to rescue a soldier whose convoy had been attacked with an I.E.D. The lead Humvee had been destroyed and numerous soldiers had been wounded. Robert had been the first to get to them and ran to the one with the worst injuries: his name tag read "Bennett" and he looked about 18 years-old. Robert quickly bandaged wounds on both arms and his abdomen but Bennett continued to fade. He guessed that there was internal bleeding and removed the abdominal bandage to check. Although there was a gaping hole, there wasn't that much blood, indicating there had to be another source. Robert assumed it must be in the chest and had no way to stop it. He further surmised that there had been a tear in one of the major arteries coming out of the heart; therefore, there was nothing else he could do except start an IV and pump fluids into the young soldier. Robert had only been in the country for a month and was not yet proficient at starting IV's but this one was surely going to die if he didn't do so ASAP. While he desperately tried the young man's veins had collapsed, preventing a catheter feed. Robert blew through catheter after catheter as Bennett bled to death; he watched Bennett die as he attempted to place a catheter for the third time.

Soon, he was ordered to stop and attend to the rest of the wounded while other soldiers came to move the dead man away. Robert then noticed a huge pool of blood where Bennett's left leg had been lying. He had bled out from a punctured artery in his leg that had been bleeding into his fatigues. The blood was soaking quickly into the sand and was obscured by the ever-present dust of Afghanistan. Robert had never checked. He was horrified to see the massive amount of blood that was inside the pant leg and on the ground as they moved Bennett onto a stretcher and took his body away. He had made a terrible mistake by assuming the bleeding originated in Bennett's chest and never checking the underside of the leg. That miss had haunted him ever since – nearly causing him to quit being a medic. He simply did not think he was up to the task. The nightmares he'd experience since the tragic incident were always the same; he would be trying to save a soldier that would not stop bleeding. The soldier would yell repeatedly "Why can't you save me?!" Robert would shoot up in bed, startled awake after seeing a huge pool of blood and Bennett lying dead in his nightmare.

Consequently, he requested to be reassigned but there was another plan. His superiors turned him down because they did not have anyone else to take his place. With no other choice, Robert decided to refocus and make himself better at his job. He recruited fellow medics to act as guinea pigs and would practice setting catheters on them. Soon, the other medics started to avoid him so he went to the soldiers. Since they had a vested interest in helping Robert improve his skills – after all, it was *their* lives he was entrusted to save – they willingly volunteered to have catheters placed. At first Robert was terrible, struggling to hit even the biggest vein and causing even the toughest soldier to fight to stay still. His platoon soldiers were soon covered in bruises but he was getting better. Within days, he was hitting the bigger veins with ease. Then he shifted to the smaller veins in the hands and feet and started hitting those too. Bennett had forced him to improve and within weeks was now the best in the division at setting catheters. No other soldier would die because of a faulty IV placement – Robert would make sure of that. Thanks to his Afghanistan experience I had a chance; he could now set an IV into a dying man in a moving helicopter. He would not allow me to be another Bennett, the angel who in spite of never knowing me, died for me on that battlefield years before.

Robert immediately stuffed another wad of gauze back into the torn skin and meat to plug the hole in my leg. Although the bleeding slowed down, it did not stop completely. It was flowing from so many places in my leg – the vein, the torn quad muscle, and the bone itself that the gauze couldn't possibly put an end to it. Additionally, blood oozed from a multitude of other places on my body; this site had been the biggest one he could identify. By hampering the blood flow here, he could buy me a few more minutes. Thus the race was on to get to the hospital before I bled out. Robert shoved more gauze into the leg wound and wrapped it in place. Even being barely conscious, I moaned from the horrific pain as he tightened the bandage. But at least the bleeding from my leg was under control.

However, I was still bleeding internally and going into shock. "Shock" is defined as the loss of consciousness and eventual death that occurs when blood pressure drops, depriving organs of the perfusion they need to function properly. When your brain doesn't get enough blood, you pass out; when your vital organs don't get the oxygen and energy they need, they fail. The kidneys are especially vulnerable, which is why kidney failure is often the cause of death for people who survive this kind of trauma.

Robert had to set a catheter.

He began to place an intravenous catheter into my arm as he talked to me in an effort to keep me awake. I needed more blood in my system to replace what I had lost; it would help stabilize my blood pressure up and perfuse my organs. In a case like mine, it is the loss of blood *volume*, not just the blood itself that is critical. I'd lost a significant amount of blood already and was continuing to lose more internally. Soon there wouldn't be enough to carry the oxygen my organs required. Robert had to replace it before my body failed. The first step in the process was to place a catheter in a vein.

As we bounced along in the helicopter, Robert started to place the IV. My veins had collapsed by now due to my dropping blood pressure and in spite of his superior skills developed in combat, he was having a tough time accomplishing this vital task. The catheters are small, flexible tubes of Teflon with needles inside. The needle makes a hole in the vein and the catheter slides off the needle and into the vessel. The Teflon is soft and flexible but stiff enough to keep the catheter from collapsing as blood rushes through the vein. It is also very smooth, allowing the catheter to slide in easily. This smooth texture slows the formation of blood clots around this "foreign" material.

But when the blood pressure is falling, there is not enough blood to fill and distend the vein so it collapses like an empty balloon. In my case, there was nowhere for the catheter to go; Robert could get the needle tip in the vein but the Teflon catheter remained outside and as he tried to feed it in, it would bend. By now, the punctured vein had started to bleed. Within seconds, a bruise obscured the site making it impossible to even see or feel the vein anymore. Robert gave up on the spot. If he couldn't place the IV, my chances of making it to the hospital fell to near zero. He had to get this done. His mind raced back to Afghanistan and the times he placed catheters as soldiers screamed and bullets bounced off the helicopter. He knew he could get one started in me.

He quickly grabbed a second, slightly smaller catheter and tried a new site further up my arm where the vein would be bigger. Having placed thousands of catheters previously, Robert was skilled. It takes a certain feel to know how to hit the vein and when to feed the catheter, especially in a moving helicopter. Luckily for me, he had the touch – much like my wife who once hit a tiny vein on a dehydrated, one-pound kitten. Seeing a quick flash of blood in the catheter, Robert carefully threaded it on in.

Once it was taped in place, he smiled and breathed a huge sigh of relief. He knew that this was my lifeline. He also knew that only a select few could have done what he had done. His *hell* of Afghanistan had saved my life.

*That one was for you, Bennett.*

Next he hung a bag of O-negative blood, the universal blood type that anyone can receive regardless of their blood type. He attached the IV line and ran it wide open. This would start to replace the blood flowing out of all my wounds. To speed up the flow, he put the fluids into a pressure bag – a simple sleeve that the unit of blood fits into. The sleeve has a bladder that can be pumped up with air, applying pressure to the bag. It forces the blood in at a much faster rate than gravity alone and is used when high volumes are needed quickly. And I needed it desperately.

Robert kept speaking to me, urgently fighting to keep me awake while blood continued to flow out – less from my leg now but also into my abdomen and lungs. I'd been bleeding to death since I left the van and he knew he wouldn't be able to stop it in spite of his best efforts. All Robert could do was impede the blood flow and transfuse the O-negative blood as fast as possible to buy me time. Placing the IV meant that he had won this round. The fight was far from over but now I at least had a chance.

Although I'd been talking the entire time, Robert now started listening to what I was saying. At first he'd assumed I was just babbling because my eyes were closed, but I had reverted back to my veterinary training and began to describe my injuries.

"I have an open comminuted femoral fracture, a fractured humerus (the upper arm bone), and a dislocated shoulder. My other arm hurts (the elbow was smashed), and I probably have a ruptured spleen since I hit the airbag so hard." I didn't remember that the rest of the family had been traveling with me in the car, so I really never asked about them (not my proudest moment as a husband and father) but my description was pretty close.

In spite of all my injuries, I was not complaining about the pain. Obviously there was a ton of pain associated with any of these injuries, much less the combination of all of them, but I continued to talk as if it didn't exist. My body had released my own pain-killers called endorphins (the body's morphine), to block it. Athletes often experience this during long, intense, and often painful training sessions. Pushed to its limits with acute muscle pain, the body releases endorphins to block it. This phenomenon is called *the runner's high*.

With athletes, this is more of a trained response to frequent, intense training. In cases such as mine, the endorphins are released to give your mind a break, to get you through the crisis. Eventually, the endorphins subside and the pain returns with a vengeance.

Lack of pain is common in major trauma. Pain is your alarm bell indicating there is a problem. With injuries like these, the brain doesn't need to sound the alarm because it is obvious that there has been a major problem. Therefore, the brain is more concerned with getting out of the situation, the *fight or flight response*. This is the time when your body is just trying to survive; pain will only interfere with getting away or fighting back. This is the reason why soldiers wounded in battle continue to fight, often not realizing that they are severely injured. When you are in a life and death situation, it is all about survival; pain comes later.

Robert looked at me a bit perplexed as I explained my injuries and asked, "Are you a doctor?" I told him I was a veterinarian and started mumbling about dogs and cats I had worked on that had been hit by cars. But as I did, my voice got softer and my eyes closed. I continued to speak but my words came slower and I started to slur. Soon I wasn't making any sense and Robert could no longer hear me over the noise of the helicopter. My eyes were closed and my skin was as white as a ghost; I was fading in spite of Robert's stellar efforts. He tried to keep me talking for a while but soon realized that I was no longer conscious. His goal now was to keep me alive until we reached the hospital. He was losing the race to save me.

My oxygen level had dropped to 75, setting off the alarms. Robert reached for the large needle and syringe he had pulled out previously. He cut my shirt back exposing a terribly bruised chest. He splashed some iodine on my ribs on my left side. My oxygen level was continuing to drop. He pushed the needle in between the ribs hoping not to hit a lung. He felt it "pop" through and immediately pulled back on the syringe. It pulled easily confirming that he was in the chest and the chest was filled with air (if he'd been in a lung, it would've pulled out air very slowly, if at all). He emptied the syringe and pulled again, sucking out more air. As he repeated the process, my oxygen levels started to rise. Soon I was up to 90 percent again and breathing more slowly. He pulled out the needle. Robert had won once more.

He did not take time to celebrate; I was getting paler and paler, indicating that my blood loss was getting to me.

Recalling Bennett, he checked my leg again. The bandage he had stuffed into my leg wound was soaked and the blood was dripping through onto the helicopter floor. He reached for a tourniquet, knowing that he had to get the bleeding to stop or else I was a dead man. He lifted my leg near the wound to get the tourniquet around it. I hadn't screamed in pain before but even semi-conscious, I screamed now. He had to get the tourniquet around the thigh above the break so he was working it under my leg trying to get it passed. As hard as he tried to keep from moving my leg, it had to move some. He pushed his hand into the mattress trying to get the tourniquet passed while the exposed nerves sent out waves of pain signals. I hadn't torn the major nerve running down the leg, the sciatic nerve, so I wasn't numb. Any movement of the leg sent a flood of intense pain through me.

Robert saw this as a bit of a good sign since at least I was feeling things. He had been concerned that I may not have been feeling my legs since I had not been screaming in pain up until this point. He'd been watching for signs that I could feel my legs, but dared not ask since the thought of being paralyzed would sap my will to fight to stay alive. Robert had seen that before with the soldiers he had treated and knew would never walk again. When I screamed as he tightened the tourniquet, he smiled. Not a sadistic smile, but one of knowing that at least I wasn't paralyzed. If I could survive, I would likely walk again.

I was done talking as the helicopter neared the hospital. It wasn't the endorphins blocking the pain anymore; I was unconscious. My blood pressure was dropping in spite of my angel Robert. The tourniquet had slowed the blood flow out of my leg, but I was bleeding from multiple other places that couldn't be tourniqueted or have a bandage stuffed in place. Blood was rushing out from nine different fracture sites and into my lungs and abdomen. A man my size had about nine liters of blood in the entire body. I had already lost half of that.

As I continued to bleed into my lungs, I started to have more trouble breathing. I was coughing up blood from both my lungs and a broken nose. My nose was moved to the side and my nasal passages were now blocked with clots, making it impossible to breathe through it. The blood flow down the back of my throat was impeding my windpipe. The body's natural reaction to any fluid near the trachea is to cough. Because I was too weak to cough the blood ran down my airway and into my lungs. Robert knew that I would soon not be able to move enough air. As I fell into unconsciousness my breathing slowed and my lips darkened to a greyish blue. Robert was losing the race.

He grabbed an endotracheal tube and a light. Without any fight from me, he opened my mouth and passed the tube into my windpipe. I was too weak to resist. This tube would be my airway. It would keep my windpipe open, allowing air to be pushed into my lungs. Robert inflated a small cuff around the end of the tube to form a seal between it and my windpipe preventing any more blood or saliva from going down into my lungs from above. This also forced air into my lungs with a squeezable bag and ensured that at least I had some air moving whether I took a breath or not. The question of having enough blood in my body to move it to where it needed to go was another story, but at least the blood I did have would be well oxygenated.

Robert continued to push air into my lungs. He could overcome some of my inability to move air on my own, at least for a while. Again, he was buying me time.

The blood in my lungs needed to clot. This was another race: would the bleeding in my lungs stop before I could no longer move air? Would the air moving out of my leaking, torn lungs stop my breathing altogether? Would my blood pressure drop to a point where my organs started to fail? Would my heart give out? Would my brain be starved of oxygen and put me in a coma? Would infection take over and kill me in just a few days? All of these questions would need a favorable answer for me to get anywhere near the man I was less than an hour earlier. Right now, there was simply no way to accurately predict the outcome.

The helicopter landed on the roof of the University of Wisconsin – Madison Hospital. This hospital has one of the best trauma hospitals in the United States. Four emergency doctors were waiting, along with sixteen nurses and support staff. I would need them all. As soon as the skids hit the roof, they charged in.

Scot Hodkiewicz

# Chapter 5

## ∞ More Angels ∞

Robert was opening the helicopter door before the helicopter landed. Three nurses ran out to get me into a triage room just inside the hospital, where the rest of the staff was waiting. He didn't have to say a word; the expression on his face told the story. I was dying and dying fast. There was no time left, I was unconscious and white as a ghost. The gurney was soaked with blood and my abdomen was bloated with even more blood. My foot lay flat off the gurney, twisted 90 degrees to the side. There was a slight bend just above the knee wrapped in a bloody bandage indicating where the leg was broken. My left arm fell to the side as they began to move me out of the chopper. It bent and rotated both at the elbow and at the shoulder, obviously broken also. A nurse grabbed my hand and set my arm back over my chest, turning the palm back to as close to normal resting angle as possible. It is hard even for professionals to see hands and feet lying grossly contorted. There is something utterly repulsive about an appendage twisted away from its natural position and alignment.

ER workers are a different breed altogether. Although they love the adrenaline of emergency medicine, I would not call them adrenaline junkies. They don't need to leap from buildings, jump out of airplanes, snowboard down cliffs, or ride motorcycles way too fast to get the "adrenaline high" others often seek. Medical professionals who toil in emergency get that every time they go to work. Ironically, I always loved emergency medicine also – save for the late hours and the necessity of getting out of a warm bed in the middle of winter. I never dreamed *I'd* be the ER patient everyone was racing to save.

By now I was near death. Robert had done everything right but I had lost too much blood. The nurses searched for a pulse on my wrist but found none. My heartbeat was audible but only barely. My heart was still pumping whatever blood was left but there wasn't much there. Since very little of that was making it up to my brain, I was unconscious. My cells would soon be dying. When blood flows too slowly through the brain, it can also form clots and lead to strokes. It was obvious that if they couldn't increase my blood pressure, I would be dead very soon.

I had seen this myself countless times before as a veterinarian: people rushing their dogs or cats into our office after they'd been struck by a car. These injured animals would be unconscious, with blood coming out of their nose and mouth. Their gums would be pale like mine. Veterinarians often don't feel for a pulse since the animals are smaller and covered with hair, making it more difficult to find. We usually listen with a stethoscope for a heartbeat. Often the heart is slowing down as it starves of oxygen before it finally stops. My heartbeat was slowing to a dangerous pace.

The hospital staff jumped to action but knew it would be a hard fight. The organs die quickly when they lose blood flow, but a few are particularly sensitive. Most organs use an entire network of blood vessels similar to a highway system: block off one road and you can detour around and still get to your destination. However, the brain, heart and kidneys are different because their blood supply is a single, one-lane road. It's also a one-way road which means if the lane gets blocked, the blood simply cannot get there, resulting in organ failure. My medical team had to get my blood pressure up if I was going to make it.

A nurse immediately began the task of setting another IV line. She wanted a bigger one that could handle a larger flow. Of course, she had an advantage over Robert since she was not in a bouncing helicopter; she was able to place another in my other arm. Still, it wasn't easy but this nurse, like Robert, had "the touch." She got the IV in on the first try. Then she immediately hung another bag of blood.

The brain, the heart, and the kidneys are the most vulnerable to a loss of blood flow. Failure of any of these usually results in death or severe and permanent disability. Obviously, brain damage is devastating and very difficult to recover from, but heart attacks and kidney failure are also common problems with severe blood loss.
I remained unconscious due to a lack of fuel (sugar) and oxygen to my brain, which had gone into hibernation and stopped working, causing me to pass out. If better blood flow was not restored, brain cells would begin to die and leave me with brain damage. Once gone, those cells would be lost forever and I would not be the same person that I had been. If extensive damage occurred, I'd slip into a permanent coma or simply die.

Blood loss also puts the heart at severe risk. The heart is a big muscle that is constantly working; therefore, it requires constant blood flow to carry oxygen in and lactic acid out. Lactic acid is the waste product of working muscles and it must be washed away continuously. When we exercise and our muscles "feel the burn," that's due to a buildup of lactic acid. But this buildup will weaken the muscles if not flushed away. The burn disappears with the lactic acid when you slow down and allow it to be flushed away – one reason why drinking water is so important after a workout or a massage. The problem with the heart is that it just can't take a rest; it must beat steadily in order to wash away lactic acid. Constant blood flow is absolutely necessary or the heart will stop beating altogether.

Though the heart is always filled with blood, it does not get its oxygen and fuel from the blood it is pumping as one would expect. It contains arteries and veins that transport its blood supply, just like any other organ. These feed into the outside surface of the heart away from where the blood is pumped. Like the brain, different branches of the arteries supply specific areas of the heart. If these arteries become plugged with a clot due to slow blood flow, I would sustain a heart attack. The muscle – starved of fuel and oxygen – would die, taking my life along with it.

My heart was beating very slowly, an indication it was getting ready to quit. Oxygen and sugar for fuel were no longer reaching this vital organ and it was growing weaker with every passing second. If more blood didn't arrive into the system soon, it would just stop. In the movies, when the heart stops someone grabs the paddles before they shock the victim once or twice, reigniting a heartbeat. Real life is different. Statistically, patients only have a 10 percent survival rate if their heart stops for any length of time. My heart only had minutes left before it gave out.

My kidneys were in trouble also. The kidney is an especially unforgiving organ and will stop working very quickly. Many trauma victims end up in kidney failure and die within a few days because of a drop in blood pressure. Loss of blood flow damages the kidneys to a point where they can no longer filter the waste from your body, allowing good things to pass out into the urine that have no business being there while retaining the bad things the kidneys are designed to filter out. Kidney failure is an ugly disease characterized by nausea, vomiting, weight loss, and even mouth and stomach ulcers. Dialysis is a temporary fix but I would likely need a transplant if mine failed.

Of course, this was a battle for another day. At this point, I just needed to survive the next hour. Therefore, the goal of my medical team was to stop the bleeding and replace the lost blood. The two intravenous catheters were supplying fresh blood into the system but it was flowing out faster than it could be put back in. Until the bleeding was controlled, the blood pressure would continue to drop.

Blood loss, however, was not their only concern. They knew I had clots everywhere; any one of them could easily break off and end up in my brain. Trauma is one of the major causes of strokes and I was a prime candidate. Usually, people prone to strokes are given "blood-thinners" to stop the blood from clotting but I was still hemorrhaging all over, and the last thing I could afford was thinned blood. I could likely suffer a stroke but there was little the doctors could do to prevent that – at least not until my bleeding was under control. Increasing my pressure would ignite blood flow (stagnant blood immediately starts to clot) so for the moment, my medical team's first priority was raising my blood pressure.

Enter my third angel of the day.

Dr. Gerry Lang is one of the best trauma surgeons in the country. Though I had many doctors that day and over the following months, Dr. Lang and I would develop a special relationship. Doctors see thousands of cases. Although every case is special to the patient, to the doctors and nurses most of them are fairly routine. As a doctor myself, I knew that even the most spectacular cases become commonplace after a while. Today I was just another guy whose family was hit by another drunk. Doctors and nurses see this all the time; I was simply an unfortunate victim of someone else's bad choices. Yet anyone who works in medicine knows there are certain cases that just stand out – the especially tough ones that demand all of our skills and knowledge. For Dr. Lang, I would be that case. He was the doctor I needed. His presence was required to save my life. In spite of my three other superb doctors, without Dr. Lang I would die.

I would later learn how talented and skilled he really was. The nurses would all smile and sing his praises whenever I asked about him (especially the younger nurses since he was handsome and ran marathons). We would have been good friends if we had gone to school together, given the fact that we were about the same age. We both loved what we did and would recount surgical cases like a high school football star recounting his experience of winning a state championship. Our kids were roughly the same age, giving us even more in common. Dr. Lang acknowledged that though he would use great skill to keep me alive, it was not all up to him; he had a great team around him and he would need every one of them today. Even so, there is always more going on than even the best surgeon can control; ultimately he could only fix so much. After that, it was in God's hands.

Right now I desperately needed all of Dr. Lang's skills. However, there was another doctor present who had seniority and was technically in charge. This doctor correctly suspected that my torn spleen was causing internal bleeding; therefore, he gave the order to get me into surgery ASAP because they had to get it out.

Although this doctor's assessment was accurate, Dr. Lang soon realized I was bleeding more profusely from the torn femoral vein in my leg. Because a tourniquet had been wrapped around it, the femoral vein was not "spurting" blood but it was hemorrhaging too quickly to postpone a surgical remedy. When Dr. Lang noticed the unusual amount of blood soaking into the sheets under my leg, he knew without a doubt that this had to be dealt with first. While the hemorrhaging from multiple areas of my body had bloodied the sheets, the area under my leg was a different story. There was simply too much blood there to ignore.

They started wheeling me down to surgery to take out my spleen when Dr. Lang stopped them, contradicting the more senior surgeon – the spleen would have to wait until the leg was dealt with. Dr. Lang took a big risk by stepping on some toes but he put me, the *patient*, first. If they did not get the bleeding from my leg under control, I would die before I got to surgery. This is where the respect for Dr. Lang originates; it takes some balls to contradict your boss for the good of the patient. And he's got 'em.

Most of the smaller vessels had already clotted by now, leaving only the big ones. A variety of defensive methods, evolved through millions of years, have saved cavemen gored by wooly mammoths during prehistoric times; these same methods would also save me in the 21$^{st}$ century. First, blood contains proteins called "clotting factors" that form a clot as soon as a vessel tears. Most of my smaller bleeders, aided by my low blood pressure, had just formed clots and stopped on their own. I would have bruises everywhere but at least some of the bleeding had already ceased.

The second defense mechanism is found in the blood vessel wall. The larger blood vessels all have muscle in their outer walls. When torn, these muscles spasm and narrow the vessels, which slows the blood loss and allows the clot to form. For many blood vessels, this will eliminate bleeding altogether. A classic example is the umbilical cord. Until recently, there was no clamp employed to put across the cord at childbirth; it broke during or shortly after delivery by either stretching until it snapped, or by being chewed in half by mom (glad we no longer have to do this!). This allowed the muscle in the umbilical cord to contract, closing the vessel and eliminating any bleeding.

Unfortunately, this mechanism does not work well in major trauma because the vessel tears so quickly it has no time to react; bleeding can be profuse.

Dr. Lang removed the bandage Robert had put in place in the helicopter and searched for the vessel that was still gushing blood. He grabbed some suture to tie it off. The leg wound was gaping wide so all he had to do was move things out of the way to locate the vessel usually buried deep under the muscles. Because our human anatomies are seldom different, a good surgeon can accurately estimate the location of a large vessel like the femoral vein; it lies next to the bone, toward the inside of the leg. In a case like this however, human anatomy is no longer normal – muscles are torn, bones are broken, and time is of the essence. The typical landmarks are gone since everything has either shifted or is no longer attached to its usual mooring.

Luckily there is a good way to find a bleeding vessel; you follow the flow of blood to wherever that may be. When dealing with trauma like this, normal anatomy becomes less important: just locate the source. Dr. Lang knew that there are two big vessels – the femoral artery and vein – running on the inside of the thigh parallel and slightly toward the back of the bone. Aware of its location and big size, he attempted to get at it.

But first, he had to get his bearings. The torn-apart muscles were in tatters, the skin was ripped open, and even the leg itself was hideously twisted and out of place; Lang ignored all of this and isolated the broken bone. This bone, the thighbone, is long and straight. The nurse did a quick surgical prep of iodine in an effort to eliminate some infection while Lang grabbed a scalpel. He quickly extended the hole in the skin so he could see and pushed back the muscle around the bone. In my case, the skin already had a large gaping hole of about six to eight inches; therefore Dr. Lang did not have to cut much more. The bone had done most of the work when it was shoved out the side of my leg.

Getting down to the bleeder was difficult. Although the tear in the skin and muscle was to the outside of the bone, the vessel was on the inside. Cutting through the other side would take too long and create more damage; the best option would be to reach the inner side of the bone through the existing hole. Fortunately, the bone was so smashed that the lower portion of the leg could be simply moved over to the side at a right angle exposing vessels on the inside of the leg. My foot was now crossing my other leg and bent more than ninety degrees. It was grotesque but this positioning pulled open the wound, enabling Dr. Lang to work. Though it might look like something out of a horror film, he knew no harm had been done; the bone was already broken. And the muscles don't care if they are temporarily bent. Bending the leg like this at the fracture opened the skin wound and allowed the surgeon more room to work.

Dr. Lang separated the muscles and moved bone fragments out of the way, shoving the various bone pieces deeper into the muscle so he would not lose them; he'd need them later to reconstruct the thighbone. A large blood clot had formed even though the bleeding had not stopped. The clot was like ice above a fast moving river – the river may look frozen on the surface but underneath it is still flowing. Like the ice, the clot had formed everywhere blood had pooled but the source – the torn femoral vein – continued to pump out more. It was now a race to stop it.

As my surgeon angel started his search, the blood was suctioned away and muscle retracted. My entire lower left leg from just above the knee was now only attached by the muscle on the back and on the inside. Dr. Lang frantically sought out the vessel. The muscles around it had contracted – not nearly enough to stop the bleeding but enough to pull it more deeply into the muscles. He searched and grabbed with clamps, but the bleeding continued. Rarely is the vessel sitting out in the open like a garden hose, just asking to be tied off. The retraction invariably pulls it deeper into the remaining muscle, which has been transformed into hamburger. Finding this vessel and tying it off before the patient bleeds out requires great skill and a little luck. Dr. Lang repeated the search-and-clamp process to no avail; the blood continued to flow.

At this point, he made another fateful decision that would ultimately save my life. After failing to find the vessel and ascertaining the rapid pace of blood flow, he realized he would not be able to clamp it before I ran out of time. I had lost most of my blood and had little left. Since I was becoming progressively weaker, he did something extremely difficult for a highly competitive person like a surgeon: he gave up on tying it off.

Instead, he called for a large lap sponge and pressed it deep into the wound directly over the femoral vein. He then packed the wound with two more sponges and pulled the leg back to its normal position to close the wound and squeeze the bandages into the hole. Finally, he quickly surrounded the leg with more wraps to keep the sponges in place and apply more pressure. For the first time since the car dashboard had been lifted off of my crushed leg, the bleeding from the femoral vessel stopped. My biggest source of blood loss was now under control. Eventually it would have to be tied off, but not today. The doctors could now move onto the operating room.

Now it was time to examine my abdomen and stop the internal bleeding. The nurses prepped my torso for surgery as they transported me into the operating room, not even waiting for the gurney to stop moving. Dr. Lang had given me the necessary time to shift focus to the second major bleed: the spleen.

# Chapter 6

## ∞ He Made Her Just Right ∞

While my fight continued, Mona and the kids arrived in the ambulance. The kids' angels, the three women who had comforted them after the crash, had wrapped them in blankets as Mona was extricated and loaded into the ambulance; these angels would hold each of them until it was time to go and then disappear, having completed their job.

Although frightened Alexa, Victoria, and Chase had heard me talking after the impact and assumed I'd be fine; I was their dad and dad was *always* alright. They were more worried about their mom. She'd been the first one knocked out and afterward as she came around, she began repeating herself, asking where she was, what had happened, were the kids ok, in an endless loop. After a short delay, she'd begin again. One of the paramedics had gotten a little frustrated with her repeated questions and snapped at her to stop talking. By then, they'd been working at the crash scene for about a half-hour and had grown tired of Mona's persistent, repeated questions. Alexa, never one to keep quiet, came to her mother's defense and yelled at the paramedic to "Stop being so mean to my mom, she's hurt!"

In hindsight the paramedic's actions were understandable as anyone who has raised a two year-old knows how frustrating the endless questions can be. However, it was probably something that he would take back if he could. Paramedics are life-savers with a genuine desire to help which sometimes requires them to be stern with patients in order to maintain control of a bad situation. Still, Alexa did not want him yelling at her beloved mom.

All three kids were pretty beat up from the impact in spite of being seat-belted. The force had compressed them against the straps and then snapped their little bodies sideways as we spun. They sustained terrible bruising of their chests and abdomens from the belts but their bones were soft and for the most part did not break. The downside was that the internal organs were less protected underneath. Internal bruising to the lungs, liver, and spleen is common in kids even without broken bones, so the paramedics carefully examined them, searching for signs of internal bleeding. Partly out of pain and partly out of sheer terror of what they'd just witnessed, they cried softly, still in shock from watching their father cough up blood and their mother endlessly repeat herself while strapped down to a back-board. They remember it all. While they largely escaped the physical injuries, they'd have to endure the psychological impact forever.

Alexa, my oldest at 10, was the only child that broke a bone when the old chicken coop they had bought hit her in the left shoulder as the van spun out of control. The impact fractured her upper arm bone, smashing the chicken coop to pieces. At first, adrenaline and shock hid the pain; now that both were subsiding, the pain arrived with a vengeance. Alexa gently tried to hold up her hand to prevent the arm from hanging because she didn't want to scare her younger siblings.

A tough kid in many ways, Alexa is far from stoic. Vaccinations usually involved an hour of wailing before and after the shot followed by days of tenderness at the injection site. She once accompanied Victoria for her vaccinations all the while telling her how the shots were "just a little poke" and "they really did not hurt." I was proud of her for consoling her younger sister who, though nervous, had never made a big deal out of shots. When they arrived at the clinic, the nurses discovered that Alexa was eligible for her next shots also. She stood for a moment in stunned silence – but only for a moment. Panic came flooding in as she realized that she too would be getting a "little poke" that "really wasn't that bad." She began to cry, then to scream; it took me and three nurses to hold her down and vaccinate her.

Now she was in real pain from the fracture in her arm but surprisingly, seemed to handle this better than the vaccinations. Though hurting, she never panicked and had the presence of mind to order her mother to unlock the doors. In spite of a broken arm, she managed to unbuckle her seatbelt and escape from the van.

For Alexa, it is the *thought* of pain that freaks her out. But in this situation, she'd had no opportunity to think about it because the crash had happened too quickly. Actually, the tears she shed had very little to do with herself and more with her precious dog, Olivia, the little Yorkie-Poo she had received as a Christmas present. On the way to the hospital, she'd realized that Olivia was no longer in the car; she was gone and Alexa had no idea where she was. Luckily, she was unaware that her pet had been ejected through the window and was still lying unconscious on the side of the road.

Now at the hospital, the kids watched as the paramedics moved their mother out, still strapped to the board and repeating herself.

They desperately wanted their mom to comfort them, to assure them she was OK and that dad would be OK too. They wanted her to promise them that their dogs were just fine, and that someone was coming to care for them until they were home. They wanted her to hold them, to rub their backs like she did when they needed to fall back asleep after a particularly bad nightmare. But instead she lay in front of them flat on a board with a strap over her head and more straps over her chest and legs. Rather than comfort her children, Mona lay there repeating the same questions over and over again, unable to console her them. All she could do was repeat the same three phrases and then slip back into semi-consciousness.

The kids' world had just turned upside down. Their parents couldn't help them anymore; they now had to rely on the compassion and care of strangers. The thought of life without parents started to creep into their minds, prompting them to cry, *not* out of pain but fear – pure fear.

I was in surgery clinging to life as they wheeled Mona into a trauma room. Some nurses took each of the kids to be examined while each experienced a surge of dread watching their mother being wheeled away. Now they found themselves alone in a new place filled with strangers, including the doctors who would examine them. It would be the first time in their young lives that they would see a doctor without one or both of their parents present. When the nurses tried to take them into different exam rooms, Alexa refused. Never afraid to speak up, she informed the nurses that the three of them would stay together no matter what. She knew it was her job to comfort Victoria and Chase; as the big sister they needed, Alexa was now their protector and their voice. In the past, we'd often worried about her strong personality, desiring her to be a bit less outspoken. But under these special circumstances, Alexa needed to be tough and unyielding. Maybe that was why God had made her that way.

# Chapter 7

## ∞ Are You In There? ∞

The spin had sent Mona flying to the right and slammed her headfirst into the passenger side door, resulting in a bruise on the right side of her head that traveled from her ear to over her eye. She continued to repeat herself, "What happened?", "Are the kids OK?" "My back is sore, can I have a pillow?" Stuck in an endless loop, her brain could formulate these questions repeatedly yet couldn't comprehend the answers because it had stopped processing any new information.

Although her back was the only injury she complained about, it was quite obvious she'd sustained a head injury also, as indicated by the ugly bruise and her nonstop questions. Mona also shrieked in pain when her left arm was moved before quickly reverting to complaining about her back. Needless to say, she was of little help in evaluating her injuries.

A doctor began to examine her left arm, suspicious of a break. As he reached the elbow, she cried out again and pulled it back; a subsequent X-ray soon confirmed it was broken. They couldn't figure out exactly how her left elbow broke when she impacted mainly on her right side but it didn't really matter; they just needed to determine the extent of the damage and decide how to repair it.

Since her back was the obvious problem, a CT scan was ordered. She was sedated, partly to keep her from moving and partly to stop her endless questions. The test revealed what they all suspected in a crash this severe – three spinal fractures, along with the broken elbow, a major concussion (hence the continual repetition of the same three phrases), internal bleeding, and a bruise on her pancreas (a likely source for the internal bleeding).

All in all, it could have been much worse. The internal bleeding was not severe and would be left to stop on its own. The doctors knew that this type of hemorrhage is usually self-limiting, with vessels clotting up within minutes; therefore, surgery is rarely necessary to find the source unless the bleeding either continues or – as in my case – is severe. Giving her fluids and a blood transfusion to replace lost blood volume would most likely work well. However, if Mona's blood pressure began to drop – a sign of continual internal bleeding – she would definitely require surgery to find the source. While confident they would not have to cut her open, surgeons monitored her carefully; in the end Mona would emerge from this ordeal without a big scar. Although not a vain person – she is as tough as they come – a large scar on the belly is hard for a woman to take. For men, it's much easier since they tend to view a huge, ugly scar as a *"badge of honor,"* something they can brag about. Not so for women. It also helps that a man's abdominal hair covers these flaws pretty well but women aren't as lucky. Of course Mona and I would be in the same boat since I'd be left with multiple scars too.

Unlike me, however, she would have a harder time psychologically and emotionally due to the way she handles adversity. In Mona's world, bad times are to be forgotten; a scar would only serve as a constant reminder of what happened. Every day, it would force her to recall the worst day of her life. Thankfully she got lucky; only a small scar from a cut above her lip would serve as her reminder.

They called in a neurosurgeon to evaluate the spinal fractures. He had already seen the three places the vertebrae had broken on the CT. Two of the fractures were on the protrusions of bone that serve as muscle attachments. These are away from the spinal canal and from the spinal cord so these would not need surgery.

The third fracture was the fracture of the vertebral body, similar to where older people get compression fractures of their spine due to osteoporosis. Now Mona had a similar fracture, not due to osteoporosis, but the sudden violent bending of her body with so much force that the bone gave way.

The danger with these fractures is that the loose bone can move into the canal and compress the spinal cord. Any type of pressure on the cord or the nerves exiting the spinal canal results in anything from numbness to weakness in the legs; to chronic, sometimes debilitating pain; to paralysis. It was determined that the fracture pieces had not moved toward the spinal cord to any significant degree. There was a narrowing in the canal but the cord had enough room around it to move out of the way rather than compress. Had the fracture moved another eighth of an inch, she would have lost use of her legs but so far she was okay.

Her neurosurgeon knew that spinal surgery is fraught with risks. The fracture can be stabilized with screws or a plate but it is not easy.

During such a surgery, the biggest risk is that the broken piece could move during placement of the screws and hit the spinal cord – making the situation even worse. The surgeons must hold everything in place while drilling a hole and placing the screws without anything moving toward the cord. All of these dangerous tasks are accomplished through a small hole, with a couple of inches of bleeding muscle pulled out of the way, while working around a spinal cord that is so unforgiving one slip could cause permanent paralysis. This is a tough, challenging operation for even the most gifted surgeon. Her team ultimately decided surgery was a last resort.

The neurosurgeon walked into the trauma room and began the exam that would truly determine the extent of her injuries. The CT revealed that the fracture was not compressing the spinal cord now, but it did not mean it hadn't done so before; there was a real possibility it could have impacted the cord when it was broken, then moved back to a better place when Mona came to a rest. Any impact to the cord, even if only temporary or fleeting, could have paralyzed her forever.

Mona complied when the doctor asked her to move her toes. Next, she felt his hand touch her toes and feet. Then, he pulled out his "hammer" – known as a pleximeter – raised her knee slightly, and hit it just below the kneecap. By striking the tendon where the kneecap is attached to the shinbone (the patellar tendon), the tendon stretches slightly, which the body interprets as the knee collapsing. In response, the body automatically flexes the muscle of the thigh to counter this perceived collapse. This is the classic reflex test with its resulting kick. Mona's foot reacted accordingly, indicating her reflexes were still intact.

While this was a good sign, it did not mean she had an intact spinal cord. Since the "kick" is involuntary the signal does not go all the way to the brain. It's simply a reflex to keep us from falling, not an activity requiring thought. As a reflex, the signal only travels from the knee to the spinal cord and back to the muscle. It never gets to the brain; therefore the test only indicates if the portion of the spinal cord involved in the reflex is working – from the knee to the lower back. In Mona's case, their concern was mainly focused on the injury further up, but since she could feel and move her toes, the doctor knew the nerves were intact.

The remainder of the neurologic exam showed no loss of nerve function. As long as this didn't change, she would not need surgery to stabilize the fracture. Instead, she would be fitted with a body brace that she would wear for the next three months. Custom-fit to her size, the brace would completely wrap her body like a corset, extending from under her armpits to below her hips. It was also hot and uncomfortable, and would be worn 24 hours per day until the bones healed together. Mona would only be permitted to remove it once daily for personal hygiene. During this time period, the muscles of her abdomen and back – her "core muscles" – would deteriorate to a point where simply standing up would be a struggle. Still, it was better than surgery.

Attention now shifted to Mona's concussion. A concussion is defined as the brain being shaken. Recently, concussions have gotten a lot of attention in sports like football where the brain is repeatedly jarred, resulting in long-term injury. The brain has a very limited ability to heal, which is why a major concussion can leave lasting effects. When Mona's head hit the side of the door, her skull stopped moving but her brain kept going. The brain floats in a small amount of fluid. As the skull stopped moving, the brain continued forward and slammed into the skull, tearing up blood vessels and disrupting the nerves. Information becomes jumbled and the brain goes into shutdown mode, rendering the victim unconscious. This severe of an impact can even pull the brain apart as lighter areas (grey matter) have less momentum than heavier areas (white matter). Separation of these areas of brain tissue result in a person being "brain dead" due to all of the connections between the higher-thinking areas being sheared and severed. Breathing and heartbeat are controlled in the more basic and protected parts of the brain; therefore a person can still be "alive" but no longer able to process any information. They are in a "persistent vegetative state", i.e. a vegetable.

Since Mona was still talking, her higher processes still worked; the doctors just couldn't ascertain how well. As a veterinarian, she could only work if her mind was clear. A concussion typically affects short term memory, so she could not remember what happened or what the doctors had just said. It's also why she kept repeating the same questions, "What happened?" "Where am I?" "Is everyone OK?" "Can I have a pillow for my back?"

This scenario would play out continuously in the 24 hours following the accident, restarting each time a family member entered her room: Mona would wake up, look around, ask the same set of questions again, and then fall back asleep.

The brain is a funny, complex machine and when it is messed up things can get a little strange. Mona would write the month of October, the month of the crash, every time she wrote out the date for the next four months. She'd consciously try to write the correct date to counteract this tendency but as soon as she stopped thinking about it, the month would revert to October. Words would be substituted or reversed without her awareness, so a Christmas recital for the kids would become a band recital, even though none of the kids were in band. She would say her sister Carla just called when she knew it was her sister Theresa.

For Mona, this was a scary reality. Because the brain does not repair well, damage is often permanent. How could she do her job if she kept saying the wrong words? Our clients would not want a doctor who inadvertently began speaking of heart disease when in actuality, their pet had kidney disease. We spend a great deal of time explaining very difficult problems to pet owners; a few wrong words can spell disaster. If Mona ever wanted to work again, she would have to straighten this out.

Unfortunately, nobody had any idea if the problem would correct itself. There is no treatment for a concussion; Mona would just have to wait it out and see if her mind would work properly again. We really wouldn't have a solid answer for months, which was harrowing because Mona had been a vet for 14 years. Practicing veterinary medicine was a big part of who she was and the means by which we both supported our family. Now it looked like neither of us would ever return to our profession again because Mona might not ever be able to think clearly and I might not even survive, much less work. Not even our stellar medical team could predict what would happen; only God knew our future.

Scot Hodkiewicz

# Chapter 8

## ∞ God's Gift ∞

By now I was in surgery – mainly an exploratory one since my medical team really had no idea what they would find. One thing they knew for sure: my abdomen was distended with blood and I would soon die if they couldn't control the bleeding. Waiting for it to stop on its own was not an option since I'd already lost so much; I had no chance of survival whatsoever if they were unsuccessful in their attempt. Although the nurses were pumping blood into me through my IV catheter as fast as they could, I was losing it just as quickly. I'd already received five units (a normal man holds about nine) and still needed more.

The surgery would explore everything – from the liver sitting up under the ribs, to the bladder down by the pelvis, and all body parts in between. I'd emerge from the experience with a big scar from my sternum to just below my navel – ruining my dream of posing with my shirt open on the cover of GQ (strike that one off my to-do list!). After shaving the hair off my bloated abdomen and doing a quick surgical prep of the skin, the area was draped off for surgery. In cases like this, there is no care given to making the incision look pretty; a small incision does not allow for adequate visualization of the various organs. Furthermore, a missed perforation in the colon down by the pelvis, or a ruptured gall bladder up under the ribs would mean a dead patient. Since you're dressed in a suit at your funeral, nobody knows, nor would they care what your incision looks like. In extreme circumstances like mine, the incision is made large; I was in no position to complain.

Dr. Lang would perform the surgery. As he entered the abdomen, taking great care not to inadvertently cut anything just under the surface, blood began shooting out and flooding onto the floor. My engorged abdomen was under so much pressure it poured out like water rushing out of a fountain. My surgeon couldn't see anything; all the organs were submerged. He called for suction but the blood flooded out much faster than suction could catch it, spilling onto the floor and splattering all over his shoe covers. He immediately extended the incision and reached for the spleen.

The spleen lies on the left side of the abdomen just below the stomach. This highly vascular organ has two main functions. First, it is an important part of the immune system since it mostly contains the cells that produce white blood cells to guard against and fight infection. Any infection or inflammation in the body releases chemicals that circulate in the bloodstream. These chemicals are recognized by "memory cells." Basically, these cells "remember" different types of bacteria and viruses that your body has dealt with before and reacts quickly to fight those infections when they encounter them again. This is the *memory* part of immune system.

It's the reason why certain diseases, such as measles, are only contracted once in a lifetime. During the first exposure the body has not seen the virus before; therefore, it can take weeks to "learn" to recognize it and mount a response. In this period, the virus has time to set up its infection and the accompanying symptoms. In the case of measles, the infected person gets sick and displays the typical skin lesions. The then body spikes a fever to kill the virus, while the glands (lymph nodes and the spleen) swell up with infection-fighting cells. Eventually, your immune system figures out how to fight this virus and develops specific white blood cells that can attack it. This is why the virus inevitably goes away in time; your body fights it off and the symptoms disappear. Once the body eradicates the virus, it stops making the white blood cells to fight against it. However, it does retain certain memory cells.

When the body encounters the virus again (and it almost always will), it "remembers" and can subsequently mount a response immediately, before the virus ever has a chance to reproduce. The response is now so quick that there are rarely any symptoms. Most people never even know that they were re-exposed to the virus. As the container of a great number of these built-up memory cells, the spleen will begin to crank out the necessary white blood cells when needed.

The second function of the spleen is to act as a blood reservoir. It holds a large amount of red blood cells – not the fluid part of blood – but a high concentration of the actual red blood cells. Blood is a mixture of about 40 percent red blood cells and 60 percent water and proteins. When a large amount is lost such as in my case, the spleen contracts and forces these red blood cells directly into the bloodstream. Basically, it provides an automatic blood transfusion.

Unfortunately, this is not a good thing if the spleen is ruptured. In that circumstance, the injured spleen contracts, pushing blood into the abdomen, *not* into the general circulation. Blood is then lost even more rapidly, negating the benefit of that built-in blood reservoir. It is like running toward a fire with a bucket of water and having the bottom of the bucket fall out: the fire rages on because your best shot at extinguishing it just disappeared. My blood was now pumping out of the spleen through a large tear and had to be stopped, or else I would bleed out on the operating table.

Dr. Lang grabbed my tattered spleen and pulled it out of my abdomen to work on it. Being a highly mobile organ, he could fully remove it and lay it on my belly while it was still attached. Now he could see it was torn completely in half. He grabbed the largest clamps available and placed one across the vessels feeding each portion of the spleen. Of course he would have to come back, tie each vessel individually, and remove the spleen but first he would arrest the bleeding so he could examine the rest of the abdomen.

Systematically, he began to check everything. The liver was severely bruised with a deep purple swelling about the size of a baseball in the lobe near the spleen. It was weeping blood but not bleeding profusely. An absorbable sponge was placed over it to slow the bleed and assist the blood in clotting. It would be left there after they sewed me up again because the body would eventually dissolve it in a few weeks. On a liver, there is really no way to tie anything off without removing an entire lobe. The liver cannot be sutured well, especially with a large bruise. Since the tissue is not tough enough to hold suture, the suture cuts right through it. Often, the suture simply tears through and falls right off, leaving in the surgeon's hand a tied piece of suture with nothing attached to it anymore. Dr. Lang decided that the smartest and quickest thing to do was to simply lay the gauze on my liver and move on.

He then examined the bile duct and gall bladder coming out of the liver, both of which held green bile, making a leak easy to spot. Both were ok. He moved on to the stomach and intestines, understanding that it's critical that neither one of these leaks. Any type of break in these organs releases bacteria into the abdomen, resulting in a deadly and incredibly painful infection inside the abdominal cavity (peritonitis). Bacteria released into the abdomen make it feel as if it's on fire; a temperature will spike and toxins will be absorbed. It is nearly always fatal but even if the patient survives, they will very likely sustain permanent digestive and pain problems, though most don't live long enough to worry about that.

The whole tract is a long tube so Dr. Lang simply began at the stomach and worked his way down, pulling intestines out, then shoving them back in until he had inspected it all. Luckily, the intestines are pretty tough and mobile; they tend to move out of the way instead of tearing. Dr. Lang did not really have to worry about twisting the intestine during this pull-out, push-in process. Think of it as a curtain that is attached at the rod; it will naturally stay untangled unless held in place by something else. Much in the same way, the intestine can be simply pulled out, inspected, and then pushed back into the abdomen without much worry about exactly how or where. In my case, there were a few areas that were severely bruised and beaten but not ruptured. These were left alone to heal. At least I would not have the added burden of peritonitis in my battle to survive.

Dr. Lang worked his way down. The blood in the abdomen had stopped refilling now that the spleen was under control. He tied off or cauterized a few small bleeders along the way but for the most part, the bleeding was stopped.

Now he checked the rest of the organs. Right away, something seemed wrong with the fluid he saw in the abdomen. Yes, it was bloody but also more watery than it should be. By this time I had received a lot of fluids so this watery appearance was only natural but Dr. Lang still suspected something else was going on. He could have easily explained it away but he followed his gut feeling: something was leaking and he had to keep looking for the source.

He immediately reached for my bladder. This is usually a fluid-filled sack but mine was empty and flaccid, containing no urine at all. Of course, most people who notice a Jeep about to hit them head-on at accelerated speed would have emptied their bladder (as well as their bowels) just out of fear alone. Mine, however, was completely empty, which is never a normal state for this organ. Dr. Lang knew immediately that there had to be a tear, so he pulled the bladder out of the abdomen and inspected every inch. A large bruise made it hard to see but, sure enough, there was a half-inch hole where the urine had blown out the side. The off-colored, watery liquid was a mixture of blood and urine. That was the reason why the bladder was so empty.

Once again, Dr. Lang's gut feeling had been right-on; this had to be repaired.

Due to its make-up, the bladder tears frequently in car crashes. It is like a balloon filled with water; a distended sac of fluid that, when impacted, has only one small outlet. With a severe body blow like the one I took, pressure will force it to burst. It probably didn't help that I drank a Pepsi on the way home and therefore it was fairly full. The good news is that urine is sterile (unless you have a bladder infection) because my bladder was now a busted balloon and I was urinating into my own abdomen.

Though urine rarely causes infection, it will quickly become deadly if your body can't get rid of your own waste. Surprisingly, death comes not from the urine itself but from an increase of potassium in the blood. The kidneys are designed to regulate the potassium levels by expelling it out in the urine. Now, with urine accumulating in the abdomen, it was getting reabsorbed and the potassium in the bloodstream was rising. Eventually, the high potassium level would slow the heart until it stopped (in fact, potassium is one of the injections given on death row with the lethal injection cocktails). Now my potassium levels were rising due to the urine leaking into my abdomen. If Dr. Lang had not followed his gut feeling and checked the bladder, I would have likely died. Because the damaged tissue was frayed and would not seal well, he had to cut it away, trimming it back to get to the more normal bladder tissue so the edges would meet cleanly. Six sutures later, the tear was fixed.

With everything inspected, the surgeon turned back to the spleen. Three major pairs of arteries and veins feed the spleen, each about the size of a pencil. Each one was separated and double-tied before cut. The spleen was thrown onto a tray and the abdomen was washed out with saline to remove any contamination, along with the remaining urine. As the saline was suctioned out, Dr. Lang moved the organs out of the way and watched the deepest part of the abdomen, where any continual leakage of urine or blood would pool. After a few minutes, he saw none. He could now close me up and deal with the rest of my injuries. I had made it through the first part but was far from out of the woods.

No major vessels or nerves seemed to have been torn in my arms so they would be splinted temporarily and wrapped to my chest to prevent further damage. Due to my unconscious state, the doctors were unable to fully test nerve function but surmised it was unlikely there was significant damage since the nerves run next to the vessels and there was no major bleeding in either arm. They had reason to hope the nerves were OK.

Because I had been under for a while the doctors wanted to get me off the surgery table quickly, knowing my weak heart could give out at any time. As they kept pushing blood in, they   started gaining ground now that the biggest sources of blood loss were all under control. Still, I'd lost a ton and my pressure was dangerously low. The average human body holds about nine units of blood; I would require 12 units that day. They simply did not have time to fix all my fractures until I was more stable; therefore, they quickly splinted my arms and wrapped them to my body.

However, the thighbone fracture presented a problem. Putting off its repair would leave the lower leg attached to my body by only by some muscle because the outside muscle of the thigh had been pierced in half by the bone. The fractured bone had broken so violently, there were at least five separate pieces to put back together. It would need a plate but plating can take a long time and I couldn't stay on the operating table much longer.

Casting was not an option since any cast or splint must extend one joint above and below the fracture to be effective. This meant the cast would have to extend above the hip – nearly impossible to do because the cast then extends up around the waist. I would still need to urinate and defecate.  How would I do that when casted up to my waist?

Dr. Schumacher now became involved as a secondary surgeon to relieve Dr. Lang, who had been working feverishly on me for hours and needed a break. Dr. Schumacher was assigned to stabilize my leg. She would later repair my elbows also. Until a plate could be put on permanently, she decided to place an external fixator temporarily on my leg. I was familiar with these since I place them routinely on animals with similar breaks.

External fixators work by placing threaded pins into the bone above and below the fracture site.  These pins travel perpendicular to the bone and are driven through the skin and overlying muscle right through the bone underneath.  They are long and are left sticking out of the skin, often on both sides. Then all the pins coming out of the skin are clamped to a rod on the outside of the leg – thus the name external fixator.  It sounds primitive and barbaric but is very strong and, in skilled hands, can be placed very quickly. There is no need to carefully realign the various fracture pieces since the surgeon only works with the larger pieces of bone. The smaller fragments were ignored for now.

This type of fixation was actually first developed in Russia during World War I. A Russian surgeon needed a quick way to repair the terrible arm and leg fractures of war. Russia was a poor country; specialized stainless steel plates and screws were not an option. The doctor improvised using bicycle spokes driven through the bones that he would then clamp to outside metal rods to hold the bones in place. For added strength, the pins would go all the way through the leg, with rods placed on both sides. It was fast (anesthetic was minimal then), cheap (no need for different plate and screw sizes), and versatile (one size spoke would work on almost all major bones). The bones would be stable enough to heal and the pins were then removed. It was a great leap forward in treating fractures that would otherwise have resulted in amputation. Of course in modern times, stainless steel pins of varying sizes with threaded ends have replaced the bicycle spokes, but the concept is virtually the same.

Dr. Schumacher grabbed her power drill and found the right size drill bit. The drill and bits are no different than what is used by carpenters except they are all stainless steel to eliminate rust. A small cut in the skin was made, muscle was separated so the drill did not grab it, and holes were drilled through the bone. Two pins went above the fracture into the thighbone – one near my hip and the other just above the fracture. Normally, a second set of pins would have been placed in the thighbone below the fracture but it was in too many pieces and my knee was broken in half. Instead, two pins went into my shinbone spanning the area of the fracture site and holding my leg in position. These four pins were clamped to a long, thick rod on the outside of my leg. Now my thighbone was secure and stable; it could not move. The vessels and nerves would not be severed by the jagged fracture ends shifting position and it could be plated when I was more stable. Not a perfect solution but a quick one.

The wound in the thigh now could be addressed. There was a hole in the outside of the thigh as big as my fist filled with glass, upholstery, dirt, and plastic deeply embedded in the tissues (Dr. Lang would later tell me it looked like a shark-bite). This would have to be meticulously cleaned out before it could be plated. Foreign material like this introduced bacteria and even fungal spores into my system. Although they'd initially intended to put in plates and screws in a few days to permanently fix my thighbone, these pieces of metal were great places for these infections to hide from the immune system and antibiotics. The bacteria can live in any microscopic divot, scratch or defect or on the plate and screws themselves, hidden away from anything that may kill them.

The body relies on blood to get the white, infection-fighting blood cells and the antibiotics to where they all need to go, but there is no blood supply to a chunk of embedded glass or a metal plate. Bacteria will colonize this material and reproduce, eventually covering part or all of it. This is called a "biofilm," a thin sheet of bacteria that is nearly impossible to cure. It usually requires removal of the contaminated material and long-term antibiotics. Of course, any infection on the plate that would eventually hold the bone in place would be catastrophic. It usually sets in before the bone is healed, interrupting the healing process. This results in a poorly healed, chronically unstable, and incredibly painful bone. Often, there is no healing at all (called a non-union) in a scenario where the bone fragments do not knit together like they are supposed to, but instead heal as separate bones. This frequently requires multiple surgeries over a period of years to resolve – and sometimes even amputation. Even worse, many of the bacteria are now resistant to antibiotics, making antibiotic use futile for these resistant bugs. These infections can spread to the heart valves, enter the bloodstream, and cause septic shock or gangrene, with amputation as the end result. The doctors would have to wait a while to plate my leg until the infection brought into my system by some piece of glass or plastic was under control – otherwise it could cost me my leg or even my life.

Dr. Schumacher removed the sponges placed by Dr. Lang and quickly cut away any muscle that was obviously dead or beyond repair. She washed the hole with a jet of saline. This removed a lot of the dirt and debris from the wound but she knew she could not get it all; glass and debris were imbedded too deeply in the wound. The end of the bone had exited the skin and was therefore contaminated; sewing the skin closed would just trap the infection. Dr. Schumacher decided to leave the wound entirely open. This would allow for it to be washed daily for continuous removal of infection and debris until it was clean enough to plate, giving the body time to "push out" any infection through the open hole. The external fixator would hold my leg in place long enough for the wound to become clean, so they would plate it a few days later (if I was still around).

There was one last thing to do: place an intra-caval filter. This is basically a big strainer, shaped like a daddy-long-legs spider. It is placed in the main blood vessel returning blood to the heart. The reason is simple; a blood clot breaking off from my thigh fracture could travel upstream, pass through the heart, and lodge in the lung. Known as a pulmonary embolism, this phenomenon kills many people after surgery or major trauma. Often, they survive the initial trauma and hours of surgery only to throw a clot into a lung and die. A clot such as this will block off a major artery into the lungs. Suddenly, blood can't get there to be oxygenated and the patient will suffocate, not due to a blocked airway, but to the blood's inability to get to where it needs to go to pick up the oxygen. It is almost instantly deadly and doctors can't predict if or when it will happen.

What they do know is that it often occurs after trauma, especially with fractures to the large bones, and the thighbone is the biggest bone in the body. It has a huge blood supply and tends to form very large clots. The marrow cavity inside the bone has large vessels draining from it – a direct line heading into the heart and eventually into the lungs. If a clot breaks loose, it *will* end up in the lungs.

Once the blood clot lodges there, not much can be done. First, it doesn't show up on X-ray and there is usually no time for a CT scan. If this happened to me, I simply would not be able to get oxygen into my bloodstream since there would be no blood traveling into my lungs to pick it up. I was already getting oxygen from a respirator, but in the event that no blood could make it to the lungs to carry the oxygen to the rest of the body, oxygen in the lungs would do me no good.

Dr. Morris was called in to address this specific issue. He was a quiet man – not the loud, cocky type you envision for a surgeon. He is an "Interventional Radiologist," that is, he uses imaging systems like X-rays and fluoroscopy (taking a series of x-rays to create a "movie," made from a series of still pictures) to place things like stents in hearts, or, in my case, a filter to catch any blood clots. The filter is placed through a vein in the thigh and fed up the venous system to just below the heart. Here the "spider legs" of the filter are allowed to open and it lodges itself in place. Any clot heading from below the heart will hopefully be caught by the filter before it can get to the lungs. This filter can stay in place for months as the body heals and is eventually removed when the risk of blood clot is gone. For me, it would be a long time.

Dr. Morris worked quickly, knowing that I could not handle much more. Luckily, the vein in the thigh heads directly up toward the heart, making placement of the filter relatively easy. The vein flows into the Vena Cava – the biggest vein in the body – through the abdomen and chest and into the right atrium of the heart. He would place the filter a few inches below the heart to make sure clots were caught before they got there. A few stitches to close the incision and I was done.

Now it was time to get me off the table. It had been 11 hours since our world had changed and my heart was still weak. They needed to end this operation ASAP.

Dr. Lang had stayed in the hospital while the other doctors worked on me, waiting to speak to my family. He had started with me when I came in and was now personally involved. Good or bad, he wanted to be the one to break the news to my loved ones. It was now 11 o'clock on a Sunday night and he was exhausted. He was supposed to have been done at noon. In fact, he hadn't even been scheduled to be at the hospital that day because he usually covered Saturdays, not Sundays.

Recently, Dr. Lang had switched his weekend schedule to help coach his son's pee-wee football team so for the last few weeks he had covered Sundays instead. This week would have been his last Sunday since the season had ended the day before; that simple decision to coach his kid had placed him at the hospital on the day of the accident to save me.

As I said, even though he was working on Sunday, theoretically he should have been gone by time I got there because his shift had ended at noon – an hour before we arrived. He'd been finishing up some paperwork and dictating notes when the call came in that we were on our way. Dr. Lang stuck around to see if he could help, putting his weekend on hold and losing his half day off for some guy he had never met.

He certainly could have left and let someone else handle it; we were just another family hit by another drunk driver and he had seen hundreds of cases like ours. But for whatever reason, he stayed. He stayed so he could be there to stop my bleeding femoral vein; he stayed to remove my spleen and suture my bladder; he stayed to get me through the ups and downs that were yet to come. He stayed because he was supposed to – not because of hospital rules but *higher rules*. God had given him a gift – the ability to save lives – and He expected that gift to be used for His will, *not* in obedience to some hospital schedule.

This is why Dr. Lang hung around. He really had no choice, though I am not sure he knew it. Yes, he could have left but his conscience prevented him from walking away. The choice was made for him when he accepted his gift as a surgeon. He stayed because, like most people that have found God's gift, he knew that he could do it better than anyone else. He would never tell anyone this, especially not another surgeon, but Dr. Lang understood the meaning behind his rare and precious talent. He wasn't about to walk away.

In that sense, he and I are a lot alike. If a dog had been rushed into my hospital after being hit by a car, I would have done the same thing. Although I employ many great vets in my practice, I had been given a gift to be a veterinarian-surgeon. Dr. Lang stayed because he knew he'd been blessed with the skills required to pull me through. There were plenty of good doctors around but my injuries demanded the very best. Dr. Lang was yet another angel in the right place at the right time, without him even knowing why. His belief that he was the only man for the job was vindicated in the end because his decision to stop the gurney, contradict the doctor in charge, and get my bleeding leg under control had saved my life. On the razor's edge between life and death, there was simply no room for error – a few more minutes of blood loss and I would have been a dead man. God put him there that day to keep me alive because His purpose for me was still not finished.

I found out later that there was another reason for Dr. Lang's remarkable competence, skill, and dedication. He was a father to three sons, one of whom had severe autism. Raising kids is hard enough but discovering your son has autism and will have to struggle in life is simply heartbreaking. Dr. Lang and his physician-wife Mary (not her real name) certainly had the means to pay someone to else raise their child; they could have easily hired a team of nannies or sent him to an institution to enable them to go on with their lives just as they had planned.

Instead, Mary gave up her career and Dr. Lang reduced his schedule so they could be with him. They accepted God's plan for them instead of trying to make their own plan work. In doing so, he became the surgeon that would save me. His autistic son taught him true dedication to others, to put his wants and needs on hold for the benefit of someone else who needed him more. Today, *I* needed him and he would stay – something he may not have done had it not been for the gift of his son. God had provided Dr. Lang with a difficult personal challenge, in order to make him stronger, to fashion him into the surgeon God intended. *Not* to improve his technical skills because Dr. Lang constantly worked on that, but to improve the other necessary traits that would mold him into the medical professional and human being God desired him to be: things like dedication, patience, attention to detail, and the ability to clearly explain very complicated situations to people whose minds are clouded with fear and shock. Dr. Lang's autistic son had imparted these lessons to him; in many ways, *he* was the one who truly saved me that day – something nobody could have foreseen when he was diagnosed with autism.

For Dr. Lang, being a surgeon was a gift from God but it had also come with a price. His conscience – God's voice in his ear – would simply not allow him to walk away. He would have been haunted forever if I'd died that night because someone else had made the wrong decision, or if the surgeon taking his place did not have his skills. He would also be reminded of his failure, his lack of dedication, every time he looked into his son's eyes. Would his son doubt that his dad would stay with him when he needed him the most? Dr. Lang could not let that happen.

If I was going to die tonight, I would die with Dr. Lang, one of the country's most gifted trauma surgeons, doing everything he could to save me. God had placed me in his hands, another angel in the right setting at the right time.

# Chapter 9

## ∞ Worse Instead of Better ∞

By midnight I was in recovery. It had been 11 hours since the Jeep had crossed the median and put me here; eleven hours since our great plan for our life had been completely thrown out the window. My wife was broken and mumbling, Alexa was recovering with a broken arm, and Victoria and Chase were bruised and terrified. All because of a loser who just had to down a twelve-pack before one o'clock on a Sunday morning as he drove around with nothing better to do in his life.

By now my spleen was out, my bladder repaired, and my leg stabilized. My torn femoral vein was packed with gauze and my thighbone had large steel pins sticking out of it, with clamps holding it in place. The gash in the muscle was tightly wrapped, waiting for me to get stronger before a true repair to the vein, bone, and muscle could be accomplished. My broken feet and arms were splinted and I had received enough blood to replace my entire volume one- and-a-half times. Although still broken, my nose and pelvis were the least of my worries. My dislocated shoulder remained in that condition due to the shattered bone that was once attached to it. The dislocations of my elbow and shoulder would have to wait until the upper arm bone was fixed. There was simply no way I could endure any more surgery tonight; I was too close to death and both my surgeons were exhausted. There wasn't much they could do except wrap my arms to my chest to prevent them from flopping around. Since these injuries would not kill me they could wait. If I managed to pull through, they could fix them later.

Our families had started to arrive at the hospital after many frantic hours on the road and Dr. Lang was ready to meet with them. My parents and three sisters were there, along with two of Mona's sisters and her brother. Mona's parents had just walked in after an exhausting nine-hour drive. They all gathered in a small room after having already visited Mona and received updates on the extent of her injuries. They had spent hours holding and comforting our kids, who were now fast asleep on the floor and on couches, completely spent from the day's activities, their youth protecting them from truly understanding the changes yet to come. Everyone was incredibly tired from the drive, yet unable to sleep due to relentless fear and adrenaline. A nurse came in and told everyone to gather around; Dr. Lang would be in in a few minutes.

As they waited for the news that would upend their lives, they spoke very little. Nobody knew what to say so they mostly prayed in silence.

Dr. Lang knocked before entering. He had now been working for 17 hours straight between his regular shift and then jumping in to work on me. After introducing himself, he sat down while our families anxiously gave him their full attention, waiting to hear the extent of the damage and an answer to the question of me ever regaining consciousness again.

*If I did, would I walk? Would I be on permanent disability?* They all knew I would hate not being able to work and would drive them all nuts if I was stuck in the house for the rest of my life. *Would they have to move closer to help with the kids?* They braced for the news about how their lives would drastically change.

Understanding they did not want small-talk, Dr. Lang got right to the point. I had survived the surgery but my chances were still 50:50 at best and things could still go downhill at any time. He explained that they would need to perform multiple surgeries to repair my various fractures over the next few days but would not put me on the operating table again until I was more stable. As for my mental status and prospects for working again, he could tell them nothing definitively. I had been unconscious when I arrived and would remain in a medically induced coma for a few days. Dr. Lang predicted a two-to-four month hospital stay and another six months in a nursing home at a minimum; I would be lucky to work again in a year. Furthermore, he warned them that the next 24 hours were critical and a lot could change. My body had taken a terrific beating and I would likely get worse before I got better. He was partially right: it wouldn't take 24 hours, it would take only one.

It started with a couple drops of blood. Not much, just a few drops. But in a strange place. Because my face had hit the airbag with such force, my nose had been relocated off to the side, with nose bleeds fully expected. However, the blood was trickling from my eye like a teardrop.

On the surface, this would seem to be a very minor problem. Surely with nine fractured bones, massive internal injuries, and cuts and scrapes everywhere, a drop of blood from the eye wasn't a big deal. But for people who work in the trauma field, such an occurrence makes your heart sink because of what it signifies. After 11 hours of work, all of the expense, surviving the surgery, and my family waiting down the hall, it was now very likely I was going to die – all from a few drops of blood.

Why?

The trickle of blood was not due to an injury. I had not bled from my eyes in the aftermath of the crash. Yes, I had two black eyes from breaking my nose, but that was not the cause of the blood currently weeping out of my eye. The trickle had started because my blood had stopped clotting. Powerless to clot, my body was now bleeding out. My nurses knew that I was now likely a dead man.

In reaction to my multiple injuries – bruises, breaks, torn blood vessels – my body had automatically started to assemble a variety of proteins called clotting factors, in series of complex steps required to form a blood clot. Now these clotting proteins were almost all depleted. Without them the whole process of clotting stopped, making it impossible to form a clot over even the smallest source of bleeding. As a result, I was beginning to bleed spontaneously and would soon be bleeding in all kinds of different areas, including out of my eyes.

Humans have learned to use this phenomenon very effectively when desired; it is how rat poison works. The poison, Warfarin, blocks a factor in this cycle and stops the blood from clotting. Anything that ingests it bleeds to death from even the slightest little bump.

Now, I was like a poisoned rat beginning to bleed with no way to stop it. Soon I would start hemorrhaging in my lungs, brain, or anywhere else. I would bleed to death, experience a hemorrhagic stroke, or bleed into my lungs and die from asphyxiation. Immediately, the nurse ran for Dr. Lang and caught him exiting the doctor's locker room after just putting his coat on to leave.

My exhausted surgeon threw off his coat and rushed to my bedside. He recognized the problem immediately, having feared it from the start. All of his skillful work, hundreds of thousands of dollars spent, a Sunday with the family lost, and he would soon have to break the tragic news to my father and mother, my three sisters, my wife and three battered children that I was gone. He was familiar with the exact words, "We tried everything we could but were unable to save him. He passed away."

They would all explode into sobs and my parents, now nearing 70, would collapse. Their lives would be ruined because they would never recover from the loss of their child and would spend the rest of their days in a sorrowful funk, not able to enjoy much of anything anymore. Family gatherings would forever be clouded with the emptiness of a missing family member. Christmas would now be about trying to act happy "for the kids" while the adults would be dying on the inside. One dead and two whole families destroyed.

Blood naturally forms a clot by what is called a "cascade." A cascade is a series of steps, each step multiplying the effect of the previous one. It is like a snowball rolling down a hill; it starts as a small ball that picks up more snow as it rolls. The faster and bigger it gets, the more snow it can pick up. A blood clot is similar. It is formed by proteins in the blood that begin to stick together causing different proteins to glom on and eventually form a clot. They are triggered to stick together by the tear in the blood vessel that exposes the underlying tissue and provides an irregular surface for blood proteins to adhere to. Each clotting protein (called a "factor" and numbered in sequence) multiplies the next protein until there is a huge amount of them all congealing together. It forms and looks much like Jell-O. Ultimately, it is a big wad of protein that sticks to the torn vessel and seals it off.

The problem for me was that I had used up one of these factors in the sequence, making it impossible for clots to form. I still had numerous torn vessels and broken bones oozing blood but there were only so many of these factors in the body at any time and I had run out. Even if one factor in the chain that makes a clot is missing, the entire process stops. Hemophiliacs can't clot blood well because they are short on a single clotting factor and thus are at constant risk of bleeding to death. Thanks to my ordeal on the interstate, I was now one of them.

The blood trickling out of my eye was the first sign. It was soon followed by a trickle of blood out of my ear. This kind of spontaneous hemorrhage is call Disseminated Intravascular Coagulation or D.I.C. It describes the making of so many blood clots that the clotting factors are finally exhausted and the blood clotting stops altogether. I had seen this in animals, either from trauma such as this or with other systemic disease such as infections or cancers. In veterinary school we used a different name for D.I.C.; to us it stood for *Dead In Cage*. I had seen it dozens of times in my practice, treated each animal aggressively, and never saved one. They all were "dead in their cage" within hours.

I had been given 12 units of blood by now but all of it contained an anticoagulant. More blood transfusions would make it worse instead of better.

There was one chance to stop the bleeding but it was a longshot: a product called Factor VIII, one of the blood clotting proteins and the one that the body typically depletes first. It also cost $15,000 dollars for the single dose. Knowing it was likely too late, probably a waste of money and most likely doomed to fail Dr. Lang ordered the Factor VIII anyway. He was not optimistic; he had used it many times before with no success; every patient had bled to death while he stood by helplessly.

After calling for the injection, Dr. Lang watched and prayed as it was administered through the IV port. Then he called Dr. Gibbs, Mona's primary physician. After informing him of my status, they both agreed; Mona should be told about my situation and allowed to come to my room. She would be able to see her husband and the father of her children before he passed away. This had to be done immediately.

Dr. Gibbs had treated Mona when she first came in and had also stayed well past his shift to monitor her. Now he had to tell her about me. Doctors are trained to deal in reality, not what they hope will happen. It was clear I was slipping away and he had to break the news to her. This was what every physician hated, telling someone that their loved one was about to die. But before he told Mona, he and Dr. Lang had to meet with the family first. They asked a nurse to find Mona's mother, Anne, and her father, Joe. It was now past midnight and they were both sleeping. The nurse found them on chairs in one of the hallways and woke them gently.

"Dr. Gibbs and Dr. Lang need to speak to you both," she announced. Sensing their fear, she added, "Mona's condition is unchanged. It is about Scot."

Joe and Anne sat with their hearts racing. They both knew that the nurse waking them up and the doctor coming in to talk to them could only mean something bad. They had already been told that their daughter had a broken back and was talking in circles, and that her husband was in critical condition with all kinds of life-threatening injuries. Although they had considered the possibility that I would die, they had not discussed it at all during the long drive to the hospital. They did not want to even bring it up.

*What would they have to do with the kids and how would they help? Should Anne quit her job to help raise the grandkids if they did not have a father? How would Mona support the family by herself in my absence? How would she work with a broken back?*

Now Dr. Gibbs and Dr. Lang entered the room and asked Joe and Anne to sit down. They were both ready to collapse as the adrenaline surged through them, with Anne starting to tear up even before Dr. Gibbs could speak.

"We have run into a complication with Scot. His blood is no longer able to clot. We call the syndrome D.I.C. I don't need to explain the acronym but he can't clot his blood, which is usually fatal. He is very likely to die tonight. We believe Mona should be brought in to see him while he is still alive."

Mona's father was fiercely protective of his family and now his instincts won out over the doctor's recommendations. "Absolutely not! She has been through enough. Seeing her husband dying will kill her."

Dr. Lang then took over, employing the patience he had developed in dealing with his autistic son. "Mr. Anderson, I understand your concern but the chances of Scot surviving this complication are only one in a hundred."

"What do you mean one in a hundred?!" Anne asked as Joe stormed out of the room.

"We have given Scot a medicine to get his blood clotting again but it is rarely successful. If one hundred people need the shot, only one will survive."

"Isn't there anything else you can do?"

"We are doing everything possible and Scot is currently stable. That is why we need to decide quickly. I do not know how long he will remain so."

"We need to bring her up. She needs to see him," Anne decided.

"We agree," Dr. Lang replied gently, "It is the best thing."

Anne left to find Joe, having come to the realization that this was necessary, and the two entered Mona's room, where she was hooked up to monitors and IV's. The huge, deep-blue bruise on her head encompassed a third of her face. She was in a back brace from her armpits to her hips and lay flat on her back unable to move. Anne gently spoke her name, asking her to wake up.

"Mona, Mona wake up." It was the same voice she had used when waking her up for school 30 years earlier.

"Mona, wake up. You need to go see Scot."

Mona's eyes slowly opened and she began to comprehend. She was still on a morphine drip and her brain was still rebooting after the concussion but this time she understood right away.

The nurses gathered around the bed to help her into a wheelchair. In the brace, she could no longer bend to get up. With her broken elbow, her left arm was wrapped to her side. Carefully yet not without pain, she was put in a wheelchair to be brought to my room.

"Why are you bringing me now? It is still dark out."

"Mona," Anne said gently, "the doctor asked that you come see Scot."

"Why? Is he dying?"

"Mona, he is very injured. They thought you should go speak to him."

Mona was still in a fog but soon realized that the doctors must be thinking I was not going to make it. Why else would they wake her up and go through all this trouble to let her see me in the middle of the night?

She arrived in my room and began to sob, having not seen me since the crash. I lay there on a respirator, my eyes shut and unresponsive. She could see all the splints and wraps and my obviously broken nose. She knew on sight that I would likely not make it through but could not even get out of the chair; all she could do was reach over and touch my hand.

I was in a medically induced coma and had no awareness of her presence. She cried softly, trying to keep it muffled so as not to wake me, knowing the pain would be unbearable if I were to regain consciousness. She did not want that for me even if it meant that I could not hear her final words. She simply said, "I love you. You saved me and the kids. You are a great father and husband. Just please keep fighting, I don't want you to leave me, we need you here."

She cried there for a few minutes. When it became clear she'd said what she needed to say, the nursing staff came in to wheel her back to her room. She was now supposed to try to get some rest – an impossible feat when you are waiting to hear if your husband is going to live or die. She sobbed in her wheelchair as they transported her back to her hospital bed.

What would she do? How would she tell the kids that their dad was not going to be there anymore? She mostly worried about Chase. As the only boy, who would show him how to be a man? Who would play football with him in the yard and teach him how to throw a baseball?

She knew the girls needed me too. They would soon be coming into their teen years when girls need a strong father figure to act as their safety net and the thing that keeps them grounded when all the boys start coming around. Dads are supposed to be that hovering, protective guardian. Now Mona knew I would most likely not be around anymore to provide that sense of protection; it was gone for all of them.

On the way back to her room she prayed. She had not had the time or mental capacity up to that point to ask God for help but now in an amazing moment of clarity, she did. Her mind cleared, making it possible for her to pray – not in an endless loop, but clearly and concisely. With all of her might she prayed to save me, begging God to let me live; there was nothing else she could do.

"God, please let him live. I don't care about anything else. He doesn't have to get back to normal, just let him live and we will adapt to anything else. I don't know how to raise these kids by myself, I need him with me. I am begging you, just let him live."

There was no reply, no booming voice from heaven. She was hoping for a comforting feeling that everything would be alright. She got nothing, just silence. It scared her even more and she felt completely alone. Although her mom was in the room with her, she still felt like her life would now be a very lonely struggle. As a 38 year-old widow, she would be raising the kids by herself. Both our parents and all our siblings were scattered all over the Midwest. If Mona wanted their help raising them, she would have to sell everything we had built together and move. The thought of uprooting the kids and starting all over scared her more than her injuries. We had just gone through the "building the business" part of things and she had no interest or energy to do it again somewhere else, especially alone. She may very well be facing the loss of her husband, her source of income, all her friends and contacts, and her home. She confronted these horrifying possibilities in a wheelchair with three breaks in her back, a scrambled brain, and no message from God that He had heard her prayer. She felt so incredibly alone.

Then her anger flared: at Jacobs who had just destroyed our lives, at God who wasn't listening, at the inability of the doctors to save me. All this advanced technology, all these highly trained doctors and nurses, and they were all standing by watching helplessly. It wasn't fair, we didn't deserve this. We had tried to be good people, we went to church on Sundays and attempted to do the right thing always. Sure, we weren't perfect but we didn't deserve *this*. Mona could do nothing to help as she lay there on a morphine drip, her mind still wanting to repeat and jumble her words. Everything was completely out of her control. Our plan for our lives had been completely destroyed.

She pushed the button for another dose of morphine – not for the physical pain but the emotional – and drifted off, assuming that upon awakening she'd be a widow before her 40th birthday.

Everyone, the doctors and nurses, and our families, stood by and waited. They all knew that the next few hours would determine whether this veterinarian, husband, and father of three would make it, whether all their work would be worthwhile or a futile waste of time and resources. Dr. Lang had apprised my family of my condition just like he had done with Joe and Anne. Now he waited to see if he would have to go through the "death speech" with them. Everyone just passed the time in quiet fear and desperation, knowing that the bleeding would likely continue in spite of the $15,000 dollar Factor VIII shot. It would probably fail and either my oxygen level would start to drop precipitously as my lungs filled with blood, or I would start to hemorrhage profusely in my brain. I would "stroke out" and never wake up. The room was quiet except for the constant rhythmic beat of the monitors signaling my heart was still beating. As long as that was going, I had a chance, though not much of one.

Margaret was the ER nurse watching over me. She had been with me from the time I left the helicopter almost half a day ago. Now she carefully wiped the blood from my eye and ear waiting to see if more came. She had to be gentle so as not to incite any more bleeding. At this point, any small bump, any disruption to a blood vessel could bleed forever – at least for the rest of my endangered life.

Blood continued to slowly drip like tears while Margaret waited, wanting to give it a chance to clot, only to see another drip trickle out. She repeated this process every few seconds with the same result, and each time her heart sank a little lower. She had seen it before dozens of times, an innocent victim cut down in their prime due to some stupid act of another. Drunk driving crashes; gunfights where only the bystanders get hit; domestic disputes where an abusive husband beats his wife repeatedly for some perceived wrong and finally puts her into a coma, resulting in death. As she wiped away tears of blood, Margaret recounted them all. She had seen the Factor VIII shot administered dozens of times but had yet to see it work. She had no faith in this last-ditch effort to save my life.

She continued for a half-hour never leaving my side, while my parents sat silently in the room. My sisters were waiting outside in the hall so as not to be in the way of the staff.

Then it happened: the tear trickled down more slowly the next time. Unsure if what she was seeing was real or a product of her imagination, Margaret did not want to say anything. She wiped the tear away again but now it seemed to take a little longer for a new tear to form. The third time it was clear: the blood was slowing down. It took several minutes to refill my eye-lid and overflow down my face. She wiped it again, not sure if the blood was going to truly stop or just slow for a while and then restart again. She did not say a word. It had to stop completely in order for me to live; a temporary slowdown would not be enough.

The next time she wiped it away, it did not refill. That's when she ran to find Dr. Lang. My parents came to my side and my sisters entered my room. Everyone began to cry. The shot had worked, the trickles of blood from my eye and ear had stopped! Margaret could not believe it. I was the one-in-a-hundred that would live after getting the Factor VIII shot.

Dr. Lang now took stock of where I was. The major sources of bleeding had been controlled, the ruptured spleen had been removed, and the torn femoral vein was packed off. The fracture in my leg had been stabilized with the external fixator, and the open fractures of my elbow and heel were cleaned, bandaged and splinted. My arms were wrapped to my chest waiting to be fixed later on; no more blood dripped from my eye. For the moment, I was stable. It was time to let me rest and go talk with the rest of my family filling up the chairs in the hallway. They had been kept updated since they had arrived and had been expecting to hear the worst. Dr. Lang gave them the good news that I had dodged another bullet and said the same words I have often told my clients after getting through a nearly fatal injury or surgery on their beloved pet, "I have done all I can do. It is in God's hands now."

My family had been praying non-stop so they did not have to be told to ask for God's help, but Dr. Lang told them to keep it up anyway. "We will re-evaluate his status in the morning. Now we all need some rest."

I had survived the crash, the loss of one-and-a-half times my normal blood volume, a torn femoral vein, and D.I.C. Nevertheless, I had a long way to go before I was out of the woods. So many things could still go wrong. D.I.C. could return, and organs could fail. My brain and spinal function had not yet been ascertained. At this point, we all just had to wait and see.

Mona was in the same boat, with the work done for the day. Anne had come to her room to tell her that my bleeding had stopped, for now. Mona's elbow was splinted, her abdominal bleeding halted or at least slowed to the point where it was no longer life-threatening, and her concussion was not getting worse. However, it would be days before they would know how badly her brain had been injured. Her back was fractured but she was in a body brace and sedated – bruised and battered but stable. Just as with me, the doctors had done all they could do; it was time to let her rest.

The kids had all been checked out also. The two youngest were bruised and cut-up but physically in one piece. Alexa had a broken arm that was now in a sling. They were not sure if surgery would be necessary since many broken arms do very well with this method; the bones are pulled into place by gravity and allowed to heal. Being only 10 years-old, she would heal quickly. She had been given pain medication and was doing OK. Mona's parents and sisters were now sitting in the same waiting room along with my parents and sisters. They all took shifts taking care of our three children.

Everyone was stable. We had made it through Day One. The only family members missing yet were the dogs.

# Chapter 10

## ∞ Where Are The Dogs? ∞

Now that the reality of what had happened was beginning to sink in, the kids started worrying about the dogs. Mona and I were in no position to ask about them but the kids knew that they were no longer with us – Olivia, our little Yorkie-Poo, and Annabelle, our rescue Golden Retriever. In all the chaos, they had not been accounted for.

Olivia was found lying on the side of the road when paramedics arrived, having been ripped from the warmth and safety of Chase's lap and thrown out the window on impact. She lay in the ditch with a fractured skull and a massive brain injury, going immediately into seizures. A bystander had covered her with a blanket to prevent the kids from having to watch their tiny beloved pet experience convulsions and die on the side of the road. It was not until all of us had left for the hospital that a paramedic checked under the blanket, fully expecting to find a dead dog. To his surprise, Olivia was still alive. She had suffered major head trauma and was in and out of seizures but alive nonetheless.

A dog lover himself, the paramedic gently picked up her eight-pound body and brought her to his vehicle, where he wrapped her in a spare towel and decided to drive her to the veterinary emergency hospital. He had seen the kids and the parents and figured their little dog would either die on her own or have to be put down but he could not bear just leave her on the side of the road to perish. Having helped to free me from the van, the paramedic was sure I would be dead soon; he also knew Mona had sustained serious head trauma and may never be the same again. As he contemplated the tragedy of these kids losing their dad and their dog on the same day, he began to tear up. At the very least, he could ease the little dog's suffering. He drove with Olivia on his lap to the animal ER.

On the way the dog had two more seizures, each lasting about a minute. Her body would tense as the seizure came over her, extending her neck backwards until it was over her shoulders, looking back behind herself. Her front legs would extend out fully and her lips would pull back in a terrible grin. Then, when her muscles were as tight as possible, the seizure would start: her body would shake violently and she would cry out. Her tongue would turn blue as she was not able to move her diaphragm and pull in any air. This would continue for about a minute and then pass, the muscles exhausted and the brain's chemicals messengers depleted. She would then relax and start to breathe again.

The paramedic arrived at the veterinary emergency hospital and presented Olivia. A situation like this always puts vets in a tough spot because we need to treat the dog but have no permission from the owner to do so. Without permission, we have no sense of how much treatment to administer. Would the owner want to do anything to save their pet or would they just want her put down? She was seizuring and obviously had major head trauma so she would most likely need days or weeks of treatment and medications before anyone would be able to determine if she'd ever function anywhere close to normally again.

From a business point of view, there was also no guarantee that the hospital would ever be paid for all their services. Nobody wants to make this decision based on money but there are real costs involved here: a veterinarian would have to examine her, determine how to best treat her injuries, and decide the proper drugs and dosages to administer. He or she would also need to monitor Olivia's response and decide if and when she needed more. Our little dog would also need an IV catheter that costs about 20 dollars, and medicine that is relatively cheap but requires someone to stand and administer it effectively and then monitor afterward. Realistically, the hospital's cost for the first day of her care would be in the hundreds of dollars. Not nearly as much as Mona, Alexa, and I were going to cost but eventually into the thousands of dollars.

Unlike human hospitals, there is no government assistance for the veterinary ER treating Olivia; the cost would come directly out of the pocket of the hospital owners if they didn't get paid. Of course, they had no way of knowing if we, the owners now broken and struggling to survive, would have a dime left to spend on a dog that may never come back from this major of an injury.

Without permission to do any treatment, they decided to administer the drugs needed to stabilize her but not do any diagnostics such as X-rays or bloodwork. They would have to keep their costs down but would do what was humane: stop her seizures and keep her pain under control.

The paramedic had tears in his eyes as he handed off our helpless pet. "Please do everything you can to save her. These kids may lose their dad tonight and don't need to lose their dog also. I don't make a ton of money but here is $165 dollars, all the cash I have on me, if they can't pay."

He was another angel sent to us that day. Not only had he been part of the team that got us to the hospital, but he had taken it upon himself to help this scruffy little dog that likely had little chance of survival. Now he volunteered to give up some of his own paycheck for a family he didn't know because he just couldn't bear to let the kids lose their dog. Yes, another angel.

The emergency hospital took her in. The vet on call checked her over and determined that there were no broken bones except for a possible skull fracture and an obvious bruise to her left eye. The bones on the side of her face felt intact but she had major head trauma. If the bones of the skull had broken, the pieces did not appear to have moved significantly and would not need surgery; they would be left to heal on their own. Dogs have much more muscle around their heads than we do and so the bones heal much faster. There was obvious brain injury with the seizures and the fact that she was unconscious, along with the history of being ejected from a vehicle onto the interstate. They would have done an MRI to ascertain the extent of the damage if they knew they would be paid for it, but for now they would just stabilize her.

The doctor ordered a catheter to be set in her front leg and a bolus of valium to be given. She calculated a dose guessing at Olivia's weight (vets get pretty good at guessing weights on dogs). The exact dose of medication didn't matter anyway since there is a wide range that can be given and, in the end, is administered until the seizing stops or the top end of the dose is reached. The doctor made a quick calculation (ER doctors know the dosage of anti-seizure drugs by heart); an eight-pound dog is about four kilograms and the middle of the dose range is a milligram per kilogram. That's four milligrams of valium, the concentration of valium in the vial is ten milligrams per milliliter so she would get about 0.4 milliliters in the IV. If the seizures continued, she could get another 0.2 milliliters until they stopped up to a total of 1.2 ml's (the high end of the dose). If this did not stop the seizures, she would administer another drug and put her into a coma. Dogs with this kind of injury often die fairly quickly as the brain swells and the seizing becomes uncontrollable. Still, they would do the best they possibly could.

After the first bolus of valium was given, Olivia was transported to a cage for observation. But before they could even place her inside, she threw a seizure again, prompting them to give her more of the drug. Afterward, she fell unconscious, her breathing slowing to a point that made everyone nervous, yet she kept going. This tiny little dog was surviving for the moment.

She was also given a bolus of steroids. The steroids used in situations like this are not the anabolic steroids that bodybuilders use but a cortisone type steroid which works completely differently. These are normally secreted by the body in response to "stressful events" and are potent anti-inflammatories. Obviously, all of us had lots of steroids in our systems with all the "stress" we were enduring but she needed even higher levels. The goal was to stop the swelling in the brain due to the injury and stop the seizures. Any swelling in the brain is a problem because it is fully encased within the bones of the skull. As the brain swells, there is no place for it to go and the nerve tissue is pressed against the bone. Pressure will damage the sensitive connections of the brain and kill brain cells, resulting in permanent injury. The worst case scenario is that the swelling gets so bad that the brain will press through the only exit point available: the hole at the back of the skull where the spinal cord exits. This is called the foramen magnum.

This phenomenon is known as "brain herniation" because the brain (actually the part called the brainstem that controls the most basic functions like breathing and heartrate) is pushed through the narrow opening and crushed. The heartbeat and breathing stop and the patient dies. This condition is *always* fatal. The vets knew they had to stop the brain swelling ASAP. They gave her the steroid injection and waited to see if it would work. They had done all they could do for her; it was in God's hands now.

The paramedic had told them about the crash so the receptionist began calling hospitals. Figuring I'd been taken to the University, she started there. She was told that, yes, there was a family brought in after a terrible car crash but there was not yet anyone available who could talk with them. They were currently working on stabilizing the parents and the family had been notified. The family was hours away yet but they would pass on the message as soon as possible. It was likely the kids would likely lose a parent today; anything they could do to save the little dog would be greatly appreciated.

Hours later, the hospital receptionist went to tell my family about Olivia. She approached my mother, Diane, who was still pale and crying from realizing the extent of our injuries, but had had some time to process everything.

"I know your son and daughter-in-law are your biggest concern but I wanted to let you know that the animal ER in town called and they have their little dog. She is alive but has a head injury. They wanted me to tell you she is stable for now but she may not survive."

My mother just nodded. She knew how much the kids loved that little dog but she just couldn't think about the family pets right now.

The receptionist turned to leave.

"Wait," Mom spoke up, "what about the other dog?"

The woman turned back to face her with a puzzled expression.

"They only mentioned a small, tan dog. Was there another?"

"Yes," she continued, "there would have been a Golden Retriever with them also."

"Sorry, they did not mention another dog. Just the one."
Grandma went to tell the kids who still hadn't grasped the seriousness of Mona's and my condition and were very worried about their dogs. Knowing that Olivia was in the hospital and alive sent them off running and yelling for joy. That is, until Victoria asked,
"What about Annabelle?"

"They did not say where she was," Grandma replied. "Maybe she is at a different hospital."

With that, the celebration was over. The kids' hearts sank as they realized nobody knew what had become of our Golden Retriever; she was still missing. Victoria had seen her take off at a full run as soon as the doors to the van had opened. Preoccupied with the human occupants, no one on the scene had stopped her. Now she was gone. Annabelle was a great dog in many ways but there was no stopping her when she panicked. She had been last seen diving into a cornfield next to the highway. Our dog was 80 miles away from home, wandering around outside in October in Wisconsin. The temperature would drop tonight into the 30s when she would normally be safe and warm inside the house. Now Annabelle was completely on her own.

All the family could do was wait. There was a good chance by morning they'd have to break the news to the kids that their parents were no longer able to care for them and that they would have to leave everything they knew behind to go live somewhere else. At the very least, it seemed more likely they would have to deal with the loss of their dad and the prospect of life without a father. Their world was now being shaken to its core. A few hours ago, their biggest concern was who got to choose the movie to watch on the way home. In the blink of an eye, one of their parents could very well pass away while the other might never walk again, and both their dogs were either injured or missing. Every face they saw had the look of dread, as if everyone around them was hiding something that they didn't want to say.

I, of course, was unaware of anything that was going on; the kids had seen it all. They would remember everything.

# Chapter 11

## ∞ Day Two ∞

The second day brought some good news: Mona was becoming more lucid. She was recognizing the people around her and had stopped repeating herself. Another specialist was brought in to evaluate her brain function. She was told at the start of the exam to remember four things seen in the room – a pen, a table, a chair, and a pillow. Then she was asked to repeat those four things. She started with the pen but then stopped, unable to remember the other three. For someone whose entire life revolved around remembering things – her job, her clients' names and cases, the animals entrusted to her care, her three children – this was troubling to say the least. *If she lost her ability to remember even the slightest details like a few objects in a room, how could she ever go back to being a vet and a mother?*

The neurologist tested a few basic reflexes before excusing herself, the exam concluded. As she turned to leave she advised Mona she'd be back in a week to retest; only then would she be able to determine if this memory loss would be long- or short-term. If Mona could pass the test in a week, great; if not, she would be looking at a very long road to recovery (if ever she ever did recover).

My wife was in full panic mode now: a brain injury would be catastrophic. If I died or could not regain the ability to work and she could not remember even the simplest detail, we would have to sell the clinic and she would have to go on disability. Since our income would plummet, she would likely have to sell the house and eventually move closer to family for help with raising the kids. She loved where we lived now and the disruption would be very hard on everyone, especially if I was dead or not the man that I had been. The *"what-ifs"* were terrifying.

Luckily, she had not yet fully comprehended all that had happened. She knew the kids were OK and under the temporary care of family. Although she'd been apprised of my injuries, her brain hadn't stored the information. She asked if I could be brought down to see her not realizing that I was presently on a respirator with multiple broken bones yet to be fixed. For the umpteenth time, her sister Carla patiently recounted the previous day's events for her. Mona had no recollection whatsoever that the doctors had brought her to me to say goodbye the night before. She was still experiencing acute pain, eased by a morphine drip that further clouded her mind. This would take a while.

The most important thing was that her spinal cord was intact and her brain function had not worsened. Yes, the recovery process would be long and grueling but she was not going to die. Our kids would have at least one parent.

As for me, I was becoming more stable but had been put in a coma and would stay there for the first three days while the doctors put me back together, one bone at a time.

First, the thighbone had to be plated. Initially, Dr. Schumacher had placed the external fixator on the leg to keep it from flopping around but the bones were not really aligned well. Therefore, in spite of the fact it could heal like this, the leg would be unable to bend at the knee, rendering it pretty much useless. It was decided that a plate would work better because it would allow the knee to bend during recovery. Since my condition had stabilized some more and the antibiotics had had some time to work on where the bone had exited the skin, Dr. Lang decided to remove the external fixator and apply a bone plate.

The thighbone had a number of problems. First, it had shattered at about the lower third of the bone and the fracture had extended down through the knee. There were multiple bone pieces present while still others were missing, having been blown out the side of my leg. The knee part of the bone was cracked in half. Also, that torn femoral vein had to be tied off once and for all.

The rule with fixing any bone is that you must stabilize the ends. It will heal as long as the two ends – in this case the upper and lower parts of the bone – are held in place without moving and have some bridge of bone to connect them. In my scenario, three inches in the middle of the thighbone that had shattered, leaving multiple shards. These were too small to be reconstructed and so would just be left loosely in place to become a framework for the new bone that would grow into the gap. This would work as long as the bone ends were held stable, because even a tiny amount of movement of the bone ends would slow the healing and/or prevent the bone from healing at all. The plate would be the best option.

Dr. Lang began by first removing the external fixator that had been placed previously. The pins that were placed into the bone and clamped together held the leg in place for the initial stabilization but now needed to be replaced with a more exact fixation. A bone plate allows better positioning of the bones and faster use of the leg. External fixators work well where the pins do not have to go through a lot of muscle such as the forearm or shin. The thigh is different – it is completely surrounded by muscle, forcing the pins to pass through all of this muscle mass before encountering the bone. This process holds the muscle to the bone and prevents its movement. Eventually, the muscle heals down to the bone and is unable to slide across it. Thus, the knee would be locked into position and useless, with muscle pinned to bone.

Dr. Lang deduced a plate would work much better. It would be placed directly over the bone and would not damage any muscle. This would enable the muscle to continue to slide and the knee to bend during recovery. I would be able to do some rehab and use a wheelchair until the bone was healed.

He removed the external fixator but before he plated the bone, he knew he'd have to fix the torn femoral vein that nearly killed me a day ago once and for all. The temporary bandage he'd wrapped into the wound had gotten me through the first day but it could not stay there forever.

Blood-soaked sponges were removed and the wound scrubbed with surgical prep to disinfect the area. Infection was a huge risk. Anytime you plan on putting foreign objects into a body – in this case the plate – you must prepare for the likely outcome of infection. Infected "hardware" is seldom cleared by antibiotics and usually has to be removed because the bacteria embed into the metal and stay there. My medical team knew this wound was contaminated since the bone had protruded out through the skin. It was scrubbed once when I first came in but they would scrub it again to remove any contamination and bacteria remaining in the area. Above all, the plate MUST NOT get infected.

The approach to the bone and vein was already mostly done. The bone had shredded the muscle on the outside of the thigh as the ends exited the leg; Dr. Lang had opened it some more when he initially tried to get to the source of the bleeding. Now he just had to follow the torn muscle to the bone ends and the torn vessel. With the external fixator off, my doctor bent my leg past 90 degrees at the fracture, leaving the foot pointing out sideways and slightly toward my head to better expose the vessel. My foot was now crossing the other leg and hanging off the side of the table, held up by an assistant. Although a grossly unnatural position, it worked. The fractured bone end was now easily exposed and the muscle bellies could be separated to find the vessel lying deep within them.

The torn vessel had retracted back into the muscle and disappeared, making it even harder to find. However, Dr. Lang had an advantage: the vein was torn but the artery was still intact. These two normally lie right next to each other so if you follow the artery it will lead to the vein. Better yet, the artery was easy to find. It was as big as my index finger and it had a pulse. Feel for the pulse and you find the artery; follow the artery and you find the vein.

The other advantage my doctor had? Many of the muscle bellies of the leg were already torn. In fact, the muscles on the outside half of the leg were completely ripped in half, creating much better exposure than he would normally have. This meant he could push the muscle further up the leg to expose the hidden vessel underneath. The skin had to be incised to see adequately but the muscle underneath was already torn away and had had a day to stop bleeding. Additionally, Dr. Lang was no longer working under the intense rush and pressure of trying to stop the bleeding before I died.

A large clot covered the entire area, filling the void where the muscle had been. It was the clot that had initially saved my life – my body's way to fight back, to stop the bleeding that had been killing me. With the pressure initially applied by the dashboard, then by Robert the flight nurse, and finally by Dr. Lang's bandage, the bleeding had slowed enough for the clot to form. It had filled the hole in the muscle forming a plug and had afforded the doctors the time they needed to save me.

But now this life-saving clot had to be removed because the torn vein could bleed again at any time – a possibility that required the doctor to secure it at last. As Dr. Lang began peeling the clot out of the defect, the blood immediately began to flow again. Within seconds, it filled the defect with fresh blood and buried the vein – making it impossible to find the source. The surgeon called for suction but it could not keep up. It was like trying to plug the end of a hose without shutting off the water; it is much easier if the water is shut off first.

A nurse applied pressure above the tear by grabbing around my upper thigh with both hands and pressing the muscle against the underlying bone. At the same time, Dr. Lang suctioned the wound and continued removing any clots. This time it did not refill, at least not very quickly. Although some blood filtered in from some small bleeders, the main source had been controlled. The nurse squeezed hard to keep pressure on the vein.

Now Dr. Lang could try to identify the vein itself. It was not easy to find because it was buried in a mass of torn muscle and connective tissue – all of which were oozing blood and obscuring the view. When Dr. Lang still could not see the vessel, he used another trick: he instructed his assistant to let some pressure off the leg. Of course, the bleeding started all over again but this time more slowly. Now with the blood clot cleared away and the bleeding slowed, he could better localize the source. The process was akin to turning a hose on and off to find the end: you stop the flow and clean it up, then turn the hose on again, narrowing down the suspected area until you achieve your goal.

The assistant applied pressure again while Dr. Lang cleaned out the wound. At this point, he could better focus on the spot from which the blood originated. The vein was located somewhere in that region. Again, the pressure was partially released and the blood began to trickle out of the vein. Now able to see it, Dr. Lang reached for a clamp. He pushed more muscle away trying to grab the vein without grabbing anything else but the clamp slipped off and the blood flowed again. Lang swore through his mask. "Suction!" he ordered, and tried again, a second time grabbing more aggressively and higher up the vein. He could feel the resistance as the clamp caught hold. The vein is large and thick and he could feel the clamp was unable to fully close because there was too much vein in the way. He had a good grip. He smiled under his mask as the assistant suctioned away the blood. For the first time since I had arrived at the hospital, the hole in my leg did not refill. At last, the moment of truth: Dr. Lang instructed his assistant to release the pressure on the thigh she had been squeezing further up the leg. No more blood; he had it.

Now it was a matter of carefully isolating the vein and tying it off. Slowly, he picked away at any other tissue caught in the clamp, moving muscle and surrounding connective tissue out of the way. My expert surgeon knew it was critical when tying off a vessel of this size that there is nothing else tied into the suture – catch a chunk of muscle in the tie and you risk pulling the suture off the vessel and having to start all over again. Not to mention having to tell the patient, their family, and all your colleagues that your patient bled to death because the suture you tied didn't hold. Of course, he would feel terrible having lost the patient, but surgeons also take great pride in their reputations among their fellow doctors and the medical staff. A surgeon whose knots slip off would be incredibly embarrassed and feel like an idiot – all because of not taking the time to ensure he did it correctly. Dr. Lang had learned to be absolutely thorough and to do things right.

He carefully placed two ties of absorbable suture material around the vessel, each separated by about a quarter-inch. He used one additional "trick" to keep the ties in place; the tie closest to the end was also "transfixed." That is, the suture was tied and then passed through – not around – the vessel and tied a second time. It could not possibly slide off the vessel since it was now both tied around and *transfixed* through the vein.

With the bleeding under control, it was time to get the bone back together, at least as much as possible. With a minimum of five separate pieces to reassemble, it was like a 3D jigsaw puzzle. Dr. Lang could place a plate across the fracture allowing screws to hold most of the pieces back in place, but he needed both ends of the plate to have at least two screws above and below the fracture line in order to be successful. Otherwise, the bone fragments can rotate around the single screw and destabilize the fracture. And unstable fractures don't heal.

The problem was that the lower part of the bone (the part that forms the knee) had split in half; there was no solid piece to hold the end of the plate. Before the plate could be placed, the end of the bone comprising the knee would have to be put back together so the plate could then be secured to it.

If Dr. Lang could screw together the pieces and reform the knee, then a plate could be placed to reconnect the knee to the thighbone. It would be critical that the pieces of the knee lined up exactly so the surfaces are not irregular and the kneecap has a smooth place to slide. If the joint is not realigned perfectly, the cartilage won't heal, creating bone-on-bone contact. The knee will be painful and never function well. Dr. Lang had to get it right.

He meticulously cleared blood clots from the pieces so they could start to fit back together and tried to squeeze them together. Try as he might, the pieces just didn't fit right; there was something in the way. He attempted to press them together harder, with no luck. If they did not fit back together perfectly, the knee would be a constant problem. He would have to make it worse to make it better.

Dr. Lang pulled the pieces apart but could only separate them by a quarter inch. That's when he called for a retractor, a small instrument that fits between the bone pieces and wrests them apart. A few clicks later and they separated, stretching the surrounding muscle and tissue. Now with his hands free, he used a probe to explore the gap, with no success. He separated the pieces further so he could get his finger in the fracture. Despite all of his fancy equipment, the best tool he had was his pinky. At last he could feel it – a small chunk of bone had broken off and was blocking the two pieces from fitting together. It was off the back of the knee away from where he was working. If he could grab it, it could be removed. He would have to reattach it if there was something important connected to it (a ligament for example) but Dr. Lang knew, based on its location, that there was nothing there but some muscle. The loss of this small bit of muscle would not be a problem. He grabbed the piece with a clamp. With a pull and a few twists to tear the muscle away, the piece was gone. It rattled when he tossed it into the instrument tray. Fixing bones is not always a delicate procedure.

Now he could put the two pieces together again. Lining them up, he removed the retractor and pressed the pieces together. Now they fit perfectly. With the alignment corrected, the jagged bones of the fracture locked back together like those aforementioned 3D puzzle pieces. A few screws would keep it them that way. Dr. Lang clamped across the entire bone and start drilling holes for the screws. Three screws were placed across the bone to hold it together with care taken to leave a spot for the plate to be attached. The end of the bone was now solid; the first step was over.

Putting the rest of the bone together would not be an easy feat since the entire middle third had shattered. Dr. Lang started to sort the pieces out. From about half way down the thigh to about three inches above the knee, the bone was completely smashed; some of the pieces were crushed beyond recognition. There was no putting Humpty Dumpty (me) back together again. Even worse, it soon became apparent that a crucial piece was missing. The bone shard had shot through the muscle and out the side of the leg. The crash had generated a tremendous amount of energy to shatter a large bone like this; one of the fragments must have torn through the skin and freed itself from of all its muscular attachments. Most likely, this bone fragment was rolling around the floor of the car somewhere. However, there was no need to see if anyone could find it because just as when a finger is cut off and unattached from the body for any length of time, it was now too late to put the bone back into my body. It would be dead. Therefore, I'd have to heal without it.

Since not all of the pieces could be reassembled, the goal would now be to hold the two ends – one from the hip to the middle of the thigh and the other at the knee – in place and let the middle part "just heal." A special bone plate was used that would span the shattered part of bone. The plate holds the ends in place until the pieces can "knit" themselves together underneath. I would have to rely on the plate to bear all my weight until the bone was healed so the team employed a bigger, thicker plate made out of titanium. Despite the strength of this plate, it still would not support a 170-pound man; I would be in a wheelchair or crutches for two- to- three months.

Three screws through the top of the plate and two more through the bottom fixed the plate to the bone. These would bear all the weight for the bone during the healing process.

Dr. Lang had one more trick up his sleeve: he wanted to help fill in the missing bone. Normally, this defect would be replaced with a bone graft. A graft is basically comprised of small chunks of bone that are placed in a gap to speed up healing. The graft is packed into the area of missing bone to act as the scaffolding for the new bone to grow into. Usually, the bone graft is "harvested" from somewhere else in the body like the pelvis or the other leg bone. A hole is made in the hard exterior of the bone and a metal scoop (it looks much like a small melon-baller) is used to dig out the soft, spongy bone underneath. The problem is that bone grafts takes time and create another site for infection – plus they hurt like hell.

Dr. Lang decided not to bother with a graft because he had a better way. He used Bone Morphogenetic Protein; this is a hormone that tells bone to grow and stimulates it to fill in what is missing. It is soaked into a collagen sponge that will eventually be absorbed. No more digging bone out of the pelvis. The doctor's assistant opened a package and shoved the sponge into the hole where the bone was missing. It took just seconds – versus a half-hour to get a bone graft. Now he have to would wait and see if bone could fill in and heal.

With the vein tied off and the bone fixed, he could now address the torn muscle. The muscle on the outside of the thigh had exploded as the bone was driven through it and remained in tatters. Much like crabmeat, there was no sewing it back together. Suture that Lang attempted to place across it just pulled through and held nothing. Although he tried numerous times, the torn muscle simply would not hold. Something different was required.

The first suture was placed across each end to the torn muscle, perpendicular to the fibers, but not tied. This allowed a second and third suture to be placed but again not tied. Finally, a fourth suture was placed and slowly tightened. The knee was kept straight to relieve any tension on the muscle and to shorten the gap. The sutures were each tied with just enough tension to pull the muscle together without tearing through. How much tension they needed to apply was all about feel. As my surgery instructor told me, "Just a little less than when it gives way." Of course he was kidding since you only know when it "gives way" when it actually does; there is no way to predict where a "little less" than this will be. It is all about when the muscle "feels" like the suture will pull through.

Dr. Lang carefully tightened the sutures one at a time, placing about a dozen. The team covered the fracture site as the muscles were pulled together as well as they possibly could but it ended up being a large wad of muscle and suture over the outside of the leg. Time would tell if it held but the leg could not be bent until the muscle was healed. Bending the knee would pull on the quadriceps and break the sutures. I would be in a splint to immobilize the knee to let it try to heal back together.

This was enough for one day. My pulses were steady but my blood was still in danger of not clotting again. It was time to get me off the table. I still had two broken elbows, a broken arm, a dislocated and broken shoulder, and a broken pelvis and nose. Dr. Lang put in staples to hold the skin together; they were not pretty but they go in fast. He then announced to the anesthesiologist that he was done; the rest would have to wait.

Meanwhile, Mona spent the day in a drug-induced haze. She was increasingly cognizant and could now really feel the pain, although morphine kept it at bay. It also prevented the realization of what had happened to fully sink in. Therefore, she didn't yet have to deal with my situation and the effect it would have on our lives.

Alexa had received some good news concerning her dog at the veterinary emergency hospital. She'd survived the night, having been medicated in an attempt to stop the seizures, and was still alive. Dr. Chris Welch, our partner at our veterinary hospital, was coming to Madison that day to see us and would stop at the ER to check on Olivia.

Our Golden Retriever Annabelle was still missing but some of the police officers who had helped us at the crash were coming back during their time off to look for her. These officers were complete strangers to us: we did not live in their community and the fields were muddy and cold. These angels went anyway to search for our lost dog.

The kids knew their mom was pretty banged up but saw she was talking so were not too worried. They hadn't seen me yet and really did not comprehend the extent of our injuries; their worry was focused on the dogs. For them, losing their beloved pets would be heartbreaking. There was nothing to tell them yet; nobody really knew the fate of our family dogs. The doctors couldn't predict Mona's and my final outcome either, but at least we were all alive.

The sling Alexa's broken arm had been placed in was causing concern among the surgeons because the bones were not in the right position but were instead overlapping. They had hoped that the weight of the arm would pull the bones back into place but that hadn't happened. The doctors had no choice but to ask Mona for permission to perform surgery.

Alexa's mother was really in no shape to make any decisions so her sister Carla had to make the call. Our daughter was only 10 years-old and surgery is always a concern. Additionally, Alexa HATES needles. Carla carefully explained to Mona that her child needed surgery and Mona nodded her head. Everyone knew that Mona was not really understanding the question but this was all the doctors needed. They allowed Carla to sign a release.

Now Carla went to retrieve Alexa, who freaked upon hearing she'd have to have an operation. She began to panic and vehemently refused. Carla tried to calm her down by assuring her it would be alright and that her arm would feel better. Alexa was in a great deal of pain with the broken arm and the pieces could be felt moving whenever she did anything. She had seen me fix a lot of broken bones at our hospital so she knew about placing pin or plates across broken bones.

Eventually, Alexa relented but panicked again when the nurses came in to set an IV. Again, Carla was there to hold her and make her look the other way. Luckily, the nurse was good and hit the vein easily. The IV was in before she knew it.

Quickly, the nurse administered a sedative and Alexa started to relax. Within 30 minutes she was being wheeled into the O.R. for surgery. With her fully anesthetized and her body strapped to the table, an assistant put a steady pull on her arm to straighten it. The muscles had tightened and the bones resisted being moved. The arm would have to be stretched until the bones could be realigned. The assistant kept up a steady pull waiting for the muscles to tire and allow the bones to move.

It took a few minutes of steady pressure but the muscles finally relaxed. The surgeon bent her arm severely at the break to get the bone ends to overlap much like Dr. Lang had done to get my broken thigh into position. He bent the arm at the fracture until the ends could be overlapped and then the arm was straightened. The jagged bone edges locked together as the bone came back together. A bit of rotation and the fracture ends lined up perfectly. Unlike my fractured leg, Alexa's only had two pieces to get together, which easily aligned. The surgeon drove three stainless steel pins from her shoulder into the middle of the bone and across the fracture and down to just above the elbow to hold it all in place.

He was careful not to drive the pins too far and force them into the elbow joint. Since the pin is buried in the bone and its end cannot be seen, he used a second pin of equal length to judge just where the end of the pin ended up. Once it was driven as far as needed, the extra length was cut off and made smooth with a grinder similar to a dremel you get at the hardware store. In Alexa's case, the pins were left outside the skin so they could be easily removed later. She would spend the next month in a sling but should heal quickly; youth was on her side.

We had all made it through another day. The risk of anyone dying was decreasing by the hour. The doctors still could not say how "normal" we would be but at least it looked like we would survive. When our families heard of the crash, they had all prayed for our survival. Nobody had dared to ask if we would return to normalcy. At this point, it looked like their prayers would be answered; we would definitely live.

Scot Hodkiewicz

# Chapter 12

## ∞ God's Will Be Done ∞

Over the next few days they would fix my elbows and shoulder. I was still in a medically induced coma and hadn't awakened since I'd arrived at the hospital. Once again, they wheeled me into surgery while my family stood vigil. They all sat waiting, knowing that my small steps forward could, at any moment, turn into a huge step back. My heart could fail, I could throw a clot and have a stroke, I could have a problem with anesthesia – so many things could go wrong that everyone held their breath every time I went in to the OR. All they could do was wait and pray. Pray that I would make it through one more day. Pray that Mona's brain would continue to improve, that her broken back would not shift, making her legs go numb. The ever-present tension of the last few days continued unabated. Nobody really slept and everyone was quiet.

As they sat in silence, the same question reverberated through all of their minds: *"Why?"* Why did this happen to *their* loved ones? We were a nice family, we never made enemies, we went to church on Sundays (some of the time), and we worked to help injured and sick animals. Surely we didn't deserve to be crushed in an auto accident by a drunken scumbag, especially one that walked away with nothing but a scratched nose. Everyone struggled to make sense of it all.

About two hours later, a nurse walked into the waiting area to announce I'd made it through another one. Another piece of *Humpty Dumpty* had been put back together. Tomorrow my arm upper would be plated and my shoulder put back into place. The day after that, my nose would be set.

I still had a couple of pelvic fractures but my medical team decided these would be left to heal on their own. Encased in muscle, the pelvis heals well. The biggest muscles in the body are in the buttocks. Because of their thick size and great blood supply, these muscles help to hold everything in place. Good blood supply and stable breaks allow for bone to heal well; therefore, they expected the pelvis to fully recover on its own in a few weeks without any medical assistance. I would be flat on my back for two months anyway; these breaks were the least of my worries.

Being in a medical coma, nobody had a clue as to my mental status. Was my brain going to work again? Would I be the same person as before or would I be unable to think or speak? This was the elephant in the room that nobody wanted to talk about.

*What if, after all this work, and all these surgeries, I never woke up? What if I didn't remember who I was or what I did for a living?*

My profession demanded the use of an incredible amount of information every day; what if I was not able to retrieve it anymore? Bones could be put back together and would heal in a few months but the brain is an entirely different thing. I had been impacted at 70 miles per hour and though I hit an airbag, it was only a one-foot thick pillow. My brain was severely concussed. I would be in too much pain if they woke me up yet but they decided to give it a try in 24 hours. Tomorrow, they would bring me around just enough to see if I was still there. For now, they'd keep me in a coma to facilitate my recovery from this latest surgery. As I slept, the rest of my family could do nothing but wait and continue to pray. Tomorrow would be the day they'd discover if they had lost the husband, father, brother, or son they had always known. Tonight it was just more waiting.

As I slept, our church pastors Mark and Mary Ann arrived. This husband-and-wife team had taken over a dying church a few years before we got to town. At the time, membership was less than one-hundred and the average age of the congregants was over seventy. Torn apart by internal bickering and a complete loss of mission, the church was in total disarray; Mark and Mary Ann had been sent to save it.

Upon their arrival, these enthusiastic pastors had great visions of cultivating a youth program. They would offer a Sunday school that was fun and engaging, along with Bible camps, and retreats for the teenagers. Their natural energy was infectious. This would be a youth-centered church.

Of course, God had sent them here specifically, which meant it would not be easy. They spent the first few weeks heartbroken, wondering if they had made the right choice. Although they had worked their whole lives with the goal of leading a church that fulfilled their vision of ministering to the youth, they had discovered that there could be no Children's Christmas Choir the first year. How could there be? There were no kids in the congregation – not one.

Mark and Mary Ann had faced what we were facing now; their plan for their lives and their church looked like it was not meant to be. How could they have a young, vibrant church when they had no kids or even young couples attending?

God had a plan; it just was not *their* plan. Their job was to accept it.

They had immediately won people over with their energy and faith. By focusing solely on the church's mission of bringing people to Christ, they completely changed the culture and ended the squabbling. With that, the church took off. Mark and Mary Ann retained the traditional service with its slow, somber hymns for the older members, but added a contemporary service complete with a rockin' band and loud, upbeat music.

At first, the band consisted of a piano player and a single vocalist. Many times they only had less than a dozen congregants in the seats. But soon, new people began to show up: word was spreading quickly about this new church that *celebrated* on Sundays. They made church fun and pertinent, focusing the sermons on real-life problems. Pastor Mark even made sure to leave a few windows open and the door slightly ajar during the more modern service. He wanted the music to emanate outside to allow people down the street to hear it – a little free advertising that things had changed.

In the six years since we had known them, the church had grown exponentially and there were dozens of kids now singing in the Christmas services. Mark and Mary Ann exuded love and compassion and had come to offer their prayers and support as soon as they had heard the news of our crash.

They walked in and introduced themselves to my family just as the doctors were leaving. The surgery to fix my elbows had gone well but since elbows are notoriously unforgiving, I would likely not get back full range of motion in either side. I would have to be in splints for a month, which would cause my joints to scar down. Before I could ever gain the use of my arms again, I would need more months of rehab and possibly even more surgeries.

When asked if I would be able to work or if the damage was too severe, the doctors just shrugged; they simply had no idea.
Pastors Mark and Mary Ann knew not to stay long. The family was under a great deal of stress and did not need a long, protracted visit from strangers. After my sister Julie updated them on our conditions,

they requested that everyone bow their heads and join hands for a prayer, prompting a slight hesitation I could have easily predicted had I been awake. My family is very conservative in some ways; we do not touch each other much. It is more customary for us to *fold* our hands for prayer, not *hold* hands. However, Mark and Mary Ann persisted until my parents, sisters and brothers-in-law awkwardly grasped each other's hands. They then all bowed their heads. As the monitors beeped and the ventilator gave me breaths, they prayed for healing and strength. Mark prayed for all of us to make it through this difficult time and accept God's will. He prayed that we'd remain faithful in our understanding that there is a higher plan – *His* plan that we cannot see or anticipate. We just needed to accept these trials and use them to strengthen our faith and bring us closer to God. He ended with, "God's will be done."

With that, they headed to Mona's room where she was now being weaned off the morphine. A side effect of those drugs is lack of GI (gastro-intestinal) motility i.e. your guts slow to a crawl. Over the last few days she had become terribly bloated and constipated as indicated by her distended abdomen. Her brain was still not functioning well and she was still in the haze of lingering morphine, which had altered her personality, making her combative and paranoid. Mona was now convinced that the nurses were sending drugs through the inflatable compression stockings placed on her legs to keep her blood moving and to prevent clots from forming. She was absolutely certain that they were all conspiring in the nurse's station to overmedicate her and keep her sedated.

Of course, the nurses were doing no such thing and even if they wanted to, they would not be infusing drugs through the compression stockings. Since Mona had an IV, any necessary drugs would be administered through that.

Mona did not care. While the drugs may have made her delusional, simultaneously her thoughts made perfect sense to her. All the consoling and reasoning of her family didn't help. In fact, it just proved that they were all in on it together. Everyone was lying to her, preventing her from getting up and going home, and keeping her drugged: she was sure of it.

As the pastors came in, she was being wheeled for a CT scan to evaluate her abdominal distension. She truly believed it was due to uncontrolled and undiagnosed internal bleeding and she was dying.

This was further confirmed in her mind because she had gotten her period (this commonly happens after major trauma) and was obviously bleeding internally.

Of course being a doctor, she would have known this was not a sign of internal bleeding and that the distension was a side effect of morphine, had she been thinking clearly. But in her altered mental state she'd convinced herself that the doctors were all sitting around doing nothing while she slowly bled to death. She was dying and they were just not telling her. She called for her sister Carla and had a long discussion about her taking the kids after she was gone.

All this was going on as Pastors Mark and Mary Ann entered the room and tried to say a prayer. Sensing that this was a bad time, they prayed with the family as a nurse came in and sedated Mona for the CT scan.

"Don't worry," the nurse assured them, "it is just the drugs talking and making her bloated. We will get her off of them as soon as possible."

Mark and Mary Ann repeated the prayer they had said for me asking for strength and acceptance that there was something bigger going on, something we simply do not have the means to understand, all part of "God's greater plan."

Knowing that this was not a great time for them to be there, they advised her mother Anne that they would visit again in a few days and keep the congregation informed. Eventually, the congregation would form the backbone of the support we needed. For now, all they could do was pray but that they did with gusto. Mark and Mary Anne spread the word that we needed prayer and the congregation responded. They not only said prayers at the services but also formed prayer chains where members asked family and friends – most of whom did not even know us – to pray also. There were people praying constantly for us, not because they all knew us or had taken their animals to our veterinary practice, but because they cared and had faith that it would help. We had worked hard to become part of the community; now the community would be there for us.

# Chapter 13

## ∞ Can I Go Back To My Coma, Please ∞

After fixing the elbows, they were ready to wake me up. They still needed to repair my shoulder but it was time to see if I was still there.

Waking someone from a medically induced coma is an agonizing waiting game. The doctors stop the drugs and wait for them to wear off while the entire family sits in the room hoping for some sign I was still the son or brother that they knew. With each passing minute and no reaction from me, they couldn't help but believe that the Scot they knew was never coming back. The thought that this was as good as I would ever get crept into everyone's minds, though no one would dare admit it out loud. They kept telling themselves that it was just the drugs and I needed more time, but the thought of permanent brain damage kept hounding them, becoming increasingly frequent as time dragged on. No response, no sign that I could feel any pain, or that I could hear their persistent voices trying to wake me.

"Scot, time to wake up," my sister Julie kept repeating.

No response.

"Scot, time to wake up."

Nothing.

My parents sat across the room, fear etched plainly on their exhausted faces. It had been four days and they had barely slept. They were both nearing 70 years-old; the consuming dread that their only son may be forever changed crushed their spirits. After all of their constant prayers for some kind of sign I'd come back, they got nothing in return.

The minutes dragged on.

It takes massive amounts of drugs to keep someone in a coma. This is not just sedation or sleep but the actual shutting off of the brain. The brain fights hard against the drugs because it is always trying to sense and feel. That's why it takes a massive dose to induce a coma. When the drugs are stopped, it takes a long time for them to disappear.

My family gathered around my bed and waited. Mona's family stood in the hallway outside knowing that the next few hours would determine their fate as well. There was complete silence except for the beep of the monitors and Julie's voice every few minutes trying to wake me up. Occasionally, someone would break the silence with some nervous chatter about their schedule and how long they could take time off from work but they all had other things on their minds. Today would determine how we would all spend the rest of our lives. If I wasn't there mentally, who would take care of me? Mona and I lived about two hours from my nearest family and eight hours from her parents; there was just nobody close by to help out for a long period of time. Rearranging schedules for a few weeks was one thing, but months or years of around-the-clock care would be impossible. They all sat and waited.

Mona was not in the room – the one who would be the most impacted by my recovery or lack thereof. She was in a back brace now and had had surgery on her elbow to repair a fracture. Under the influence of heavy pain medication she was sleeping soundly in her room, unaware that they were trying to wake me up. Her concussion was resolving and her brain resetting but she was confined to the bed. Her back injury made it very difficult to move her because every time she was taken out of bed there was a chance that her spinal fracture could displace and cause paralysis. Getting out of bed was not an option. Additionally, she was still on a lot of morphine and though able to answer questions, did not truly comprehend what was going on around her. So it was decided that Mona would not be present when I came out of the coma. Her sisters stayed with her while her brother and brother-in-law kept the kids busy. My family watched and waited.

It took about two-and-a-half hours after they stopped the drugs. They kept the morphine going so that I would not come out screaming but stopped the drugs that kept me unconscious. Because morphine specifically blocks pain, I would definitely still need it, but they had to let my brain start working again.

The doctors stood ready to see if I could breathe on my own. If not, they would re- insert the tube and put me back on the ventilator. They would also know that I would likely be a vegetable. Breathing was one of the most basic brain activities. If I couldn't do that, I wouldn't be able to do much else; I would likely never wake up.

As I came around, my body first realized that there was something in my throat. I began to gag and cough as I tried to expel the tube they had inserted to keep me breathing. The nurse gently pulled it out and the coughing abated. I took my first independent breath since Robert had inserted a tube in my throat on the helicopter flight in. Everyone in the room was excited. At least I could breathe on my own and would not need a respirator. But the doctors reiterated that this did not mean there was no serious brain damage; I could still be a vegetable for the rest of my life. Still, at least that part of my brain was working. So far, so good.

It took about 20 minutes for me to start moving and emerge fully out of the coma. I started with a groan. My sister Julie, a year older than me and my closest sibling in age, continued saying my name and asking me to wake up. This would be my first memory since leaving the cabin three days earlier. Julie was a social worker who specialized in elderly care so she knew how to communicate with people with decreased cognitive function. She kept it very simple telling me only what I needed to know. As my eyes opened she said very plainly, "Scot, you are in the hospital. You were in an accident but Mona and the kids are alright."

At first, I didn't really comprehend what she had said. She repeated it again, "Scot, you are in the hospital. You were in an accident but Mona and the kids are alright."

Slowly, it started to sink in. I was on my back looking at the ceiling. The walls looked like a hospital room, very clean and plain. To my right was the monitoring equipment, an ECG for heart rate, and a pulse oximeter for oxygen level. We used these daily in our hospital so I recognized their rhythmic beep immediately. There was also an IV stand with a fluid bag attached. I was sure that it fed into a catheter somewhere in my right arm.

As my brain processed where I was, I began to take inventory. From the time I was a child, I could only see well out of my right eye. My left eye was so bad that I could not make out the E on the top of the eye chart. I was always terrified that I would lose my good eye and end up legally blind. I looked around taking it all in. I could see pretty clearly so I knew immediately that my one good eye was working. At least I would be able to see.

Julie asked me to squeeze her hand. In a bit of a panic, I thought, "They are asking if I can move, this must be bad."

For me, paralysis had always been another huge fear. I concentrated hard and squeezed. Julie smiled and said, "Good job." I knew that hand worked. She reached over me and held my other hand.

"Now squeeze your right." Again she smiled and said "Good job." She knew I could not only work my hands but that I was understanding her simple instructions also.

Both my arms felt extremely heavy. I was flat on my back and unable to raise my head; I couldn't see that both arms were splinted. I could feel my fingers so I knew the nerves must be working down to my chest.

Next, she asked me to move my toes. I quickly realized that they were checking for paralysis. I concentrated and sent the message for my toes to move praying that they would respond. First, the left toes moved. Then, the right toes. A wave of relief swept over me – I could move all my limbs! I could not comprehend why my arms and legs were so heavy but I didn't care. I knew that as long as I could feel them, the nerves were working. I had no idea how bad everything was but as long as I could feel them, I had a good chance of using them again.

My family watched the process and with every movement felt a wave of relief. By the end, they were all smiling. All the prayers for me were paying off. Not only could I move my limbs, but I could follow instructions. This meant that I was hearing and processing information. I could see; therefore my one good eye must be working. These were primitive tests but at least my brain was functioning at some level. I may not be completely back to normal but I sure could be worse.

I soon found out that there was a downside to being out of the coma: the nurses arrived in my room for the sole purpose of changing my sheets. I had a urinary catheter in place that drained urine into a bag so that was not a problem, but I had numerous open wounds that had to be kept clean. Using a bedpan was out of the question since that would require them to lift me over it; consequently, I had to defecate in the sheets. This wasn't a problem yet since I hadn't eaten for three days but the sheets had to be changed. The two nurses who'd arrived to do it got on one side and rolled me over, pushing the bedding underneath me. My left arm was still not fixed so as they rolled me, I felt (and heard) the bones moving. Being on a high dose of morphine, the pain did not really register but having felt hundreds of broken bones in animals, I remember thinking, "Boy, that's a bad fracture," as the jagged ends of the broken bone in my upper arm popped and ground against each other. It suddenly hit me that what I felt moving were MY bones and that it was MY arm that had this bad fracture. I hadn't realized that my arm was broken until now. I wished for the coma again.

Having established that I could see, hear and think, the nurses gave me more sedation. I needed to rest because there was more surgery scheduled for tomorrow.

My family was thrilled and my mother rushed to tell Mona the good news. I had a long way to go but had cleared another hurdle. At least I would not be a vegetable.

Scot Hodkiewicz

# Chapter 14

## ∞ Please, No Shortcuts ∞

It was time to fix my broken and dislocated shoulder and Dr. Lang would finally finish putting me back together again. His specialty is shoulder surgery so he was in his comfort zone.

He spent over three hours putting the ball of the shoulder joint back into place and then plating it onto the bone. After the bone was reassembled and everything back in place, Dr. Lang worked to reassemble the torn muscles and ligaments. These tears are the "torn rotator cuffs" that people talk about in baseball players. If not fixed, they will lead to pain and loss of movement. My surgeon carefully checked every muscle, tendon, and ligament and carefully repaired anything he found. That took another hour but Dr. Lang wanted it done right. These structures, like the muscles of the leg, have to slide and move to allow normal range so it was vital that they be repaired properly. The doctor knew that this was his chance to get it right if I was to have a good outcome and was determined to do what was best for ME in spite of the long surgery – not what was easiest or quickest for him.

Dedication to his patient is what makes Dr. Lang a *great* doctor, not just a good one. This quality also makes a great teacher, attorney, plumber, builder, etc. You become great at what you do when you do what is right for the one you are serving; you become bad at what you do when the job becomes just a job. When you put your needs – in this case the need to get on to the next surgery or home to the family – in front of the needs of your patient, the recipient of your skill and services. Reconstructing my shoulder would take longer than expected and set him back for the entire day; he would skip lunch to catch up and be over an hour late in getting home but he was going to do it right to enable me to live with as little pain and with as normal a shoulder as possible. He would sleep well tonight knowing that he had done everything he could, that he had taken no shortcuts. How I would turn out was largely out of his control after the surgery; that depended on my physical therapy and some luck, but he had done his part and done it well. It was time to wake me up.

In four days, I had had four major orthopedic surgeries, repaired three dislocated bones, had my spleen removed and bladder repaired, nearly bled to death a few times and been in a coma. Needless to say, I had had better weeks.

# Chapter 15

## ∞ Monkeys In The Room ∞

Every day I got a little stronger but there were still more surgeries to go. My medical team had to clean and debride some wounds and straighten my nose; however, these were relatively minor compared to everything else I'd endured. Mona was allowed to come and see me but neither one of us could move enough to do more than touch hands. Still, I could see she was also going to take a long time to heal. I also knew that, for the time being, she and the kids were on their own. As parents, we would not be able to do much to help our kids get through this hardship. We'd have to rely on family to support us; fortunately, we both had strong ones. Until we could get back to them, the kids would be with grandparents, aunts, and uncles. At least they could have people they trusted around them to make Mom and Dad's absence a little easier.

We decided not to let the kids see me in this state, with two casted arms, two casted legs, major black and blue eyes, and a feeding tube coming out my broken and bandaged nose. They'd already been through enough and didn't need to witness this spectacle; talking on the phone would have to do. My kids were still young enough to believe their dad was indestructible and I didn't have the heart to steal that from them, although I certainly didn't feel indestructible anymore.

My night nurse's name was Andrew – a very dedicated and caring individual whose personality fit perfectly with a night shift. Not only was he professional and kind, but he worked independently. This was critical since he often had very minimal help during his shift. Some people need others around to get all the gossip and social interaction that make work enjoyable, but Andrew did not. He looked to be in his mid-40s and was simply past that time of life when all the gossip and office politics mattered. To him, the patients were of utmost importance and, like Dr. Lang, Andrew believed that *he* needed to be there for them since only *he* could do the job as well as it truly needed to be done. For me, he was yet another angel sent to guide me through my hell.

I was now out of my coma but still on heavy doses of morphine, which began to do some funny things. That night I decided that I had had enough. I distinctly remember telling Andrew that I was "leaving this dump and nobody could stop me" as I pulled out my IV and got up to pack my clothes.

Of course, this memory was a dream. It is one of my most vivid memories of that first week but it never happened. I had both arms and both legs in casts and was weeks away from sitting up, much less walking out the door. Still, I was convinced that I needed to leave, I didn't NEED any of these quacks, even though these *quacks* had saved my life.

A few hours later I apologized to Andrew for my outburst and for calling his hospital a dump. He just smiled because he had seen it before. He advised, "Come find me when the drugs wear off. Then you can tell me if you think this place is still a dump."

Due to the heavy morphine doses, I was only lucid at times. In spite of the steady stream of visitors and well-wishers who came in to see how I was doing and give me words of encouragement, I remember nothing. While I appreciate their intentions to this day, I have no recollection of anything.

Even when I appeared to be there, I wasn't. One of my best friends that I grew up with traveled all the way from Atlanta to see me. We talked for hours and he fed me ice chips to keep my mouth moist. He told me later that I was making perfect sense and we talked about everything from the crash to politics. Yet I don't remember *any* of it, not even a second. Later on, his visit completely forgotten, I would wonder why this good buddy had never even called to see how I was doing when in fact he'd traveled 800 hundred miles and spent several hours in my hospital room with me. I still don't remember him being there.

Unfortunately, all these people in the room were keeping me awake. In fact, I had not slept much since coming out of the coma over 36 hours earlier and my mind started playing tricks. My family was working in shifts to ensure that someone was in my room at all times. This was very nice and demonstrated their incredible loyalty to family but it was preventing me from getting much-needed rest. Finally, with my sister Julie monitoring me, I very nonchalantly told her to "watch where she sat, there were monkeys running around the room." I was seeing monkeys climbing over my bed and swinging from the curtains.

Julie looked confused and asked, "Did you say there were monkeys in the room?"

I said, "Yes, but don't worry, they are nice monkeys".

She paused momentarily, then replied, "I'll be right back," before she quickly ran to the nurse's station to alert them about this latest development. About 15 minutes later another doctor entered my room and introduced himself as Dr. Jacobs from psychiatry. Yes, within 15 minutes after seeing the monkeys, they sent a psychiatrist to evaluate me – pretty good service!

Dr. Jacobs said, "I hear you see monkeys running around the room."

"Yeah, they are kind of fun to have in here," (I was oblivious to how insane that sounded).

In response he asked a simple question, "Do you see the monkeys when your eyes are open or closed?"

I looked around. Not seeing any, I closed my eyes and the monkeys reappeared.

"I guess only when my eyes are closed," I answered, again oblivious to any connection to reality.

He smiled and advised, "Get some sleep and call me if the monkeys are around when your eyes are open."

Then turning to Julie, he plainly stated, "No more visitors except family. And only for two hours a day. Scot needs his sleep."
Julie replied, "I have known him his entire life and have never seen him sleep more than eight hours in a day. In fact, he usually only sleeps about six."

"Not anymore," the doctor ordered. You heal better when you sleep. Any visitors – family included – are only allowed in his room for a maximum of two hours a day. He will probably be sleeping for 18-to- 20 hours a day for a while now."

Realizing the good sense in the doctor's words, Julie agreed and quickly informed the family and the staff at our veterinary practice who called our church pastors so they could announce it at the services. All of these people were advised to send cards and emails but not to come to the hospital. As hard as it was for them to hear it, they conceded to the fact that it was best for me and my recovery. My many well-wishers, although trying to be nice, were unintentionally making things worse. *Two hours a day*. That would be it.

The next day, the doctor who would straighten my nose entered my room. My sisters, not having to be in the room anymore, had gone home. My mother and father came in with the doctor not knowing if I was conscious enough to comprehend what she was going to tell me.

She pleasantly introduced herself but I could tell she was all business. After quickly informing me about what she was going to do, she asked if I had any questions.

"Just one," I said. "I always thought this nose was a little big. While you are fixing it, could you take a little off and make it more like Brad Pitt's?"

My dad broke out into laughter while my mother just stood there shocked. The doctor stared at me in bewilderment.

"I think I will just put it back where it is supposed to be instead of smashed over to the side like it is now." With that, she turned and walked out of the room.

Dad looked at Mom and remarked, "His brain is working well enough to be a smart-ass. The crash didn't knock *that* out of him."
I smiled for the first time since the crash and it hurt. I didn't care; I was starting to come back.

## Chapter 16

### ∞ Where Is Annie? ∞

The day had also brought some good news regarding the dogs: Olivia had stopped seizing. Dr. Welch, our partner at our vet clinic, had come to Madison and taken her back to the office for monitoring. The doctors at the ER had recommended that she be put down when she first arrived due to her brain injury and non-stop seizures. Dr. Welch had made the decision that to keep going and give her a chance to recover; he had kids of his own and knew that ours would be devastated to hear about the death of their dog right now. Instead, he would take her back to our hospital, where our staff would nurse her along until she either improved or died, but she would *not* put her down. They had lots of drugs to use and could put her in a coma if needed; essentially she would be given every chance to live. They set up a schedule with either a doctor or a trusted technician in charge of monitoring Olivia every night. Our dedicated staff alternated taking her home at night in a little carrier to watch her for seizures. If she had one, they had meds at the ready that they could administer. Dr. Welch told them all to call him anytime if there was a problem.

Despite all of this excellent care, it would be very tough for our little dog. Even after she stopped seizing, she could not get up since her balance center was thrown off. She would try to sit up but get dizzy and fall over. Because she couldn't eat or drink, she was on an IV. Three times a day they would hold her up to a bowl of wet food or chicken in an attempt to get something into her. She would try but then get dizzy and fall to the side, unable to swallow or chew more than a few bites. They were not sure if they could get enough food into her and considered placing a feeding tube, but as she was gradually able to eat more and more, they decided to wait. They kept this up for a month, rolling her from side to side to prevent pressure sores and hand-feeding her until she could finally eat on her own and start to sit up.

A whole bunch of angels.

Annabelle, our Golden Retriever, was still missing after three days, having fled the crash terrified and confused. She'd been hiding in a cornfield, afraid to approach anyone. The police and the farmer who owned the field had walked the area for days calling for her but she would not come out. Soon the farmer would need to harvest but was delaying it, fearing Annabelle might get into the machinery and be killed. He had never met us or our dog but had seen the damage to the van and heard on the news that there were kids involved. He waited to harvest the field because he did not want to cause more pain for these people he didn't even know.

On the fourth day, the medivac helicopter called in and said they thought they had seen her in a field and gave the location. They were the same crew that had flown me in previously and had been watching the area as they flew over on another run. The fact that they would even think to look for her, as busy as they are and without knowing our family at all, was amazing enough. That they had found her was a miracle. More angels.

Now knowing her location, my father and father-in-law decided to go look for her. They had been out every day up until this point with no luck; Annabelle was just too afraid to come out of hiding. The evening temperatures had been plummeting down to below freezing and rain was expected. She would be hungry and freezing tonight. Our Golden Retriever would not survive much longer out here alone.

As they were leaving, they had an idea; they would bring along eight year-old Victoria. They stopped at a store on the way to buy her a pair of boots because it was muddy and cold in the field. When they got there, they handed Victoria the leash but stayed in the car. Our little girl walked along edge of the corn calling for her dog. She walked and walked but got no response.

The dads drove up to get her as she started to cry. Poor Victoria had been so hopeful that Annabelle would be found; she knew how cold it was getting and how wet everything was. She could sense that this was their best chance of finding her dog, and it had failed. Furthermore, she knew about coyotes since there are a lot of them around our home, and that they would easily gang up and kill a dog like Annie.

The dads tried to coax Victoria into the car but she refused. She wanted to walk a little farther into some woods nearby just to check. The dads once again sat in waiting.

Victoria continued on calling for her dog, becoming more and more desperate.

Then she heard it, a rustling in the woods. Something was moving in there, probably just a deer or a squirrel. She called again and the rustling got faster. Whatever it was, it was moving toward her. Then thought of the coyotes returned and she started to panic a little: she was just a child and all alone. What if this was a pack of hungry coyotes? When Victoria looked back, she could not see the car anymore; she had gone too far.

Then she spotted it: a flash of wet, muddy hair in the trees. Her heart raced as she called again. Out of the brush it came at her at full gallop. It was Annie! She ran up to Victoria and almost knocked her over. Her tail beat wildly and she rubbed up against Victoria's legs doing circles around her and smearing her with dirt. Victoria had found her and she was okay!

They ran back to the car and Annabelle leaped in, muddy feet and all. My dad looked at Joe and smiled, "Glad we took your car, not mine."

Although Joe was a fanatic about keeping his car clean, to him this outcome had been worth any inconvenience. He was a true dog-lover having bred, raised, and trained hunting Labradors for most of his life. The pure joy on his granddaughter Victoria's face was something he would never forget. Time to take Annie home.

# Chapter 17

## ∞ Let the Mind Games Begin ∞

Now that the surgeries were winding down, the psychological battle was ramping up. My family kept telling me how lucky I was to be alive, and I could see that was true. Still, it was hard to feel lucky in my condition. Both arms and legs were in casts and I was coping with constant pain on a morphine drip while contemplating the possibility of not being able to support my family again – at least not by doing the job I'd spent the previous 20 years learning to do. It is hard to feel lucky when your doctors tell you that you will be in the hospital for two- to-three months, and then in a nursing home for six more. I had been an active, 38 year-old man in good shape; now it would be a miracle if I ever walked again.

Upsetting me even more was that I was forbidden to see my kids. I looked so scary I would give them nightmares; I had two black-and-blue eyes and a bandage over my nose, in addition to a feeding tube up my nostrils since I would not be able to eat on my own for a while. My wife had three breaks in her back that could paralyze her, or at least keep her in chronic pain. Aside from the fact that back pain is one of the hardest types to resolve, she might also be facing the inability to do the things that she loved to do – work as a veterinarian as well as tend to her horses and goats. We had been the only car to get slammed on a crowded interstate as Jacobs drove headlong into oncoming traffic. He had hit us hard and nearly killed us all; we were going through and suffering from enormous pain, both physically and emotionally. The doctors refused to predict the extent of my recovery – not because they didn't want to, but because they had no way of knowing. Yes, the bones would heal but the messed up the joints were a whole separate issue; there was a real chance I might never be able to use them again.

If the joints locked up they would be useless. At the very least, all the breaks in the joints would likely lead to arthritis in both of my elbows, and possibly my knee and shoulder. All the rehab and surgery in the world would not fix trashed joints, so I could very well face multiple joint replacements and years of pain. Of course, even this scenario was based on the assumption I didn't throw a blood clot in the next six months and die. Or, I could contract some terrible infection – resistant to all the antibiotics – from being immobile in the hospital for months with my multiple open wounds, healing incisions, and pieces of metal embedded in my body. It also assumed my heart and kidneys would not shut down after losing so much blood, and that my brain could still function at a high enough level to get back to work and earn a living. A helluva lot of things had to go exactly right in order for me to return to anything close to normal.

Beyond the physical healing, this best case scenario also assumed that Mona's and my relationship could survive this kind of ordeal. Many couples – over *half* – that live through this type of major crisis end up divorcing because the stress and pain take a toll, not to mention the loss of income and mounting hospital bills. The disruption of one's life is more than many can bear. Mona had been working part-time but kept both the business and the home running on a day-to-day basis. At the office she handled a lot of the tedious but necessary things – from ordering supplies to dealing with staff issues – in addition to seeing clients. At home she kept the kids where they needed to be, the house organized, and the bills paid. It was truly amazing the amount of tasks my wife could complete in the course of a day. Now we weren't sure if she could even be weaned off of the pain meds or if she would spend the rest of her life lying in bed in a haze.

My job at the animal hospital was to perform the major surgeries that so many of our clients had come to expect. Those long, complicated procedures distinguished our hospital from most others and brought in a significant portion of our income. It was our bread and butter. Now I didn't know if I would ever be able to walk again, much less stand over an operating table and concentrate for two or three hours at a stretch. The crash would force both of us to change our roles – at least temporarily – and dramatically reduce our income, which would impose an incredible amount of pressure, leading to much resentment and frustration. Soon we would be fighting with each other and miserably questioning if we'd made the right decision by getting married in the first place. Divorce would soon follow.

Was I lucky to be alive? Yes. Did I feel lucky? No.

For the first few days after waking up, I had very few emotions. I drifted in and out of consciousness, still in shock that this could have happened to us; I had had our lives all planned out and this crash just wasn't a part of it. I didn't know if I really believed that this was real.

*Maybe it was just a dream?*

But reality was starting to settle in. I had been in the bed for nearly a week with various family members rotating through. Although my parents still drove down every day to visit with me, conversation had just about stopped; there was just nothing else to talk about and I was on so many drugs I couldn't think clearly. My visitors had been restricted to just a few hours a day to allow me to get enough rest and I was sleeping 20 hours daily. Mona was permitted to come in once a day for a few minutes, but it was risky and difficult to move her – not to mention incredibly painful.

I went through the gamut of emotions. First up, joy that we all had survived and the kids were not severely hurt. That joy quickly turned to anger at Jacobs for being such an asshole and driving around drunk on a Sunday afternoon. *What did he think was going to happen?* Then, as I started to comprehend the extent of my injuries, fear would take over as I envisioned what my new, post-accident life was going to be like. There was real dread that this was now going to be my new normal – crippled and lying in bed. I had worked hard for the preceding ten years to build a business so that I would not have to work as hard when I hit this age; now I wasn't sure if I or the business would survive. If I did pull through, I figured the business would be much less valuable than it had been in the past and I would no longer be able to pull my own weight.

The partners would tolerate it for a while but eventually reality would hit home: if I would not or could not produce, I'd have to step aside. Our veterinary practice simply couldn't sustain the dead weight of a veterinarian who couldn't stand on his own two feet, move around, and treat patients. With the amount of damage to my feet and legs, I couldn't visualize myself standing long enough to perform the long, complicated surgeries that had built our practice. The reason why many of these surgeries were done at our hospital was because the pet owners did not have the money to take their dog or cat to a referral practice where these same surgeries cost thousands of dollars more to do. If I was physically unable to save them, these pets would instead be euthanized. Consequently, our practice would be just like any other, and our patients and their owners would start to go elsewhere. I would be half the man I was before, crippled and in pain for the rest of my life, living on disability. I would be a failure.

For me, the thought of not working, of not doing the job I knew I was perfectly suited for – the one I had been born to do – scared the hell out of me. I had never intended to be unemployed; boredom would kill me. Spending the rest of my life watching TV on the couch while my kids played outside was as frightening as anything. I would get lazier and lazier, and my mind and body would wither away. All the years I'd worked to hone my skills as a vet, as the "fix-it guy" around the house and office, and as the "fun dad" out running around with the kids had been for naught. I had worked hard to stay in reasonable shape to maintain good health  and the ability to handle the long days on my feet with no lunch break. But now, it would be months before I could stand and nobody could predict if I would ever be close to normal again. So much of what I had worked for was now gone. I felt my spirit and drive start to waver as I felt the first onset of depression.

I kept telling myself I was lucky: I survived, and my wife and kids had all survived. But I just didn't *feel* lucky. My life was now in turmoil and not because of anything I had done. I simply didn't deserve this. Why was this happening to me? I hadn't done anything wrong. Why did I have endure so much pain? Despite the high doses of morphine, pain dogged me relentlessly: every move – even the simple act of breathing – hurt terribly and it wasn't looking as if that would end anytime soon. These injuries – shattered elbows, a dislocated and broken shoulder, and severe leg and foot fractures – might not ever heal to the point that they were no longer a source of intense discomfort. These were joints and they needed to move. Bones needed to slide against each other, something mine might not never be able to do again now that they had been broken and pulled apart. The drugs certainly helped but I did not want to spend my life on narcotics, which at best only lessened the pain. It had never really ceased since I woke up; it was just less intense when I was still and worse when I moved. I could not even lay on my side with both feet and both arms wrapped in heavy bandages. And the simple *thought* of pain kept me immobile; too scared to move at all.

The worst part?

Realizing the pain would be around for a very long time. When you experience excruciating pain from hitting your thumb with a hammer, at least you know it's temporary. If you can handle it for a few minutes, it will quickly subside and go away completely in a day or two. My kind of pain in the aftermath of the accident was dramatically different – not only because it was much more intense, but because it had no foreseeable end. It wasn't going to dissipate in a few minutes or even a few days; it could very well menace me for the rest of my life. This debilitating pain was completely sapping my will to fight. Every move I made involved a long thought process weighing the cost in pain versus the benefit of motion. I even tried not to urinate or defecate, which I had to do in my sheets since I could not lift myself to void in a bedpan. Afterward, the nurses would have to come in and roll me side to side so they could change my sheets and wipe my ass. Needing a 22 year-old nurse to first insert a suppository to enable a bowel movement (the morphine was making me terribly constipated), then come back to change my soiled sheets and wipe my butt like a baby was absolutely humiliating. I wasn't sure that I could just "tough it out" and handle the pain or the embarrassment. What if Mona, or God forbid *the kids*, would have to do this for the rest of my life? No way could I live like that.

As for Mona, I figured she would walk again but might have back pain forever. I knew in all probability she would not function like she did before. She loved riding horses but that part of her life was almost certainly over. Neither of us would likely be able to work like we had before either, causing our business to suffer. It had been 10 years since we'd built a large, modern hospital with lots of staff and all the newest "toys" for helping our patients but now I figured we'd be lucky to keep it all afloat. Modern toys in medicine like ultrasound and digital X-ray are necessities for diagnosing and treating diseases but they come with a big price tag. We had just upgraded the X-ray from plain films to digital to the tune of $50,000, which did not include the X-ray machine itself (another $35,000). Without Mona and me there to see clients, our income source would dry up. The debt payments however, would hang around and eat up a large portion of our take-home pay. Owning a business is great when it is going well but there is no guaranteed income. We did not have a pension that would continue to finance us and our expenses; we were reliant on generating income by doing our job as veterinarians. As owners, we were the last ones to be paid. If a business fails to make a profit, the owners don't get paid at all. If I couldn't get function back in my arms and legs, I would be forced to sit home collecting disability for the next 40 years, bored out of my mind. With the business failing, I would be unable to sell it for even half of what it had originally been worth. Anyone interested in buying it could just patiently wait while it continued to wither away and buy it for next to nothing. Or, worse yet, just set up next door and outcompete us. All our work for the last ten years would just circle the drain, taking all of our plans with it.

I would hate this new life. I can't even stay on vacation for more than a week without going stir-crazy. Now I'd be confined mostly to bed, unable to do my job and without a viable business to support the family. *Would we lose our house in the country? Would we have to move into town and give up the horses, goats and chickens the kids loved?* I dreaded the thought of losing the life we had worked so hard to attain.

I sank deeper and deeper into depression. I could feel it happening but didn't really know how to stop it; I'd just wait for the next dose of morphine so I could fall back asleep and get through another boring day of watching TV while trying not to move.

My depression evolved and grew as time went on. It changed from sadness at what had happened and what I had lost to hate for the man who had caused it. As I became more able to understand what people were telling me, I absorbed more details about what had happened. I had no recollection of the crash or anything that transpired for three or four days afterward.

Mark Jacobs, the drunk who'd slammed into us head-on at high speed, was about my age but that was probably the only thing we had in common. We were as opposite as could be: I was married with children; he was unmarried with a child out of wedlock. I worked hard to support and provide for my kids; he was years behind in child support. I taught my kids the importance of always telling the truth regardless of the consequences; he ran away and left us to die rather than face what he had done. I had been employed continuously since I was sixteen years-old and my employers always wanted to hire me back; he could not hold a job because of his endless drinking. He was an alcoholic who couldn't stop; I had never faced addiction and regarded it as a failure of will by a pathetic human being. To me, it was simply an indication of a lack of strength to be addicted to anything. Real men would suck it up, get their life back in order, and quit screwing up. Jacobs' addiction meant he wasn't a real man but a weak, sniveling wuss.

The man that did this to my family was everything I despised. In fact, I have a hard time calling him a man because I believe a man takes responsibility for his actions and supports his family. Jacobs did none of this, therefore was not a man by my definition. He was easy to hate and I hated him through and through.

In many ways, hating Jacobs was natural and expected. My family despised him also; I could tell when they talked about him. I felt I *should* feel hatred for him after something like this. *Isn't it right to hate the man who could do this to an innocent, perfect family, one with a perfect plan for how their lives were supposed to go?* Jacobs had screwed everything up.

Thus, I alternated between depression and hatred. Being brought up in a family that did not show much emotion, I kept my feelings to myself. When I talked to visitors or family, I did what I had been taught to do when I was growing up: I smiled and said I was doing *fine*. I didn't complain about much and did not want anyone to create a fuss over me. Not eating was OK because I was being fed and nourished through a tube; my pain was a three out of ten when it was more like an eight. I told everyone I was positive I would get back to work in four or five months when the doctors were telling them I would spend at least two months in the hospital and six months in a nursing home, with no guarantee I'd ever go back to work again. I'm not sure if this is a Midwestern thing, a Polish thing, a male thing, or a combination of all but I didn't think complaining about my condition was acceptable. I would not show anyone I was in trouble; I just had to suck it up. I had handled everything else myself; this would be no different.

Whatever I did or said on the outside, on the inside I was alternatingly depressed or angry. As my condition improved, I spent more time alone. I was getting past the risk of dying and the surgeries were mostly done. I just needed time to heal. My parents were still there every day but I was sleeping most of the time and there simply wasn't much that they could do. My bones were still too unstable for physical therapy. My sisters needed to get back to their own families and lives, and I would be in the hospital for a long, long time. Mona couldn't visit much with her broken back and seeing her only fueled my anger at the man who had caused her so much pain and anguish. The kids were at home with Mona's sister, Carla while her other family members would rotate through for weeks at a time to care for them. They were trying to get back to some normalcy but were over an hour away and not coming to visit any time soon.

I was caught in a cycle where the more I thought about what had happened, the angrier and more depressed I became. My pride and stubbornness prevented me from asking for help since I thought I should be able to handle this myself. Having never been through anything this bad, I figured that I did not need help from anyone even though I was in a hospital with psychiatrists on staff. All I had to do was stop telling the doctors I was fine and they would send me a doctor specifically trained to help me navigate through the emotions of what had happened. I was too mule-headed to ask for help. Instead, I became more isolated as I struggled to hide my hatred, depression, and fear. The isolation just forced me to focus on it more and more, while my anger increased exponentially. Round and round it went, getting worse every day.

# Chapter 18

## ∞ My Plan ∞

After all of the surgeries I was moved out of intensive care. At this point I mostly needed time to heal but the doctors were talking months. I was going to survive but still had no idea what my new life would be like. My bucket list had included things like fishing in Canada, touring Australia, and hiking the Grand Canyon – all active things that required a sound body to accomplish. Now mine was broken and those dreams looked impossible.

I had now been in the hospital for a couple of weeks and spending most of my days alone. Mona had been discharged and gone home to be with the kids. They were over an hour away and with the coming winter and Mona's injuries, travel was difficult. We talked nightly but they were seldom able to visit. My family was an hour-and-a-half away and could not be at the hospital every day anymore either. My sisters had families of their own to care for and my parents knew they couldn't do much to help me. Consequently, I had all kinds of time to stew on just how much this sucked – all due to some inconsiderate asshole driving around completely drunk at one o'clock on a Sunday afternoon. What a complete LOSER! I hated him more and more each day.

The sheer hate, depression and boredom were taking a toll. These emotions were making me want to sleep more just so I could wake up and have another day behind me, but I was finding it harder and harder to sleep because I could not do anything when I was awake. I was just never really tired. The more trouble I had sleeping, the more irritable I became and the more the hate and anger grew. I relied on the pain medicine increasingly when I should have been needing it less and less often. But when I got the next dose, I felt no pain and zoned out, plus I could escape the hate and sadness for a while. So I kept asking for more and more. The doctors were very aware of the drug-seeking that often occurs after severe trauma and remained cautious. However, I had a great excuse for wanting pain medication and was still in the recommended dose range – just nearing the top with every request. I found myself overstating the pain level to get "enough" OxyContin. They would ask to rate my pain on a scale of one to ten, with ten being the worst. I found myself "rounding up" whereas before I was always "rounding down." I would tell them six when it was really a four. I told myself that I was blocking the physical pain but, in reality, I was medicating the emotional pain. I was on the slippery slope of drugs. It had begun.

My family saw it too. I was interacting less. I wasn't speaking about when I could get back to work or when the fractures would be healed. I was speaking in *"ifs"* – "if" I would get back to work and "if" I would walk again. Although they noticed the change, they did not breathe a word about it as per our family's way of dealing with things. They needed to stay positive and avoid the negative vibe I was emitting. It was natural for me to be hateful and angry; maybe it would just pass.

The change in me was quite evident to the nurses also. I wasn't the self-confident, "I can beat this" person I was before. I was broken, both physically and mentally. How could I be confident in the future when my plan for it had been completely torn apart? I had figured out every step in my life and up until now, had been executing each step perfectly along the way. I had never thought about not being healthy and having to stop working. I had no plan for *this*.

I had lost all control of my life when control had worked so well for me before. I had been the boss, and a bit of a tyrant at that. My staff was intimidated by me but the business had prospered so I wasn't going to change. I had excelled at everything in life so I must be *really* smart and *really* blessed; God must like me, right?

Now I wasn't so sure. I had failed at things in life before but not anything that I had genuinely put my heart into. I had failed at being an athlete but that hadn't bothered me because I was born with only one good eye and had no depth perception. Without that, catching or hitting a ball was nearly impossible. Sports were not my focus. I had failed at playing a musical instrument but that was not how my mind worked. Music required feel, not logic and my brain was purely analytical. Definitely not for me.

In the end, I was good at remembering facts and using logic to figure things out. Plus, I worked incredibly hard. I felt that what I lacked in physical and musical talent was compensated for by my smarts and work ethic. From high school on, I had just memorized everything I could and out-worked everybody. I had brains and drive so I was *supposed* to be successful at the things that required those qualities; things like medicine.

Now everything I was good at was in jeopardy. Since my body was a mess, out-working everyone was no longer a guarantee; my job could not be done at a desk. My mind was fogged, maybe with drugs or maybe due to bouncing my brain into an airbag at 70 miles per hour; therefore, I just couldn't be sure if I would be able to think the way I did before the crash. My family's modus operandi was to simply state that everything would be fine, but I was a long way from that. Though I would never admit it, I was just plain scared.

It was all Jacobs' fault. He should rot in for what he did to me. I was sinking deeper and deeper into the hole of hate and self-pity.
I had never had to deal with something like this; my life until now had been pretty easy. There was no precedent to follow; I honestly didn't know how to get out of my downward spiral because I had never had to do anything like this before.

I needed revenge: the sweet revenge I thought would make me whole again. I needed to get even but I knew I couldn't do that physically. I couldn't break his bones like he broke mine, but I could work to send his pathetic butt to jail for as long as possible. Jacobs had been caught after literally running away after the crash. He'd taken one look at Mona and me bleeding and dying in the car, and our terrified, crying kids in the back seat, and fled like a coward. He disgusted me.

One day, two of the policemen from the scene showed up in my room to update me on Jacobs, who'd been arrested after the crash. Another motorist who had driven around the wrecks when they opened a lane of traffic had been heading down the next off-ramp when he'd spotted a man walking on the side of the highway. Jacobs turned to look at him as he drove past and the driver noticed blood on Jacobs' face, quickly surmising that this guy was probably the other driver involved in the crash. When he pulled over to ask the hitchhiker where he was going, Jacobs told him his house was a few miles away. The savvy driver replied that he needed to drop off his girlfriend but then would give him a ride; he left her at the nearest convenience store and came back for Jacobs. Meanwhile, his girlfriend called the police, who were waiting at Jacobs's home when they arrived. He was arrested and given a breathalyzer. Over an hour after the crash, he blew a 0.22, almost *three times* the legal limit.

It was critical that this driver picked Jacobs up. Not only did this assure his arrest, but it prevented Jacobs from using the trick so many repeat drunk drivers know about: when you get in an accident, run to the nearest bar or get home and start drinking. It then becomes impossible to determine if the drinking occurred before or after the incident, creating enough reasonable doubt that they avoid the DUI. Jacobs couldn't use this tactic since he had no opportunity to drink after the crash. The police had taken pictures of the open beer cans and the half empty case in the back of his car. They had even taken DNA swabs off his airbag where he had left blood in order to prove that HE and not someone else had been the driver. Good police work.

They had arrested him on the spot for his eighth DUI; he was on probation from his sixth and seventh already. More importantly – the policeman smiled as he informed me – he would be charged with three counts of "Hit and Run with Great Bodily Harm" because he fled the scene with three of us injured in the car. The eighth DUI in Wisconsin would come with a maximum of six years in jail, of which you serve four. However, each count of hit and run carries a maximum penalty of fifteen years; therefore you serve ten. With three counts, the loss of probation from his sixth and seventh DUI, and the eighth DUI, Jacobs faced over 40 years in prison. Nearing 40 himself, he would likely never be let out. Surely, this was the revenge I needed to stop my descent into darkness.

After the policemen finished speaking, I smiled and thanked them for their great work. My mother was in the room and nearly jumped with joy. *This was the news I needed to hear, right?*

Somehow the news didn't change a thing. Deep down, I knew it wouldn't. I told my mother this was great and served him right but my smile was fake; I felt no joy. I kept telling myself I got even and I should be happy. But like everything else since the crash – including the facts that I'd survived and would eventually heal, the news that Jacobs was caught and would be sent away for life did not make me happy. Nothing did. That is, nothing except the OxyContin.

I began to wonder if I would be joyful again without pills. *How could I be?* My life would now consist of living on disability and waiting on the couch for a check to come in the mail that I really didn't earn. *Would I be sitting there consumed with anger at no longer being able to do my job? Would I hurt every day and no longer be able to play with my kids?* My son was four and I didn't know if I would ever throw the football with him again. *Would I be the strong rock of a father figure, something that is so important for my girls to have growing up, or a hobbled, weak shell of my former self stuck in the house watching TV, popping pills and getting weaker, dumber and fatter?*

I looked at my casted arms and splinted legs and doubted my recovery. I had destroyed a knee, both elbows and a shoulder, and knew that joints rarely heal well. I felt the anger bubbling up inside of me again and figured that being in a constant state of anger, being a victim, was now my life. Yes, it was better than being dead but not by much. After my mother left for the night with a big smile on her face, I cried for the very first time. I was losing hope that I would ever be close to the man I was before Jacobs literally crashed into my life; I was also angry at God for putting me through this because I deserved better. I had done everything right – been a good person and gone to church when I could, and yet I was still in this mess. It wasn't fair.

The next day I had a meeting with the hospital staff about my long-term care. I was no longer critical and had to leave the intensive care unit even though I could not even sit up and required months of rehab. I was just starting to eat on my own but could not take in enough      calories and was still losing weight. When I began this ordeal, I weighed in at about 170 pounds but was now at just over 145 pounds. The staff was talking about the best nursing homes for me.

I was too drugged to participate in the conversation and too depressed to care. Sure a nursing home; great, *whatever.* It was just another reason to hate my new life.

Thankfully my sister Julie stepped up and acted as my advocate since I was too destroyed to form an educated opinion. In her career as social worker, Julie placed the elderly in situations where they'd receive the level of care they needed: stay at home, assisted living, or a nursing home. She knew all about these facilities and the type of care they could provide. There was no better angel to help me with the next fateful fork in the road.

The hospital staff was convinced that a nursing home would be the best option. They had round-the-clock staff and the equipment and staff to care for me.

Julie was adamant that she could do better. Nursing homes are basically set up to help people in the last stages of life; to guide them through their inevitable decline toward death. Patients there are not really seeking to get back to the activity level of a man less than 40 years of age.

I needed a different goal in care: intense rehabilitation to regain the strength I had just a few weeks ago. My sister knew I needed to be in a hospital in order to heal and receive the physical therapy designed to push me and push me *hard*. She felt I could take the more intense regimen she had in mind, completely unaware that I was beginning to believe the intense rehab wouldn't help. I was starting to believe I was done and my body wasn't going to get much better. I had lost my drive.

They just looked at her like she was crazy. A nursing home was the only option based on my level of care needed. My broken body demanded intense care for months, not weeks and was in no shape for rehab yet because my bones were nowhere near healed. They wouldn't come out and admit it but they really didn't think I would get much back either. I could not even start rehab for another few weeks when my bones were more healed, so they did not want me to take up space in a rehab unit. Other patients who had a better chance of recovery might need it more than I did.

Julie and the staff argued as I drifted in and out of sleep. They left the room to allow me to rest and sat down in a conference room, where the fight became intense. Julie is a consensus maker; her job is to work with distraught families about their ailing loved ones. Now she was on the other side as she fought like hell to keep me out of a nursing home.

The hospital brought in a third staff member to argue their side but Julie held fast. She had it all set up; I could go to the hospital where she worked in my hometown. My parents and two sisters all lived there and she had arranged a place for me on the rehabilitation unit. She had already spoken with the physical therapist she wanted to handle my case. It was all arranged; she just needed this hospital to sign off on it.

The hospital argued that I was not ready for rehab; I still could not bear weight on my leg or lift either of my arms.

After an hour of arguing, the staff gave up. I was moving out of their facility and would be someone else's problem; I'd be transferred by ambulance at the end of the week. My sister's boss had signed off that my rehab would start immediately even though at this point I could not even sit up in bed. Julie was doing more than stretching the truth about my condition and in the process, putting her job and career on the line. By getting me into the rehab unit when I was not physically ready, she could easily be fired if the insurance company refused to pay. Yet she trusted in the Scot she'd known all her life; the guy who would do whatever was necessary to get better.

At least that was who I was *before* the crash. I was not at all sure that this was still true. I knew the rehab would be hard and painful and had started to doubt that it would be worth the effort. My body was so badly damaged it seemed unlikely that I could get it back no matter how hard I tried.

Finally, the hospital gave up and signed off on the transfer; I would be someone else's responsibility if it didn't work out.

Every day got worse as I sank deeper and deeper into depression. I watched endless TV and had realized that 90 percent of the shows were just stupid. It hurt every time I tried to move which wasn't much. I had splints on both feet and both arms so I was stuck lying on my back like a turtle. It seemed every day the casts and splints got a little looser; I knew I was losing muscle quickly. Great! *If I ever got home, I would not only be a useless, pill-popping, disabled couch potato, I'd be weak and scrawny too.*

I needed to find a way out of the depression but didn't know how or where to begin. I had never dealt with depression before and such things were not discussed in our family, where everyone was expected to just deal with bad things and not whine about them. I'd always been taught to toughen up and get over it; depression was for wimps who couldn't handle it when the going got rough. Now I was discovering it wasn't about being tough; I was depressed because I was confronting major problems in my life that I might not be able to fix. That made me sad, incredibly sad.

I needed a new plan since my last one had not worked out as intended but how could I plan out my life now? I couldn't really do so until I knew how much progress I could make along my path of healing and rehabilitation but I had no idea how I would end up physically and mentally. Months of rehab awaited me without any clues or guarantees as to how well I'd emerge from the experience when I was done. They were talking six months to a year. I couldn't plan anything until I knew if I would walk, run, be confined to a wheelchair, or live with chronic pain. I just didn't know.

I had never been without a plan before; my life was on hold, which just added to my depression. It wasn't fair that my life was in such shambles because I'd figured it all out years ago and my plan had been perfect.

Then I heard it.

It was a whisper; not a booming voice that you hear in the movies or from behind a burning bush, but I heard it clear as day.

*"It is not your plan."*

The still, small voice stopped me dead in my tracks. My mind had been racing; I hadn't been able to sleep more than a few hours because I kept trying to figure out my life. But as I lay there, the thought kept reverberating through my head.

*"It is not your plan."*

I tried to ignore it but it wouldn't go away. Instead it grew louder, if a thought could be loud.

*"It is not your plan."*

It blocked out everything else. I concentrated on it fully, trying to determine if it was real or imagined.

*"It is not your plan."*

I didn't get it at first. I was always in control of my life. How could it not be my plan? It was *my* life so I was in control, wasn't I? I was the one who made the decisions in my life and if not me, then whom?

*"It is not your plan."*

# Chapter 19

## ∞ But I Want It To Be My Plan ∞

"It is not your plan."

This repetitive thought in my head wouldn't go away; I couldn't make it stop or conform to what I wanted. I wanted to be in control but the voice was stopping me. *Why?*

At the same time, I sensed I'd heard this voice before, although I couldn't place where or when: I was just certain I had heard it previously. It was familiar.

*"Well, of course its familiar,"* I told myself, *"it's in your own head. It must be you. It's your own thought."*

But I didn't believe what I was hearing: after all, *I* was in control of my life. Up until that asshole slammed into me, I had made all the right decisions. I sure as wasn't about to let anyone else control my actions.

The thought persisted, over and over again. It was loud and clear and wouldn't be denied.

As I sat alone in my hospital bed, hooked up to IV's, immobilized in splints and casts with the TV tuned into a Judge Judy episode I'd already seen three times, my mind raced. *What did this mean? Why couldn't I get the thought out of my head?*

I fought to deny the simple truth the thought conveyed. *I* was in control! It was *MY* life!

I was railing against the obvious and the inevitable.

Could this *really* be the voice of God talking to me? God doesn't *actually* speak to us with a voice like that, does He? I had never been *that* religious before. I went to church and called myself a Christian but never figured God would address me directly. Of course I'd heard of other people who claimed to have "spoken to God" but I always rolled my eyes and figured they were "Bible-thumpers." In their zeal to have a true experience of God, they'd convinced themselves He'd spoken to them, creating a self-fulfilling prophecy. I figured they had so little going on in their lives that "speaking directly to God" was their way of making themselves feel more important than they truly were.

But I was far from a Bible-thumper. Truth is, I had never even read the Bible. Yes, I attended church but rarely listened to the messages imparted through the services. *Why should I?* I had it all figured out and used that hour in the pew to plan out the day or refine my next great idea. While I could recite the Lord's Prayer by heart, I had no clue what it meant. I wasn't even desiring to talk to God, nor had I even bothered to consider listening to the prayers that Pastor Mark and Mary Anne were reciting; I was too drugged up and arrogant even as I lay in my own feces and urine. I hadn't even thanked God for keeping me alive. I hadn't thanked him for Mona avoiding paralysis and for the kids being alright.

Why?

I was too busy worrying about what was going to happen to *me* and how I, the smart guy with the plan, would handle it. I was completely self-focused. After all, I was the strong one who had beaten the odds and survived in a situation where everyone else would have died. That meant I was simply better than most. *Right?*

What an ass!

In spite of my selfishness and ingratitude, I was getting the help I needed to start my recovery. It was like when I was a kid and had a problem I couldn't figure out: my dad would walk in as I floundered and solve it with a few words. Then I became a teenager and *I* knew better, I didn't need my father's advice anymore. Of course, like most teenage boys, I had made mistake after mistake because I thought I knew it all. Could this be God, my other father, solving a problem for me with just a few words also? *Could this be me, the arrogant teenager once again, not accepting His wisdom and trying to do it all myself?*

It soon became apparent that the thought wasn't going away no matter how much I resisted. My belligerence wasn't going to prevail over it so I stopped fighting the voice and said, *"OK God, it is not my plan. It must be yours. But what is your plan? I need to know why this happened and how I am going to make it through, so tell me what your plan is for me."*

Silence.

I asked again, expecting God's voice to answer my questions. I was such an important and special person; I had just heard His voice so I must have a direct line to God.

"What is your plan God?"

Silence.

OK, I guess I didn't have a direct line to the Almighty after all. He wasn't on my speed-dial. But I thought about His words, "It is not your plan." I got it; it was *His* plan.

Maybe I wasn't in control as much as I thought. I kind of felt like the Grinch who stole Christmas when he realized "Maybe Christmas doesn't come from a store, maybe Christmas means a little bit more." I almost felt my heart "grow three sizes that day," just like the Grinch. I smiled for the first time since the crash; I was getting it.

Although I wasn't in control like I thought I was, I was beginning to realize this was OK with me. I had always said that I would only worry about the things over which I had control but it was becoming obvious that I wasn't in control of much. Moreover, as I lay there unable to even roll over, I realized that I had *never* been in control. With respect to the accident, I'd been in control of my car yet could do nothing to stop this drunk driver from hitting us. I had controlled my veterinary hospital but now it was functioning without me. For crying out loud, I didn't even have control of my body: each limb was immobilized, I couldn't eat much yet, and they were feeding me through a tube. I couldn't even use the bathroom on my own; I just voided in the sheets and called for the nurse to clean me up like I did for my mother when I was a baby. I smiled as I figured out that God was making his point by reducing me to this, "YOU ARE NOT, NOR HAVE YOU EVER BEEN, IN CONTROL, I AM AND I ALWAYS WAS."

Even I, the arrogant, follow-my-great-plan guy, could see that I had been wrong – nearly dead wrong.

Now it made sense; this was the reason I had survived. It wasn't that I was special or Superman; it wasn't because I was such a great person that God didn't think the world could survive without me. It was because He had decided I would survive. It was *His* call, not mine. He had a reason even if I did not understand what it was. I had no control over my survival because it was His choice whether I had lived or died that day – whether I lived or died every day.

That night, I finally slept well. I had fallen to the bottom of the pit of depression and vengeance and I had lost. My life would turn on how I dealt with this – something I had never had to deal with before – a total lack of a plan. But I knew if I stayed like this, struggling to regain control, I would never pull myself out of the pit and my life would continue to be crap. But I had changed: this voice, this simple thought, had led me out and all I had to do was what I was struggling to do. All I had to do was listen.

Once I understood and acknowledged it was God – not me – who was in charge of my life, I realized the same was also true for Jacobs. God had allowed all the steps to align perfectly in order to put our two cars, the van and the Jeep, in that exact spot at that exact time. It was He who had permitted all of those things to go right that day to keep all of us alive.

I had been mad at God for letting this happen. Really? Did I honestly think *I* knew better? After admitting He was in control of my life – including the accident and recovery – did I still want to question HIM? Was I arrogant enough to think *I* knew better than *Him*? I just couldn't be *that* self-centered anymore; I just couldn't declare that *I* had a better plan than *God* did. What a selfish prick I had been! Not anymore.

Now I felt I would find peace. I wasn't entirely there yet; I still became angry every time I thought about the drunken man who hit us, but I knew I would be alright. It still bothered me that I couldn't recall when or where I'd heard the voice but for tonight, I had had enough. I sensed I'd turned a corner. Tomorrow would be a better day, all because I had accepted the fact that I couldn't control anything; my life was in *His* hands, not mine. I accepted the fact that this had been true from the very beginning, in spite of my long-held, misguided belief otherwise. God was in control.

Scot Hodkiewicz

# Chapter 20

## ∞ The First Step Out ∞

I woke up determined to get stronger each day. I began sleeping less and becoming increasingly cognizant of my surroundings. The staff wanted to wean me off the feeding tube and try getting me to eat again. Although it had been providing some nourishment, it is nearly impossible to feed enough calories into the body through a tiny nasogastric tube, which has to be small enough to fit through the nasal passages, down the throat, and into the stomach without causing a gag reflex. At the same time, the high caloric fats and proteins traveling through the tube are thick and tended to block it up. The end result? I wasn't getting more than 800 hundred calories a day and losing weight quickly.

Even though the doctors could also put a little glucose (sugar) in the IV, there are simply not enough calories in that to make a difference. Additionally, glucose in the fluids reacts with many of the drugs running through the IV. This reaction between the sugar and the drugs  often forms solids that can settle out, creating a potentially deadly scenario as these particles then flow into the bloodstream where they could block a vessel and cause an embolism (a blood vessel blockage in the lungs or brain). The risks of placing sugar in the IV outweighed the benefits of those few extra calories it would provide.

They discussed using a liquid diet which would be higher in calories; this is the IV feeding often used in coma or cancer cases, but it is very difficult to maintain. These liquid diets must be very high in fat, and fats are very irritating to the blood vessels where the IV line is placed. Within a day or two the vein becomes inflamed and painful, so the IV has to be pulled.

The only way to administer IV nutrition was through a PICC line. This stands for "Percutaneously Inserted Central Catheter." It's a very long (about a foot and a half), large bore IV catheter that is fed through the skin of the upper arm (inserted "percutaneously" or "through the skin") and into a large vein. It is placed using ultrasound guidance to avoid hitting the large artery pulsing next to it, then fed up the vein where it enters the heart (into a "central" not "peripheral" vein). Only when fed into one of these large vessels that dumps directly into the heart is the blood of high enough volume that the fats and proteins are diluted quickly enough so as to avoid destroying the vein.

My medical team wanted to avoid all of this: it was time for me to eat on my own.

I had not only lost about 30 pounds but most of the muscle around my arms and legs; my face looked skeletal. A large part of the problem was the OxyContin pain medicine that had shut down my gut, creating a stalemate of sorts where nothing was moving. Also, in the two weeks since the crash, my stomach had shrunk to a third of its normal size; I simply could not eat a large meal even if I wanted to. Now was the time to slow down the pain meds and try to get calories in.

The thought of intense pain made me very nervous. In reality, I was becoming addicted to the meds and did not know if I could make it without them.

Here's where I swallowed my pride and asked God for help. I understood the whole "not my plan thing" and had given up on trying to do this on my own. I knew I needed His help in order to wean myself off of the drugs.

*"God, please help me handle my pain better. I want to eat and get stronger. Then I can heal and follow your plan. I will follow wherever You lead. I know that it is all up to You."*

This was a 180-degree swing for me. Relinquishing control? Giving up on having everything figured out because I was soooo smart? I had not been without MY plan since I was in high school. To now accept that I was not in control was tough. Still, God had proven to me that my control was an illusion; in spite of what I believed, I had never really been in control of much of anything. God had just led me down my path. Now, when my life was much tougher and uncertain than it had been, I reached out my Creator for help, seeing clearly that the next few months or years would be more than I could do alone. The long, painful healing, the fear of being permanently disabled, of not playing with my kids anymore – these were all too much for me to bear by myself. I needed a Father.

I knew I had to take fewer pain meds but I was also aware that I could not just stop all the drugs *cold turkey*. The body doesn't work like that. I still needed pain meds; it had only been a few weeks since the horrific crash and my bones were still broken. At the same time, the drugs were keeping me in a daze and sapping my will to do anything. I was just waiting for my next pill and the blissful sleep that would soon follow.

This was not me; it was time to started weaning off. I started by just taking less, cutting the dose down by 25 percent. Then I waited for the pain to come.

An hour later, I noticed the pain wasn't so bad. It was comprised mostly of a dull soreness as long as I didn't move. Since both of my arms and legs were still splinted, it wasn't hard to stay in one spot. I just laid there on my back watching TV. Boring, yes, but at least I knew I was healing.

I dozed off for a few hours; Judge Judy wasn't real exciting today. When I awoke, I felt hunger pangs for the first time in two weeks. The pain was manageable and I was ready to eat. I looked up to the ceiling and offered, "Thanks."

I buzzed the nurse and asked her to have the cafeteria send up a cheeseburger and fries with a chocolate milk shake. I wanted calories. In a half-hour it was delivered to my room. By this point, I was starving. The tantalizing aroma of the fried food was overpowering; all I wanted to do was wolf it down and then ask for more. I knew the more calories I could take in, the faster I would heal and the stronger I would get. With gusto, I dove into the burger with large bites.

For the first time I discovered God has a sense of humor. While this was the one time in my adult life when I could eat as much of anything I wanted – ice-cream, pizza, cheeseburgers dripping with grease – my stomach had shrunk considerably. I savored the taste as I started to eat, forcing the food down but I could not eat more than a few bites of anything. One half of a burger and I was stuffed full. I couldn't even finish half the fries and a quarter of the milk shake. I smiled. It was "God's little joke."

Now I had to figure out something else. I needed the calories but I could not eat the volume of food required. Therefore I decided to add more calories to the food I was consuming. Foods with the most calories in the smallest volume are fats, and the best source of fats is cream.

While God may have a sense of humor, He was also willing to give me a great way out of my predicament. I loved ice cream and started adding it to just about everything. For breakfast, I would order sugary cereal and add in two big scoops. It was cold, chunky and overly sweet but I got the calories I needed. For lunch I would add more ice-cream and even more at dinner, and as a bedtime snack. In fact, I ate so much ice cream that I soon became sick of it. I could hear God laughing at his little joke again; the one time I could eat as much ice-cream as I wanted and I no longer wanted it – real funny!

I had decided that it was time to start working on getting back to normal. My kids deserved a father who was as physically close to what they'd become accustomed as I could possibly get. I played a lot with my kids – baseball, football, and soccer depending on the season, even though I've never been a big soccer fan. I just didn't get the sport at all and watching it bores me to tears. Yes, I know there are a lot of soccer fans in the world who are just as into it as I am into football, but I can't stand it. Nevertheless, because the kids liked it we played it a lot in the backyard. At least we used to.

My goal was to get back to the physical condition I was in before the crash. I didn't know how close I would get to my goal, but I knew I had to give it my all. I would not want my kids to ever think I could have done more but chose to do less.

I decided that every day I would get a little better; work to get just a little bit closer to normal. Unfortunately, "normal" was a long way away.

The Chinese have a great expression, *"A journey of a thousand miles starts with a single step."* It was time to start the journey. It was time to take that first step.

The first step wasn't a step at all. I had been flat on my back for weeks and now they wanted me to sit up. "No big deal. This will be easy."

A group of nurses surrounded me. "Wow, what service," I thought, reverting to my arrogant ways, "they must really like me."
Then I found out why they were all there. Each grabbed an arm and they started to raise up the bed. I reached vertical and was sitting up, not on my own but just with the bed being raised (my first step). I was sitting upright and figured I would soon be ready to try to walk down the hall. I would be home in no time.

This lasted all of about 10 seconds.

Then the room started to spin and everything went black. I had passed out and the nurses were waiting to catch me before I fell out of bed.

I was back to in a few seconds with a dazed look on my face and flat on my back again. One of the nurses smiled and said, "You did great, you made it ten seconds." I had never fainted in my life so I wasn't sure what had happened.

She explained, "You have been down for all this time. Your heart doesn't remember that it needs to pump harder when you sit up to get the blood to your brain and you passed out. Keep trying, your heart will have to learn again."

I couldn't believe it. *My heart has to learn to pump correctly?* It has been doing this for almost 40 years and it forgot in a few weeks?

But the body will adapt to what it needs in the moment. It hadn't needed to pump harder so it lost the ability – a classic "use it or lose it" response. I would have to work on it a few times each day and each day it would relearn some more. Yes, I would get nauseous and nearly vomit each time I passed out but I had to keep trying if I would ever sit up again. The more I lay flat, the harder it would be to get up.

Wow, did I have a long way to go! It seemed like I really did have a "journey of a thousand miles" ahead of me.

They let me recover and then tried a second time with the same result; I was passed out in about ten seconds.

"You did great," she complimented, "we will try again tomorrow." With that, they all left the room.

*This was doing great?*

I could not even sit upright. That's when it hit me just how weak I had become. The frustration I'd been holding in for a long time now came flooding out. As a man, I was taught never to cry but my world was now upside down and I didn't really care. If crying was what I needed, then I would wail away. I was alone in my room and did not want anyone to be there to console me. It was time to let it out and I did. I had been told that crying was normal and I should let myself indulge. Of course, I, the arrogant bastard I was, thought the rules did not apply to me. I was stronger than everyone else. I was a man and I would handle this without sobbing like a baby.

Now I knew crying was part of the healing process and part of releasing the arrogance. It was God breaking me down enough to accept Him and accept Him fully. Now I was ready and I decided to let it fly, no holding back.

I cried and cried and cried.

After what seemed like forever, I realized I was feeling done. The crying stopped. The room was dead quiet. "God, help me. I have such a long way to go. I can't even sit up. How will I walk again? How will I run with my kids again?"

I was finding out just how hard this journey was going to be and my will was already starting to falter. Maybe I could just learn to accept lying in bed? Everyone would understand that my injuries were just too much to overcome.

After hearing His voice before, I waited for it again. I heard nothing.

This time I didn't get angry or ask again. Instead, I thought about why I hadn't heard a response. Finally, I said, "God, I am in your hands. I will work as hard as I can and be satisfied with what you give me. It is your plan, not mine, so what I get back is up to you, but I will put in the work. I know you could heal me in a second but you want me to go through this for a reason. I need to learn to fight, to push harder. Getting strong again will be the toughest thing I have done but I will do it. I will do it through You."

Nothing. I smiled anyway; I knew He had heard.

Over the next week, they kept coming in to help me sit up. Each time I got stronger, first 30 seconds, then 50, then a minute. Soon it was five minutes and they were moving me to a chair instead of the bed. My heart was remembering how to get the blood to my brain. There were times when I dreaded it because each time I passed out I would want to vomit and was nauseous for hours but I kept going. I had taken the first few steps in my thousand-mile journey.

## Chapter 21

## ∞ Thud ∞

As I mentioned, the only family that still visited daily by this time were my parents. Having returned to their busy lives, my sisters were stopping by less frequently, and of course, Mona and the kids were home. I spoke to them at least once a day but noticed we talked very little about the crash; whenever I brought it up, they would quickly change the subject. Even Mona, whom I faithfully called every night, avoided any discussion of it. After a while, I asked my father why. He noted that every time we talk about the crash, everyone ends up crying and angry; it was just easier to avoid the topic altogether. Exhausted physically and mentally, we hated what we were going through, thanks to Mike Jacobs, the loser drunk who'd hit us then run away. We couldn't even watch the news reports they had recorded about the crash because everyone would break down in tears.

Dad continued, "I hadn't cried in years and now I am crying every day. It's just hard to face the reality of how close you came to dying and how much work is still ahead of you."

He was right: I was facing months in the hospital followed by months of rehab just to walk again – maybe. Whether I could get back to work and support my family again was a 50/50 shot at best. I didn't even know if I could make love to my wife after all this. My life would be a giant struggle for the next year or two – possibly forever – and I hated the man who'd caused us all of this misery.

This anguish had continued unabated for weeks now and I realized something had to change. Understandably, every time anyone thought about the crash, it resulted in anger and sadness. There was no escaping it; it was now a part of all our lives. God knew, I certainly couldn't get away from it because every time I gazed at my bandaged arms and legs, or felt excruciating pain as I tried to move it was a constant reminder. I had never really hated someone before, having been raised not to hate anyone but this guy deserved it: eight drunk driving convictions – probably countless others where he didn't get caught – dereliction of his child support obligations, no interest or ability in keeping a job; an easy guy to despise.

While hating Jacobs came easily, in my heart I also knew it was wrong. I had seen other people in my situation before where something terrible had happened and now they were mad all the time. Nothing is ever good enough; nothing ever goes right; they are always being persecuted and unfairly deprived. Not surprisingly, they end up divorced and alone, which just confirms that the world is against them.

Now I was becoming "that guy," the downer that nobody really wanted to be around. My family would tolerate me for a while but slowly find excuses to keep their distance. And really, who could blame them? Nobody wants to be around the "angry guy" whose only emotion and attitude is one of bitterness.

That's when I decided I didn't want to be that resentful person anymore. One of Mona's favorite sayings is, "happiness is a choice." No matter what, you can choose to be happy or you can choose to be sad. Anything else and you are a victim; you have given up your power.

It was time to put those words into action. We had talked the talk but could we walk the walk? A tragic, devastating event had wreaked havoc on our lives, but I still had the power to choose whether I would let it control me or whether I would put it in my past. Bad things would happen in the lives of my kids; they already had. *How could I tell them to fight through it and not be a victim if I was acting like one myself?* Victims stay angry, they thrive on hate. Yes on the day of the crash we had been victims, but that day was over.

I was told once that when you change in the way God intends, He changes your name. When Simon became the disciple of Jesus and chose to follow him, Jesus changed his name to Peter, meaning "the Rock," and told him that He would build His church upon him.
Now, if we let go of the anger and accepted God's plan, we would no longer be "victims" but "survivors"; our names would be changed. It was time to start acting like survivors, it was time to stop the hate. Since it was my choice, I chose happiness – right in that moment.

Excellent plan, right? There was just one catch: I wasn't sure how to do it. I had taken the first step already when I had accepted that God had a different plan for us, but Jacobs' stupidity and inconsideration still made my blood boil. *How could anyone be such a loser? What did he think was going to happen that day?*

Though my family did not want to talk about it, I knew that ignoring the elephant in the room wasn't going to work anymore. If they were ever going to return to normal, the kids would need to talk about it, as would Mona and I. The hate we were holding for Jacobs would eventually destroy both of us, our marriage, and ultimately, our family. I decided I wasn't going to let Jacobs destroy any more of our lives. He had already inflicted more than enough damage.

I tried to tell myself that there must be something positive about the guy and that it wasn't his fault. Yeah, that sounded nice but I am a big believer in personal responsibility. Jacobs made the choice to drink that morning and drive around. He'd also decided long ago to evade responsibility for his alcoholism after four stints in rehab and five years in jail. No matter what had happened in his past, he repeatedly chose to make the same mistakes over and over again, which ultimately resulted in a head-on collision with a car full of kids at 70 miles per hour. It *was* his fault; trying to make excuses for him only pissed me off more. This cycle continued for days. I just did not know how to get past the hate.

Then as I lay there watching the news alone in my room trying to figure this out, a story was broadcast from out in Pennsylvania. A local crazy had gone into an Amish school with a gun, where he ordered all the adults and boys out before tying all the girls up on the floor. Turned out that his daughter had died shortly after birth some nine years earlier and he hated God for putting him through that tragedy and grief. He just had to kill these innocent school girls because in his twisted mind, this would "punish God for taking his daughter."

The adults had called 911 (some in the people in the school were not Amish and had cellphones) and the boys and teachers huddled together outside and prayed for their classmates. The girls inside the room, ages six to sixteen, asked the gunman to pray with them. Instead, he lined them up against a wall and shot them one-by-one in the back of the head, killing five out of the ten girls before killing himself. His anger over the death of his daughter had destroyed him and a room full of innocent children; his hate had rotted his mind to a point where he thought killing innocents would make things right.

As I watched this horrific report, I realized that I was on that same path; I had to find a way off or I may have just as well have died on impact. If I couldn't let go of the hate, my life was over one way or the other. I would be like the gunman, exclusively devoting all of my time to plotting my revenge and driving myself to insanity.

Next, a reporter interviewed a father and mother dressed in simple Amish clothes who had lost a daughter in the shooting. She asked what they thought about the man who killed her and her schoolmates. Their response shook me to the core.

"We have forgiven him and our child is now safe in the arms of Jesus."

The stunned reporter followed up with, "You have forgiven him? Forgiven the man who just shot your daughter?"

Equally stunned, the parents of the murdered child looked at her and replied, "This is what Jesus teaches us to do, 'forgive us our trespasses as we forgive those who trespass against us.' We must forgive him."

Then I understood. It was like someone had turned the light on in my darkness. For the second time, I had heard the voice of God, this time in a news story out of Pennsylvania. It now made perfect sense. This family could only deal with the tragedy – a much greater tragedy than mine – by forgiving the man responsible. It was only through forgiveness that the hate would go away. I had tried to bury it, to not speak of it, to live with it, but it was clear that none of this was going to work. The only pathway available to me was the hardest and most unnatural; I had to forgive the idiot who had nearly killed my entire family, nearly paralyzed my wife, and put me in the hospital for the foreseeable future. I had to forgive him even though he did not deserve it or even asked for it. It wasn't fair and did not seem right but I knew it was the only way.

That day I decided to forgive; I would no longer hate. Jacobs was a despicable human being who didn't deserve forgiveness but I would forgive him anyway. I told myself that this was not my plan and that God must have used Jacobs for some other reason; I just was not able to see why. In the end, I didn't need to see why since it wasn't MY plan but HIS. I didn't need to *understand* it, I only needed to *accept* it.

Could it really be this easy? *Could the Amish, stuck in the simple ways of two-hundred years ago, have figured it out so much faster than someone like me, schooled in the modern world with all this information at my fingertips?* It seemed pretty obvious that they had. The scripture they had quoted was from the Lord's Prayer, something I had repeated since I was four but somehow had never given much thought. I just recited the words by rote without ever contemplating their meaning. Those people were smarter than me because they really meant what they were saying. They followed God's word exactly and it was leading them through the darkness of their tragedy. Now, it would lead me through mine. They were angels, grieving a terrible loss 300 miles away, saving me from my hatred and anger.

With that, I felt the hate start to go away. It was like coming through a tunnel and emerging out into the light. The tunnel was cold and dark, the light was warm and bright. It was the joy that comes with letting God back into my life. I felt happiness returning. I felt the hate dissipating. I could envision the devil himself, a demon that was living inside of me, being driven out by the simple words of the Lord's Prayer, *"forgive us our trespasses as we forgive those who trespass again us."*

As I thought about it, I figured that Jacobs would be so much better when he realized that I had forgiven him. I would be seen as a great guy who could forgive the man who did not deserve it. I would be seen as a role model for forgiveness, a really special human being. I stopped. The anger started to come back. Why would I care if Jacobs felt "better?" His feeling better about what he did would only compel him to repeat it. I wanted him to feel terrible about what he had done for the rest of his life. If we had to be in pain, so should he.

Whoa, back up! I thought about it again. Once more, I was thinking of myself, not really following what Jesus would do. I was wrong, I wasn't getting it. I realized I couldn't really forgive Jacobs simply because others would see me as a hero. Since he hadn't been tried in court yet, I was banned from speaking to him; I could not tell him that I had forgiven him even if I wanted to. Most people would think I was crazy to not be mad at him anymore. They would probably see me as weak and gullible, not a hero. They wouldn't get it, they wouldn't see why I had to forgive him.

In many ways, my forgiveness would ultimately be kind of selfish but in a good way. While it was possible he might be happy to find out that I no longer hated him, I was doing this for *me*, not him. I was starting to get it; forgiveness is the path through tragedy. It was my way out. Maybe Jacobs could see it as his way out too.

I realized that hate is the barrier that stops everything; a wall we put around ourselves that ultimately becomes our prison. How many times have we heard of two people who hate each other but neither one can remember exactly why? Maybe something was said or done by one person and completely misinterpreted by the other. As a result, they never spoke again for 30 years. Hate does this. It clouds the memory and distorts the truth. Now, it was preventing me from being thankful that we all had survived; that my kids came through with relatively minor injuries, and my wife would walk again. The hate was depleting my drive to do the rehab; it was pushing my family away; it was even making the nurses hesitant to come check on me in my room as often. Hate was a wall I had built and was now just in my way. Since I alone had built it, only I could tear it down.

I discovered an interesting thing about forgiveness; it has just as much or even more impact on the *forgiver* than the *forgiven*. It is like giving a gift; the giver feels just as good – or even better – than the one who receives it. In this case my gift to Jacobs was forgiveness. I *had* to do it if I wanted to survive, to get back to where I was *before* the crash psychologically more than physically. I had to do it whether anyone else knew about it. God had arranged it so that it would be done without others knowing (I legally could not speak to Jacobs). No witnesses would be there to admire me; that was too arrogant and self-serving. It had to be done because "that was what Jesus teaches us to do."

Hate is the lazy way out. It is just so easy, much like a drug; it makes you feel superior and strong but soon takes over your life until all you can do is hate. It is a temporary fix that makes you feel good for a moment but ends up isolating you from everyone, with only your anger for company.

Forgiveness, on the other hand, is the opposite of hate. It is not our natural response but a learned behavior (the Amish did it easily because they are taught from day one to forgive others). For most of us, it takes work and effort. It brings people together, it makes people happy but it is hard to do. How tough is it to call that no good brother-in-law you haven't spoken to for a year and apologize? Forgiveness takes work. It's not a drug; drugs are easy. Forgiveness is more like a "runner's high"; it takes a ton of effort to experience but is well worth it. Have you seen runners? Their chiseled bodies and endless energy make us all jealous.

I had to choose: did I want to keep hating or did I want to forgive?

I decided that today the loser who nearly wiped out everything I cherished in my seemingly perfect life would be forgiven. I asked God to help, knowing that I could not do this myself. There had been many times in my life when I'd asked for and received forgiveness (I was taught that Jesus forgives all our sins); now I would forgive Jacobs. No, he hadn't asked to be forgiven and did not really deserve it but that didn't matter. I needed to complete the process of forgiving Jacobs so I could move on with my life; I wasn't about to wait for an apology from him. I asked God to help me forgive him regardless. I wanted to let go of the anger and bitterness.

Again I wondered, "Could it really be that easy? Could it be that if I forgave him, with all his faults, that *I* would finally be happy again?" Once more, I remembered those words I had repeated since the first time I went to church, "Forgive us our trespasses as we forgive those who trespass against us."

But this was not a simple "trespass"; he had nearly killed my entire family including three innocent kids. Still, the words were simple and this was the Lord's Prayer, the prayer that Jesus instructed us to use when we spoke to God. There were no qualifiers as to whom or what should be forgiven. It just said to forgive, period.

I *had* to forgive Jacobs if I wanted peace. Like that Amish couple dressed in their simple clothes without buttons had stated, as if they were speaking directly to me, "It is what Jesus tells us to do." If I wanted Jesus' help getting through this, I had to do what He wanted me to do without question. Nothing is free including happiness.

With that, I forgave Jacobs. I would no longer see him as evil. I would no longer hate him. I would put it in the past.

Immense relief washed over me. It felt like I had finally dropped a heavy weight I'd been carrying around and I could almost hear the thud as the baggage dropped. I felt physically lighter though I knew I wasn't. I had been carrying this bag of hatred and anger around for almost a month. Now it was gone and I knew I could go on. In that moment, I knew I would not fail at this.

For a month, I had walked through hell. While I knew the journey was far from over, I could now see my way out. It was like I had been lost and now saw something I recognized; I knew I had found my way. For the first time since the crash I felt like I was going to get my life back – maybe not physically, but emotionally and spiritually. We would be OK.

# Chapter 22

## ∞ Trust in Me ∞

Forgiving Jacobs was like turning a page in a book: the dark, terrible chapter in my life was over and a new one was beginning. This chapter would be one of recovery now that the weight of my anger and hatred was gone, along with the depression and *"Why me's."* Sure, there would be times when they'd come back for a visit, but each time I could take heart in the words that had initiated my recovery, "IT IS NOT YOUR PLAN."

I found comfort in my belief that there was a reason for all this – a reason I did not fully understand – but a reason nonetheless. I could now focus on my recovery and rehabilitation, not my sadness for being stuck in a hospital, or the pain with every movement, or the injustice of being the victim. I reminded myself that I was no longer a victim; I was a survivor. God had changed my name.

I had started fresh. I wanted to write the next chapter, one that just had to be better than the last, and I was excited to get on with it. I envisioned my life as a really good novel where I couldn't wait to turn the page and discover what comes next. Content that the last adventure, whether for good or ill, was done, I would look forward to the succeeding chapter in this unfolding story.

I was coming to realize that there was an explanation for why bad things happen; I just wasn't smart enough to see it. God was not going to give me the details of His plan because He knew if I had advance notice of what was in store for me, I would then try to change it to fit my perception of what the plan *should* be. But my vision was far too narrow; I would not know how it should really play out. This was His plan, not mine and I did not need to know anything more about the future; I only had to accept whatever it was just like I had accepted the past.

Absolute faith in Him was required, pure and simple. When he put me on this course, I was lacking in the faith I needed but it was now growing inside me. I was beginning to understand if I just placed my trust in Him, I could follow His plan for my recovery and the rest of my life without fear. I could relax about the details of why it was happening, stop complicating everything, and just keep moving forward.

Truth was that I had to submit to Him, to allow someone else to direct my life. I had spent my entire adult life trying to be in control. Now I had to completely allow God to take the reins, something that I had never really done before.

The fact is, bad things happen to all of us – good people and bad people – it is not about who deserves it. When horrible events take place in our lives, our natural inclination is to search for a reason. But in the end, the answer is simple: bad things happen to you because you are alive and they are part of life. I had to accept that I was on this earth, susceptible to both good and bad developments. This acceptance included the facts that people are not always going to be nice to me and that even the most carefully orchestrated plans are not always going to unfold as I like.

Much like what I was dealing with in the present, there will be even more times when I'd come out on the short end of the stick and it won't be fair. Yes, very true. What happened to us wasn't fair but a lot about life isn't. If I was waiting for life to be "fair" or to "get even" with those who have wronged me, I would always be disappointed. "Fair" and "getting even" just don't happen in this life. I had to accept this reality and move on. Looking back and asking "why me?" would not help me walk again, especially not when I had to endure the pain of rehab. The "why me's" and the "this sucks" were dragging me down and eroding my will; just more unnecessary weight I was hauling around. I had realized that the idea I didn't *deserve* the car crash or someone else didn't *deserve* the disease or the downsizing or the abuse had no relevance. It is likely true that I didn't deserve what happened but it happened anyway. It wasn't fair that Jacobs had walked away with nothing but a scratch but I figured that there were things in the past that had happened to him that were not right either. *Yeah Scot, life isn't going to be fair; tough shit, you need get over it.*

Although I might not have deserved it, maybe I needed it. Maybe it was a vehicle for me to get stronger, to have more faith, to change course. I don't know. What mattered now was that I would live my life in a different way – a better way. Would I learn the lesson God meant to teach me or would I wallow in self-pity? In the end, that was the choice I had to make.

I decided I was not going to fold. It was my time to *man up*.

It sounded harsh as I lay there with both arms splinted and both legs immobilized, unable to even roll on my side. I still could not eat much or even use a bedpan. Nobody would ever tell me, as I lay there, that I wasn't tough enough; that I needed to suck it up and deal with it but I knew I had to. Others may be afraid to say this to me but I could say it to myself. I knew it was true. This wasn't going to be easy, it never is, but the healing and the months of rehab was what had to be done. It was the mental toughness that I needed now. Physically, I had a long way to go but I first had to get strong mentally and spiritually; that was the next step on my road to recovery.

I decided this was not going to beat me; I would not let it. I began to see my recovery as God's challenge for me and decided He had given me an opportunity – yes *opportunity* – to see what I was made of. I had been the "smart kid" and never been particularly tough. Growing up, I was always afraid of getting into a fight on the playground and would usually back down. I was of average height and skinny; I had stopped playing football in eighth grade and wrestled for only a year. At my large high school, the other kids were just bigger and faster. In college, I worked out regularly and was no longer as scrawny, but I had never really been physically stronger than average. Now I would have to work harder than ever to regain my strength: it was time to get tough.

I started to see this event as a great challenge. I, like most people, had not gone through a really tough time had always wondered how I would respond. Soldiers going into battle always wonder about how they will act when the real bullets start flying. This crash became my war, my test of character.

Malcolm Gladwell refers to this in his book *David and Goliath*, in what he calls the "near-miss" phenomenon. It was seen in the English during World War II when London was bombed for 59 days straight in "The Blitz." There was great fear among the leaders of England, Winston Churchill included, that the civilians would panic if bombs started falling from the sky on London. The government did not even build bomb shelters because they were afraid civilians would not come back out, fearing the English people would not have the courage needed to make it through the toughest, most horrific parts of the war.

Instead, the opposite happened. Bombs fell but there were no civilians running through the streets in a panic; after a while people barely even looked up. It is a strange part of the human psyche: we are all afraid of how we will react to a terrible event but once we make it through, the fear starts to go away. In London, the people who survived the bombings (those in the "near-miss" group) began to feel invincible, as if not even bombs could touch them; they'd drop on someone else but *not* them. They had been "chosen" to survive, therefore the bombs would miss them time and time again. Fear of the bombs diminished and was replaced with resolve. The Londoners defiantly went on with life to show those German bastards they were tough. Screw the Nazis – let them drop their bombs, the Londoners were invincible. Funny thing was that those who survived were right. The bombs did not hurt them. They *were* invincible.

I began to feel the same. I had *nearly* died but this had been my "near-miss." It was not going to beat me. Screw Jacobs, I was better than him and I would prove it by walking again. He would not keep me down, I would win. I had survived against all odds, I was invincible. Let the bombs come.

I would push myself harder than I had ever pushed. I would get back as close to normal as I could so that my kids would never question my effort. They would know that, even if I didn't get back to where I was physically before the crash, it would not be because I gave up; it would not be because I was weak. Healing is seldom perfect; there is always something not as good as the original, but my effort would be full-out and I would try every avenue from traditional to non-traditional. I would research things I had never put much faith in before like meditation, acupuncture, and nutritional supplements. Of course, I would also get serious about my relationship with God.

Only one thing still bothered me: I had heard that voice before, that voice that kept telling me, 'IT IS NOT YOUR PLAN" but I couldn't remember where. I had figured it must have been some other life-changing event but there hadn't been any until now. I just couldn't place the voice.

Then it hit me.

The voice hadn't been some "burning bush" like Moses in the desert – my life wasn't nearly as dramatic and I certainly wasn't Moses. In fact, it hadn't been a "voice" at all, just a thought. Like the *'It's not your plan,"* thought it was accompanied by an urgent feeling that I should listen; I intuitively knew this one was important, that I needed to pay attention. Although I wanted to dismiss it as random, I sensed clearly that this thought was crucial, and that I should remember it. The realization sent chills down my spine.

It had occurred the night before the crash and was one of my few memories still left over from the weekend. I was alone in a bedroom at the cabin getting ready for bed when the thought popped into my head out of the blue for no particular reason, seeming completely out of place. The words were simple but clear, "IF A CAR COMES ACROSS THE MEDIAN, YOUR JOB IS TO KEEP IT FROM HITTING THE KIDS IN BACK."

At first, I had kind of laughed it off thinking in my usual know-it-all manner, "That was a strange thought. Why would I be thinking about car crashes? Besides, cars come across the centerline, not the median. Medians are there to keep cars from crashing into each other in the first place. There's no way a car would cross the median and hit us!"

But, it wouldn't go away; this persistent thought kept reverberating. Eventually I had to stop and think about it.

*"If a car comes across the median, your job is to keep it from hitting the kids in back."*

Yes, I was the dad: it's my job to protect the family at all costs. That meant that if a car was coming at us, I would prevent it from hitting the kids. I guess it makes sense but it just would never happen. Of course, at the time I had no idea that less than 24 hours later, a Jeep driven by a drunk driver would careen across the median and collide head-on with our van.

Now I understood. With that thought, God was just instructing me how to do as He commanded: keep the car from hitting the kids and He would take care of the rest. The voice I had heard was just a seemingly illogical, out-of-place thought that advised me how to survive a crash that's usually fatal. I just needed to shut up and listen. I needed to do what He said.

I don't remember the crash and don't know if I did anything in particular to protect the kids. I doubt that I consciously thought about anything; there was no time. All I do know is that we were hit in just the right spot to be injured but not killed. The impact was incredibly hard and we had all "nearly" perished but in the end we all survived, even the dogs.

Our family had a "near-miss." Mona suffered three spinal fractures and a major concussion but was not paralyzed or brain-damaged. In spite of my multiple, serious injuries I had survived. We'd made it because we collided at just the right spot at just the right angle. Jacobs' car had hit mine at the driver's side headlight at about a 30-degree angle. It had sent us spinning, thereby dissipating a great deal of the energy. A few more feet to the left and he would have hit on the side by my door – and three inches of a van door would not have stopped a Jeep coming at 70 miles per hour. My head would have snapped to the side into the door instead of forward into the airbag; this would have certainly broken my neck and fractured my skull. Jacob's thousand-pound Jeep would have collapsed the side of the van and landed on me.

In that case, not only I but also my son Chase, who was sitting behind me, probably would have been killed or paralyzed instantly. Instead, we all shot forward first and were stopped by our seatbelts, while Mona and I hit the airbags. The forward, not sideways, impact kept our necks from breaking. The deadliness of a sideways snap of the head is like the rope in a hangman's noose; when placed correctly, this noose is always to the side and not directly behind. The sideways pull will snap the neck and ensure a quick kill, just like a side impact in a car crash. Colliding at high speed, we needed to hit *head-on*, but not *straight* head-on, in order to survive. The location of the cars' collision allowed the front of our car, with its heavy engine, to absorb the impact, in between us and Jacobs' Jeep. If he had hit us further to the right or at less of an angle, Mona and I would have taken an even bigger blow and likely been paralyzed or killed. I would have broken my right leg in addition to my left. We would have suffered a more direct and forceful impact to the chest and abdomen. We had barely survived the injuries we sustained; any more would have certainly killed one or both of us.

I had subconsciously done exactly what I was told to do, exactly what I *had* to do for all of us to survive, remembering the persistent thought from the day before, *"When a car comes across the median, your job is to keep it from hitting the kids in back."*

I don't think there was any conscious effort on my part but I had been guided by God's voice; the voice that had seemed like just a random, illogical, unrelenting thought. In the end, God rewarded us for my obedience. Mona and I would still get hurt badly, there was no way around that, but we would survive. And we would emerge from the experience stronger, perhaps not physically, but mentally and spiritually – which was ultimately more important. It proved that God had a plan for us. Some would call it "luck" and no doubt we had been lucky but why, *if it was just plain luck*, was I given a warning the night before the crash? God had informed me in very simple terms, "Don't swerve. Do what I say and I will take care of you. Have faith and trust in Me."

## Chapter 23

### ∞ Angels, Angels Everywhere ∞

After about three weeks, Mona was discharged. She joined the kids back home, having been fitted with a solid plastic body brace that went from her armpits to halfway down her thighs. It was sweaty, hot, and confining (it completely encircled her) and she had to wear it for 24 hours a day. As you can imagine, it made sleeping very uncomfortable with many fitful nights. Mona's broken elbow was splinted, making that arm totally useless since she couldn't bend or lift it. Her body ached all over due to the violence of the crash which had inflicted multiple muscle and tendon damage when her body first slammed forward, only to be abruptly stopped by the seatbelt and airbag, and then thrown to the side as we spun. Little wonder pain ravaged every part of her.

Of course, they'd prescribed OxyContin to ease her suffering but it made her sick to her stomach and constipated so she was rarely able to take it. Most days it was simply Tylenol as her sole pain medicine; *Tylenol* for three spinal fractures, a broken elbow, head trauma and severe soft tissue damage all over her body.

Most people who have not been through it have no idea what it is like to cope with unrelenting, long-term, chronic pain. It's debilitating and saps the will of even the toughest person, knowing it will hound them every minute of every day for months, with no escape. Mona had already proven her toughness so it wasn't a matter of being tough; it was about getting to the point of wondering if life would be worth living like this. Life with this kind of pain would be no life at all.

But she was a mom to three little kids with a husband who might not be of much help anymore; she had to persevere and keep her family together. The maternal drive to protect the kids kept her strong and determined. She had no choice but to get better. Since I was not around and probably wouldn't be coming home for a long time, the kids needed her. She simply prayed for the pain to subside.

However, daily maintenance of family and home activities was a real struggle for a variety of reasons. First of all, Mona could not be left alone. She couldn't drive in a brace so transporting kids to school and running the typical household errands were out of the question.

Her injuries made even simple chores like laundry, vacuuming, and preparing meals impossible. *How do you make dinner when you can't stand for more than a few minutes or even drive to the grocery store?* The kids could get themselves on and off the bus but they couldn't participate in after-school activities. Still, we did not want them sitting around watching TV for months while their dad was convalescing in a rehab facility and their mom confined to bed.

Enter more angels. Mona's family had rushed to the hospital when they heard about the crash. Now, with Mona and the kids back home, her mom and sisters stayed with her in two-week shifts, putting their own lives on hold and using up vacation time to help us out. Her sister Carla came first for two weeks, followed by her mother Anne, and finally, sisters Theresa and Denise. Their assistance was invaluable in feeding the kids and getting them to school, keeping animals (Annabelle the dog, three cats, goats, chickens, and horses) fed and watered, doing the laundry, and shopping for groceries. Some normalcy returned for the kids as they got back into the routine of school and friends, taking their minds off of all the trauma and putting them into the swing of fall.

At just ten years-old and her arm in a sling, Alexa stepped up to the plate. She was a lot like her mom in that she just focused on what had to be done and did it. When it was time for her mom to bathe, Alexa would help her to the bathroom and in and out of her back brace. When Mona needed anything, Alexa ran to retrieve it. She even helped feed and dress Victoria and Chase, ensuring they were ready for school every day. This experience forced her to grow up and take responsibility, which she did without complaint. She proved to be one tough kid, and as I said, very much her mother's daughter.

Victoria was only eight but she did what she could, mainly babysitting Chase to enable whoever was there to help us to focus on other things like meals and laundry. Even though Chase was only four, he realized that things had changed and took over a lot of the animal care. He also helped with the laundry. It was amazing to watch these kids rise to the occasion. They saw that they were needed and thrived on it. At that time, without any at home nursing care, we had to rely on the kids and family to help out.

And they did. Because they were angels too.

The assistance we received from our community was a bit unexpected but simply amazing. We hear so much about the bad things people do in the world but those we knew – and even some we didn't – consistently demonstrated kindness and generosity in the aftermath of the accident. They were truly angels among us. We'd moved to Lake Geneva ten years earlier when we bought a very small one-person veterinary practice with Mona as the only veterinarian and a single employee named Karen. We'd worked six days a week, including seeing emergencies, which required being on-call every night and every weekend for the first five years. Our diligent work ethic ultimately paid off in the form of a new building and a four-doctor veterinary practice that served thousands of clients and pets.

Initially I'd believed that all of that sweat equity was for the sole purpose of building the practice and paying the bills; now I realized it had yielded so much more than that. These clients had become friends and we had become an important part of the community, helping all these people when they needed us. Now, it was the community's turn because we needed them. The facts that our kids attended the public schools, had lots of activities and that we as a family attended an active church had given us the opportunity to meet a large percentage of the population – even those who didn't have pets or, *God-forbid*, took them somewhere else for medical care.

Due to the nature of our job, we tended to get to know our clients very well. Often, we'd see them through some of their toughest moments as pet owners. When someone who has just watched their beloved dog get hit by a car comes rushing into your facility – usually in the middle of the night – and hands their pet over to you with trust and confidence, it creates a bond. In many cases, we were the ones who diagnosed and treated some problem in a client's animal or ended their suffering by putting them down when we could do nothing more. No matter what, we had always made an effort to assure our clients knew that we cared and were doing all that we could.

Because of this, many people felt a close bond to us. Being the person who can help someone else when they are at their lowest and most frightened forges a relationship in ways that few other professions do. I would develop the same type friendship with my surgeon, Dr. Lang.

Now we were the ones at our nadir and people rallied around us.

Word of the crash had spread quickly, even though it had not been broadcast on the local news channels but in Madison (60 miles away) where it happened.

Nonetheless, Lake Geneva is a small town so news travels fast. Some of our clients had relatives in the Madison area who'd called them when the news reported a "terrible crash involving two veterinarians from Lake Geneva." The crash had taken place on a Sunday and as soon as our office opened up on Monday, calls began flooding in.

*"Was it true? "Were Dr. Scot and Mona really in a crash?" Are they going to be alright? How are the kids?"*

People were not asking when we would be back to see their pets, or when we could help *them* again; they were asking how they could help *us*. Angels.

Friends and clients arrived to assist. One of our neighbors plows snow in the wintertime; every time a snowflake hit the driveway he was at our house. He'd plow out the drive while his teenage son would shovel the walk. His son even brought out a broom and swept any remaining snow to prevent anyone from slipping.

A client who owns a dry cleaner and laundry mat called the office and told them to have our family assemble everything that needed washing; they would do our laundry for free. Once Mona and the kids were home, the dry cleaning office would call the night before to inform us that someone would be there in the morning to pick up the laundry and bedding. That same night, they'd return it washed, folded and pressed. They did this twice a week to help us keep up.

A local pizza place delivered lunch to our veterinary office every Friday, knowing that the staff was overworked and could use a good lunch. The owners were a young couple with a    big Lab whose shoulder I had fixed. During the process, we'd become friends. We shared some things in common in that they also had a business that required lots of time, dedication and late hours. Their restaurant was the local favorite, known for its great food. It was packed every weekend and most weekdays. Despite being so busy, they never failed to deliver lunch to our staff every week.

Another friend came and installed a wheelchair ramp and a handheld showerhead to enable Mona (and eventually me) to shower sitting down. He also installed handicapped bars around the house to give us something to hold onto.

One of our clients had a daughter Alexa's age. Since the two girls were friends, we'd gotten to know the family over the years through school and 4H activities. They owned a gas station in town and offered free gas to anyone coming to visit us – basically donating $50 to $80 dollars each time someone needed a fill-up. Gas stations make little profit on gasoline but instead the chips and sodas we all buy; this money essentially came straight out of their pockets. But they did it anyway....for months.

We also had an angel named Earl, who lived down the street. He may have been in his upper 60s but he had the strength and determination that characterized so many of his generation. He rarely sat still and would normally take care of the horses, chickens, and goats when we were on vacation. Now, he showed up twice a day to feed and water them as well as maintain the barns. It was winter, which meant he had to carry five-gallon buckets of water out daily for the animals over snow and ice. Here was a man, close to 70 years of age, hauling water up and down ice-covered hills to make sure Mona and the kids didn't have to. Earl knew that Mona could never accomplish such a task with a broken back and that our kids were hardly big enough to carry anything that heavy. But he knew it was winter and the animals needed water. Having already been taking care of them for us while we were at the cabin that weekend, he just kept on coming once he heard about the crash. This incredibly generous man even made sure the maintenance was done, fixing latches and shoveling doors so they would close. We always paid him for his services but now he would accept nothing.

There were also the people who own a small farm where Mona had purchased our goats. These goats were just pets and not much work but they still had to be fed and watered. We kept them in a little shed at night to protect them from the coyotes; therefore, we had to go out twice a day to let them out or lock them up. Goats are also somewhat ill-mannered and tend to jump on people, especially if there is food around. Obviously, Mona was in no condition for that.
Hearing about our injuries, this family came, got the three goats and brought them back to their farm. They cared for them for six months until we could handle them again. We did not even have a good way to transport the animals so they picked them up and dropped them off for us. Again, they would accept no payment.

One of my favorites was my barber, Bill Huntress. Bill was born and raised in Lake Geneva, a bachelor who smoked fat cigars, had been divorced twice, and sported a bumper sticker on his truck that said, *"If they call it Tourist Season, why can't you shoot them?"*

For nine dollars you can get a great haircut and all the local gossip you can take in. Bill owned the classic old-time shop on Main Street with the red-and-white striped pole out front and an old TV that seemed to always be playing *Gunsmoke* reruns. He came across as a tough guy that loved to hunt and had even named his best dog *"The Loser"* because she had once failed to find a bird. Of course, she was about four months old at the time and just learning how to retrieve but she became *The Loser* from then on – even after she'd retrieved hundreds of birds since. Of course, Bill would also spend 20 minutes after each hunt with that dog in his lap, picking out burrs and combing through looking for ticks. But that was just Bill.

He called me in the hospital and asked to come up because he wanted to give me a haircut. This man drove two hours to the hospital to give me a nine dollar haircut and then refused payment. I don't know if anyone ever called Bill an angel before but he *was* one. A gruff angel with a bit of tarnish on his bent halo, but an angel nonetheless. More proof that they come in all shapes and sizes.

The church also jumped in quickly. Our pastors Mark and Mary Anne visited us two- to- three times a week to pray with us and our families – over an hour's drive each way for two very busy people. They did it anyway. After they announced what had happened at all three services the following week, they kept the congregation informed of our progress. They led prayers for us in church and also organized prayer chains where people prayed for us then asked their friends to pray for us also. Many of the folks participating in these prayer chains had no idea who we were – they'd never met any of us – but they didn't care. They prayed for us anyway. We literally had hundreds, maybe thousands of people storming heaven and we'd probably never even met half of them.

Mark and Mary Anne provided more than just spiritual help. Though they believed in the power of prayer, they recognized the real-life challenges Mona and I were facing and were determined to do more than pray. The church organized volunteers to deliver dinners to the house as soon as Mona and the kids were home. Though the prayers were important and helped us heal, the food saved the day. People cooked fantastic meals so Mona and the kids did not have to make many suppers. They enjoyed lasagna, meatloaf, even fresh caught Alaskan salmon a friend had just brought home from a fishing trip.

The food was delivered by five o'clock every night and was one of the greatest gifts we received. Having meals delivered allowed Mona to rest and heal at a time when it was a struggle to even sit up in bed. Alexa would meet the people at the door, take the food and thank them. Those delivering the food had been instructed by the church NOT to come in; they did not want Mona to feel pressured to get out of bed and try to keep herself "presentable" for guests. Their instructions were to hand the food off and keep any conversation short. It was all about making life easy for us, not about the volunteers getting recognized for what they did. Since Alexa rarely knew the person delivering the food, it was a lesson in anonymous giving and the pure joy that accompanies it. Our pastors made sure everyone understood this, too. For many, it was the first time that they did not receive recognition for their good deeds. It was a lesson in giving freely with no expectation for repayment and the ensuing joy that results – a lesson most would not soon forget.

One of the angels delivering food was a 20 year-old college student named Sara. She had signed up to deliver a meal but had run late at a class. When she called the house in a panic, Mona's sister Carla answered.

"I am running late," she apologized, "and I don't have time to cook anything."

"Don't worry," Carla replied. "We have plenty of food for the night."

"No, I *want* to deliver something," Sara insisted. "If you don't mind, I will pick something up. My sister has little kids and they love Happy Meals. I know it is not very fancy but would the kids want that?"

Carla laughed and yelled to the kids "Do you want some Happy Meals tonight?"

The news that they were getting McDonald's for dinner sent the kids screaming. Sara laughed on the other end of the phone. A half-hour later she delivered the bags of food that the kids loved – maybe not for the food itself, but for the prize inside. She also brought two meals for Mona and Carla who, after trying to eat healthy for the entire last month, enthusiastically dug in.

This angel college student had just dropped 20 bucks on people she barely knew. It was probably the equivalent of two-to-three hours of work for her. Most likely, she was broke. Yet she chose to spend the money on us; people she did not really know in a community she had not really lived in for years. Incredible.

One group of ladies within the church optimized the efforts to help. They met multiple times each week to make quilts and shawls for the sick, those leaving for college, the newly baptized, and those entering military service. These quilts were given so that each individual would have something to wrap themselves in when they felt lonely or depressed. They symbolized the love of Jesus and the community wrapped around them, and offered an amazing amount of comfort. As a quilt is hand-stitched, these women pray for the person for whom it was intended, asking God to keep them safe or to heal them. These wonderful ladies made a quilt for each member of our family, customized to us as individuals. Mona's, of course, had horses, mine had fishing and hunting, the girls' had various animals, and Chase's had cars and sports.

The strange thing was that each of us used the quilts every night without really thinking or talking about it. We all had plenty of blankets to keep us warm but each one of us, acting independently, wrapped ourselves in those hand-made quilts instead. It was something that brought great comfort knowing that we had a community of people thinking of us. We all automatically held them close, absorbing the prayer and love put into them. It was another one of those "God moments" we needed to survive. It felt like His arms were wrapping around us with those quilts. In fact, they were.

The veterinary community also came to help. The veterinary field is a relatively small profession and so we get to know each other pretty well. Dr. Mike Aushwitz was one who had graduated with Mona; he was also one of my best friends since my second year in undergrad. I was in charge of his floor as a Resident Assistant and lived right next to him. We had followed similar paths to veterinary school, both spending three years in undergrad before getting into vet school at Wisconsin. He was even the best man in my wedding. When he found out about the crash, he came to visit and soon realized that we would not be able to work for months. Knowing how hard it is on veterinary practices when one, much less two, veterinarians are out, he decided to do what he could do; he came to work at our office. Mike had every Thursday off so every week he drove the hour down to our place and worked for us. He would accept no pay; it was just his way of helping out. The clients and staff loved him because of his upbeat attitude and his hard work. He took on every task without complaint so our other two vets could take a lunch or simply slow down for a while. We never asked him to do this; he took it upon himself.

Mona's classmates, Dr. Chris Holder and his wife Dr. Tracy Kusik, sent their little girl to stay with her grandparents and came down to help us for three days. They lived over two hours away and each ran their own busy practices. Chris was a solo practitioner, which meant he had to close his office, while Tracy had to pay a part-time vet to work extra hours – all because they wanted to do their part. Like the other angels, neither one would accept any payment for their time.

Dr. Jeff Korosec, a veterinarian from a neighboring practice, scheduled himself to come in to our office and perform some surgeries that simply could not wait. This was in spite of the fact that these clients would likely have traveled to his practice for the surgery since he was just a few miles away. He came to our facility anyway – sacrificing the thousands of dollars he could have made had these clients come to him instead. He also refused any compensation for his good deeds.

Every single one of these people were angels, stepping in when they were needed to  help us survive. We could not have made it without them.

Of course, our office staff had also been plunged into a huge mess because suddenly, without any warning, we were two doctors short in a four-doctor practice. For months, the other vets, Doctors Chris Welch and Kay Stratton, would be asked to work a boatload of hours including every Saturday. They would be on-call every other day and every other weekend. Between vets, receptionists and technicians, we still had a staff of about fifteen people to support and did not want to lay anyone off, knowing these people still needed their paychecks. Appointments and surgeries would have to continue.

Dr. Welch, a one-third partner in the business, now had to run the whole show. He also had a wife, Kelly, also a veterinarian, and three very small children including a newborn. He would work all day nonstop, run home to see the wife and kids for a few hours, then run back to the office, fill out records, and call clients after the kids were in bed. Mona and I had done this during our start-up years, and I knew how exhausting the pace could be. Yet, Dr. Welch soldiered on, keeping the business afloat and paying the bills.

Dr. Kay Stratton was our associate veterinarian working part-time. A level-headed woman, she takes all things in stride. Her husband Steve is a jovial salesman who is constantly making people laugh. Their two children were about the same age as Alexa and Chase. Kay had been working part-time for us and part-time for another practice 40 miles away, where they lived. In the aftermath of the accident, she decided to quit her other part-time practice in order to work full-time for us. We had been considering offering her a full-time position anyway but had been waiting to do so until spring when our caseload usually got busier. However, the crash had accelerated this process: we needed her NOW.

But moving closer would be no small task. It required selling their house and transferring their kids to a new school. Any parent who has ever had to do this knows just how    disruptive it can be, so they decided to wait until the school year ended in seven months. In the meantime, Kay commuted two hours roundtrip to our office daily. By joining us full-time she took a huge burden off of Chris. Together, their hard work enabled the practice to continue employing all staff members and keep up with payroll.

We were fortunate to have very well trained and dedicated people working for us. Our office manager, Karen, had been with us from the start. She had been our first employee, coming with the practice when we bought it from the original owner, Dr. Smith. Karen is one of the few people I have ever met who is always happy; she has an attitude where she can handle anything with a smile. Life has not always been easy for her but both our clients and the staff she manages love her. When we first took over the practice, we had no idea what a blessing she would be. In the very beginning, Karen was the liaison between suspicious clients who still wanted the original owner, Dr. Smith, and the two new young vets in town – Mona and me. Although we were strangers to these clients, they trusted Karen; if she said we were OK, then we were OK. Now she faced this latest challenge with her usual smile and upbeat attitude. She was the one clients called for updates on our condition; she dealt with ordering the myriad of supplies needed each week; she handled the staff issues that invariably arise with 15 women and one man working together suddenly, under the stress of fewer doctors and a cloud of uncertainty. Karen smiled through it all, drinking lots of coffee along the way.

The rest of our staff took it upon themselves to do as much as they could so that Chris and Kay could tend to their next appointments. They learned to set the catheters for the surgeries and in-patients; they took the X-rays and ran the bloodwork. The doctors would examine the patient and tell the technicians what they needed. The staff would get it done and the doctors would move onto the next patient. Everyone was forced to become more efficient and take on more duties – and each one did without complaint. In the end, it forced the hospital to run much more smoothly and efficiently; ultimately, we would continue the changes that they had instituted from then on. In the end, the extra stress and work had forced the staff to grow and improve to the point of transforming themselves into some of the best veterinary workers I have ever been around.

Most importantly, the staff put its personal issues on hold – no bickering and/or office politics – they knew it just wasn't the time for that stuff. If the practice was going to survive and thrive, they had to pull together. And they did, knowing that Mona and I had other things to worry about, and that Chris, Kay, and Karen had their hands full. Nobody needed more drama. Therefore, everyone did their work and kept their complaints to themselves.

This was especially important for Chris, the only remaining practice owner who could work. Not to be sexist but out of our 15 employees, Chris and I were the only men. Throughout my years as a veterinary practice owner, I've discovered women just think differently. Chris and I had a real hard time relating to the office politics, even though men deal with politics, too. However, our brand differs from the women's so we found it nearly impossible to understand women in the workplace (and elsewhere). It took me years to arrive at the realization that I never really would *get* them. There would be days when the entire staff was upset with me. Of course, I had not noticed and had no idea why; Karen or Mona would just relay the information. A typical conversation went like this:

"Do you know the whole staff is ready to quit?'

"No, why?"

"Because you said this. . . "

"No, I said this…"

"But you meant this…"

"No, if I meant *that*, I would have said *that*. I didn't mean *that* and so I said just what I meant which was *this*…"

"But it was the *way* you said it that they are upset about."

It took me years to figure out how to express my thoughts in a way that the women around me would take as intended. Although I mostly just asked for things in a nicer way, I said "please" and "thank-you," a lot more often. Not a bad lesson to learn anywhere in life.

Now our staff pulled together and pitched in to help; a genuine testament to their character. They were a truly great group of people. More angels among us.

Every one of these people provided a big lesson for us. When others are down and out, they need more than words of support, they need actions. Cards and letters are great and I read them over and over as I lay in the hospital bed, but the wonderful actions of these people truly spoke louder than words. Not having to cook dinner, do laundry, or shovel a walk when we were physically unable was incredibly helpful, especially since we never had to ask. They just did it. They sacrificed their own time in order to do all of these things for us, fully aware that there are just so many details in life that are impossible to do when you are in seriously impaired physical condition. I thought of how tired I used to be after a normal day of running the business, managing the house, and charging after the kids. Now, accomplishing these tasks when the simple act of standing on your own two feet was an exhausting struggle after just two minutes was downright impossible. For the first time in our lives, we simply could not physically do things on our own; we needed help.

Yet we were both reluctant to accept it because we had never needed it before. One day, Mona called and to tell me we were getting a donation from the local Boy Scouts. They had sold pizzas downtown on a terribly cold winter day to raise money for us. How do two professionals who had made a good living accept money from a group of young boys who could use it themselves? A few months ago, they probably would have been coming to *us* asking for a donation; now they were raising funds on our behalf.

Mona wanted to know about sending the money back. I wasn't sure what to do so I told her I would think about it follow up with her the next day.

Pastor Mark walked in a short time later to check on me and I mentioned our dilemma. He, of course, had a great story to share in response.

Mark began, "There was a man who had great faith in God. He was stranded on his roof during a flood. With his great faith, he prayed for God to deliver him and save his life as the water got higher. A boat drifted by but he did not jump in, telling them 'I don't need your boat, God will save me.' In a little while, a group of firemen came by in another boat and told him to jump in but he again refused saying 'God will save me.' Next, a helicopter hovered overhead with the water now nearly up to his feet and yet he still refused to leave stating, 'I have faith that God will save me.' Finally the water got too high and swept the man away. When he reached heaven and saw God he asked, 'God, I prayed to you to save me and you let me drown. Why didn't you save me?' God replied, 'You prayed and I sent a boat, a team of firemen, and a helicopter, yet each time you refused my help. You died because you expected something different and failed to see me in the people I sent to you. I was working *through* the people I sent. You were arrogant and thought you knew what I would do to save you. You did not know my ways; nobody does.'"

His story made perfect sense. These people were sent by God to help us like the firemen sent to save the man trapped in the flood. Turning the Boy Scouts away, refusing to accept their gift – or the gifts of others – is turning away God's help. As hard as it was for us to take charity, turning it away would have been pure arrogance. For now, we needed help and people were willing to assist any way they could. We would use the charity for its intended purpose: to get us back on our feet. There was no shame in that. We'd be careful to only use the help of others until we no longer needed it and then we would pay it forward with the next ones down the line. Otherwise, there *would* be shame in accepting help.

After Pastor Mark left, I called Mona and advised her to accept the gift from the Scouts. "It would be a slap in the face to those boys to refuse their generosity. We had helped them before and now it was their opportunity to help us. Accept the money and the help. We will pay it back somewhere down the road."

Indeed, in the aftermath of tragedy there were angels all around us.

Scot Hodkiewicz

# Chapter 24

## ∞ A Long Road to Normal ∞

With my sister Julie's help, I was transferred from the intensive care ward in Madison to the rehab floor in Julie's hospital 80 miles away in Fond du Lac, our hometown. My parents still lived in the area, along with my sisters Julie and Kim. Since I was in no shape to return home and Mona was in no shape to care for me, it was decided that I would go to the rehabilitation unit in the Fond du Lac hospital. There, my family could take care of me while Mona's family took care of her and the kids at home.

Now at a new hospital, I would begin rehab. I was excited to finally be starting the process of learning to walk again. Although I wouldn't be able to put any weight on my left leg for another month, I could start rehabbing the rest of my body as soon as I recovered from the move.

As they wheeled me into my new room after the hour-and-a-half trip in an ambulance, a nurse walked in.

"Scot, do you remember me? It's Renee, we grew up a few houses apart from each other."

Indeed we had. Renee and I had known each other since kindergarten but lost touch after graduating from high school. I had no idea she was even a nurse – much less worked on the floor I'd be residing on for the foreseeable future.

"Renee! Great to see you."

"Love to say that you look good but you really don't."

"You should have seen me a few weeks ago. I was really a mess."

"I heard. Your sister filled me in. Sounds like you were pretty lucky to still be here.

"Yeah, I feel more blessed than lucky."

"Julie told me you were coming today. Don't worry, we will take good care of you."

"Thanks Renee. How is the family?"

"Everyone is good. You rest, we will catch up another time."

"Yeah, the ride really knocked me out."

"Tomorrow we will get you into a wheelchair and out of the room for a bit. If there is anything you need, just hit the button. I will take extra good care of you."

Having been in bed for three weeks and sick of being confined to a room, I was excited to get into a wheelchair; visions of racing down the hallway and popping wheelies danced in my head. I settled into my new room, still shivering from the brief trip outside in the cold moving from the ambulance to inside the hospital. It was November in Wisconsin and the ten seconds I had been outside had left me feeling frozen. I buried myself under the covers and waited to warm up.

As I snuggled in the warmth of my bedding, I thought about Renee: I hadn't seen her since we were teenagers and now she was my nurse assigned to watch over me. Yet another angel sent to guide and help me through all of this.

The next day's rehab started pretty simply. The first goal was to get me out of bed and into a wheelchair. Renee came in with another nurse and a board used to slide from the bed to the chair.

*"Piece of cake,"* I thought. "I just need to slide down the board."

Renee put the board between the bed and the wheelchair and told me to move up onto the ramp. I struggled to get myself up, raising the bed as much as possible to get to an upright position. I pushed and fought to hoist myself onto the board to slide into the wheelchair but could not do it. My arms were still too weak to shift my butt even half an inch to get onto the board. It was unbelievable how much strength I'd lost and how far I needed to go. But having accepted this devastating injury as something I may not have wanted but something God said I needed, I could now laugh it off rather than do the "this sucks" thing. At this point I was so weak, there was nowhere to go but up.

The nurses helped but they did not want to do too much for me; they knew I had to get stronger. After three tries, I was finally able to get onto the board. By then, my arms were shaking and I was starting to sweat. I slid down to the wheelchair, nurses on each side to keep me from collapsing. With a lot of effort, I got myself into the chair. My arms were now exhausted. I had no chance of cruising around the hospital and popping wheelies – not yet anyway.

As I sat in the chair trying to get my strength back, Renee wheeled me over to the sink and helped me take off my shirt. Part of rehab was learning how to live at home with my new body and they wanted to show me how to do a sponge bath in the sink (I wouldn't be showering for a while). When I looked in the mirror for the first time since the crash I was shocked at what I saw: I had lost about 35 pounds and my face was gaunt and hollow. My body looked like that of a 12 year-old; skinny with no muscle at all. I had bony legs with knobby knees and arms so thin I could almost encircle my biceps with my fingers, something I hadn't been able to do for almost 30 years. Although I was never a huge guy, I had worked out hard from high school through college to develop some muscle and now it had all disappeared. All those years of trying to stay in shape and it had all disappeared in a few weeks. I had gone from a healthy, vibrant, hard-charging man to a skinny, weak, invalid who couldn't even get out of bed without help. I felt my will starting to fade. I had so far to go; it looked like an impossible mountain to climb. Running between three exam rooms and doing ten surgeries in a day seemed a distant memory.

Renee helped me do a quick sponge bath and I was freezing again. The side effect of losing this much weight was that I had no fat to hold in the heat. Even though the water was warm, my wet skin quickly got cold. Once I told Renee I'd had enough, she quickly put on my shirt, noticing that I was starting to shiver and my teeth were chattering – totally expected when she saw how thin I was. She quickly helped put me back into bed.

Once there, I pulled the covers up tight while my teeth continued to chatter and the rest of my body shivered uncontrollably. I hadn't been this chilled for a long time. Now I understood why so many women complain about being cold, especially if they are thin. With no fat and little muscle, it was nearly impossible for me to stay warm. This was something I had not expected but here it was, another battle to fight.

After shedding a few more tears and rededicating myself to rehab, I drifted off to sleep. I put myself in God's hands and thanked him again for all of us surviving. I would put up with the pain and struggle: it would make me stronger, and I would be thankful for any little advance. It had started to make sense. If I wanted to get my stamina back, I would have to do the conditioning and push my body. If I wanted my muscle back, I would have to work them and work them hard. Nothing would come back by me lying in the hospital bed feeling sorry for myself. It would not be easy or fun but I would have to put in the work if I wanted to have a better life than this. I would have to get the strength to be on my feet all day if I wanted to do my job – the job God had designed me seemingly since birth to do. I knew it would be hard, *really* hard. I would go through but it was the only way; the only way to get out of this predicament.

I had done the "long struggle" thing before: becoming a veterinarian took a tremendous amount of work and study. I'd put an incredible amount of effort into my chosen profession, spending countless hours studying and practicing techniques until I got them down. I would read veterinary articles until I fell asleep at night instead of relaxing and watching TV. In school, I would be looking through a microscope alone in the lab after everyone else was gone because I wanted to be the best. It has been estimated that you must put in about 10,000 hours to master anything. No matter what it is, 10,000 hours applies to everything from music to business to medicine, whatever. It takes about that many hours of practice and study to excel at any given skill. It had taken about that much effort but I had become very good at my job and had reaped the rewards of the hard work. I thought I was far beyond this kind of struggle and could now live the rest of my life on cruise control. Of course, I was wrong again but my past struggle had prepared me for my current one: I would push my recovery just like I had pushed in vet school and it may very well take just as long. I would dedicate the time and work at it every day, with the confidence my devotion would be rewarded. If I put in the work, I would get better.

Getting stronger would take tremendous effort, but so what? I wasn't going anywhere for a while so I had the time. Fact was, if I took it easy and did not fully dedicate myself to getting back to my normal, I would end up weak – spiritually, mentally and physically. Reaching the finish line with an even stronger mental and spiritual outlook was more important to me than the physical aspects of my recovery. Looking back, I couldn't think of much in my life that was both valuable and easy. My kids were my greatest blessings but parenting was tough and I needed to keep working at it to improve as a father. Being a veterinarian was tough but offered great rewards. Maintaining a healthy marriage took a lot of effort but was well worth it. Running a marathon (something I had never done) required tons of incredibly hard training but runners are in great shape and admired for their dedication and perseverance.

This situation was the same: It would be a huge amount of work but I was no stranger to that because I'd done it before. If I put in the time and endured the pain, it would be worth it in the end to run around outside with the kids again. With broken heels and a smashed femur, I doubted that would include running marathons, but I would not have run a marathon before the crash either. At least I would know that if I couldn't run with the kids, it would not be because I laid in bed feeling sorry for myself.

Maybe I didn't deserve this but who in this hospital deserved to be here? Wars were still waging in Iraq and Afghanistan; how many of those soldiers would have it so much worse than I? None of them deserved it either. I was done whining. I had survived; time to be grateful, anything from here would be a blessing.

The next day I woke up ready to hit the rehab with everything I had. My sister had lined up a physical therapist named Jeff to take on my case. I would soon discover he was another one of my angels. It wouldn't be easy and it would be painful but I was ready. Time to get to work.

Unfortunately, though I could now sit up, all I could do was some minor range of motion exercises. My arms were still splinted and my leg was too weak to support weight. Learning to stand or walk was still out of the question.

Rehab at this point consisted of sitting up in a chair and stretching. I had done this routine for the last week at the other hospital and it was all I could do. The first week at the rehab unit was no different; I just stretched some and sat up in bed. I was ready for more but my body wasn't. I had to be patient.

At the start of the second week in Fond du Lac and a month after the crash, the doctors removed the splint on my arms and the cast on my feet, replacing them with lighter, more flexible wraps. I was instructed to take it easy but I could start using them. My left leg was not splinted but I was instructed that I could not bear weight on it. I was now ready, physically and mentally, to start rehab.

About 20 minutes into my 40-minute session with Jeff, after stretching and doing range of motion exercises, I stopped.

"What's wrong?" Jeff asked.

"We need to start pushing it. I'm ready. It's time to get me up and going. I want you to push me every day. Don't be nice. I don't need you to be my buddy. I don't even need to like you. I need you to get me back to where I was before this happened and I don't care how you do it. I will take anything you can dish out just push me so I get better. I won't walk again by just stretching; my muscles need to work. I have made my peace with what happened. I have made my peace with Jacobs. I understand that this is just some mountain I have to climb so let's get going."

Jeff replied, "Julie told me you had the drive but I wasn't sure. Now I see it. Some of this stuff may hurt and you may not like it. By the way, I can still be your friend. You don't have to hate me."

"I have a ton of pain medication so I can handle the hurt but I will only be your friend if you get me walking." Of course, that was a lie; Jeff was hard not to like.

The next four weeks were grueling as Jeff pushed me harder and harder. We did some stretching at first but even that was painful and tough. He wanted me to get better range of motion in my joints. Having been broken and splinted for weeks, all the joints had started to freeze up due to scar tissue. If I wanted to use them again, that scar tissue would have to be broken down without breaking apart the convalescing bones.

We also were working on other things. I couldn't do much with my legs yet but he wanted me to start strengthening my upper body. I would need to be able to push the wheelchair and eventually use crutches but right now my arms were so weak I could do neither.
We used weights – two pounds to start – just lifting them off the bed. These were the "girly weights" that I used to move out of my way to get to the *real* weights when I was working out. Now lifting them was a struggle and a bit humiliating. Humility was another lesson I was learning but after having to defecate where I slept for weeks, this humiliation was minor. My elbows and shoulder were still healing so I was very limited in what I could do. Still, I could do something and that felt great. The stretching was necessary but I wanted to get strong. Unfortunately, the doctors did not want me even to stand on my plated leg or lift much with my plated elbows and shoulder for another month or two – much less "work out." The "girly" weights would have to do.

Jeff was in a real predicament. How do you strengthen a man who can't bear weight on his legs or lift more than two pounds?
His solution was to start with what he could rehab. At first, this entailed just getting up from lying flat on my back, if that was all that I could do. Soon it transitioned into a modified sit-up with my back

on a raised mat and my feet on the floor. Then Jeff added balance exercises and more core work.

Slowly, day by day, I got stronger. At the end of the first week I could sit all the way up from a lying down position. Even though I could only do it once and it hurt like hell, a single sit-up was progress. Though I couldn't stand on my leg, Jeff got permission from Dr. Lang to try to bend it. It had been immobilized for weeks to allow the torn muscle and broken bone to heal and was now stuck in the slightly bent position it had been in when I was lying in my bed. He sat me on a chair and grabbed my ankle. Before he could push, I stopped him.

"You aren't going to break this thing are you?"

"Guess we will see."

"Real funny."

He pushed down to flex the knee and my foot moved an inch before it stopped dead. The knee was frozen. Jeff pulled a goniometer out of his pocket. This tool – basically a couple of plastic legs joined at one end – is used to measure the angles. He placed one side of it along my thigh along the other along my shin. "Fifteen degrees," he observed. "A knee can normally bend about 100."

"Wow, really? I have a long way to go."

"We figure that if we can get 90 degrees of bend, you will be functionally normal."

"So how do we get it to bend?"

"We will do some stretching exercises and some other tricks I have."

"You are going to just push on it until the scar tissue breaks up aren't you?"

"Yeah, you got it."

"I bet that is going to hurt like hell."

"Remember, it was your own sister who asked me to help you."

"I don't remember ever being *that* awful to her growing up."

"Well, you must have done something to her. Unfortunately, that is what we need to do if that leg is ever going to bend again."

"I figured brute force was the only way to tear down the scar tissue."

"There is not any other way that I know of and the sooner we start the better."

"Are we starting now?"

"Tomorrow. I want you to take some extra pain meds before our session, Okay?"

"That bad, huh?"

"I will get more done if you are a bit doped up."

"Deal. I don't think I want to feel this anyway."

"Don't worry. You will feel it."

The leg muscle of the thigh, the quadriceps, had been torn apart during the crash. Muscle is nearly impossible to suture back together so it was basically left to form a big scar. Scar tissue forms from the blood clot that filled the gap in the muscle. All the proteins and factors that make up the scar start in that clot; it just needs to organize itself into the scar. Unfortunately, the scar grabs onto anything in the area and starts tying it all together. Because the bone was broken and I was not allowed to bend my knee for the first three weeks, the scar got stronger and stronger. By now it was a solid band of immobile scar tissue keeping my knee from bending.

As part of the healing, it had even started to calcify (laying down new bone in addition to scar tissue) but the new bone was in the muscle a few inches away from the thighbone. This happens frequently in major trauma and I had developed some more of it in my chest muscle also. The tendon to the shoulder from the chest had been stretched and damaged when my shoulder was dislocated. Now there was a perfect outline of the calcified tendon on my shoulder X-ray as well as what looked like a second thighbone in my leg muscle. Both of these I could feel as rock-hard masses where the tendon or muscle should be.

Of course, calcified tissue (bone) doesn't stretch so if I wanted to move those joints, I would have to work to free them up. A surgeon could not remove it since they would have to do more damage, but by starting to do the rehab I would try to limit how much formed and how much it would tie up the other structures around it (the other tendons and muscles in the area).

Later on, I would break this extra bone in my shoulder during rehab. I was working the chest muscle when I heard a "pop" and felt a jolt of pain. An X-ray would later reveal a crack in the abnormal bone and leave a large, painful knot for months.

I did not have a choice but to try to stretch my knee because a knee that doesn't bend is worse than useless – it is in the way. Even getting into a car is impossible without bending your legs; you can't get your foot in the door. If I couldn't get it to bend then I would be better off having it amputated. A "frozen shoulder" from that calcified tendon made even getting a coat on difficult. Both needed to gain mobility if I was to get anywhere back to normal. I would have to break down a lot of scar tissue and I realized this would involve having to endure an incredible amount of pain. The knee would have to learn to bend again if I was going to get better but right now I could barely bend at all. A hundred degrees of bend was normal and here I was at fifteen. I couldn't imagine that I would ever get there. When I got back to the room, I contemplated the long road ahead.

I was staring down my path through just hoping that at some point I would find a way out. "Right now, all I could see was the long road ahead of me, without a finish line in sight. I could not see an end to this pain, this suffering, this *Hell*."

"God, I asked you to help me through this. Please help me through the pain and get my leg moving again. I told you that I would put in the work and now it is time. I just ask for Your help getting through the pain. I am scared. Please help me if You see fit. Your will be done."

With that I felt peace. The pain would really suck but my desire to be active again compelled me to soldier on. The ensuing sense of peace I felt after my prayer assured me God was with me. It would be alright. Not fun, but alright.

The next day I arrived at my therapy session psyched up and ready to hit it. I had taken some extra OxyContin to help with the pain and I was raring to go. Jeff began with some upper body work to strengthen my chest and arms and some simple stretching of the leg. When he tried bending it, it would stop at 15 degrees. There was no give; it just stopped. Jeff looked at me soberly and asked, "Are you ready?"

"Go ahead" I replied.

I sat on the bench and gripped the sides. Jeff put his shoulder into my shin and pushed. I just about flew off the table as the pain shot through my leg. Early scar tissue is comprised of many nerves and mine had all just gone nuts. The pain was horrific as Jeff bore down, trying to bend my knee. After ten seconds he stopped; I was already sweating. He simply stated, "Let me know when you are ready to do it again."

"Again?" I thought. "I don't think I could possibly do this again!" Yet I also understood that every day we waited, the scar tissue would only become stronger and better organized. If it was going to get broken down, it would have to be now.

"God help me."

After a minute, I was ready again.

"Let's go," I told him. Jeff grabbed a hold again and pushed. Again the pain shot through my leg as the scar tissue let me know I was going to pay for disturbing it. I screamed and Jeff stopped. "No," I ordered. "Keep going!"

Again he pushed down and held for a count of ten. After a minute he repeated it for a third time. The pain was greater than any I had ever experienced since I didn't remember the crash. Now I would be enduring it daily for the foreseeable future.

We did this exercise every day for the rest of the week: stretch and work on upper body strength, then try to bend the leg. Little by little, the scar tissue began to release. I never felt it give way (this was good since it meant the muscle had re-torn); all I could feel was the pain and soreness of my leg. At the end of the week we measured the angle again. "Twenty degrees," Jeff declared.

All that pain and agony had moved the leg an additional five degrees. To get back to useful, the leg would have to bend to ninety degrees. I did the math; five degrees a week, seventy more degrees to go, that would be fourteen weeks. Three-and-a-half months of this agony just to return to "functional" – not "normal" – just "functional." This is when I knew I had a very painful road ahead.

Again my spirit started to sag: I never realized the rehab would be this painful and take this long. I had expected to be rehabbing for weeks and now it looked like it would take months or even years. I also knew that the first week was likely the easiest since the scar tissue had not fully matured yet. The stretching would probably get harder as time went on so it was likely to take much longer than the three-and-a-half months I'd figured. I wasn't sure that I could handle this amount of pain every day for another week, much less four or five months.

The next day, I asked Jeff if he could push harder and get this over with.

"Relax," he said, "your bones are not strong enough to push any more than we are doing. If we push too hard, the bone will break."

I knew he was right. The bone in my thigh would take another two-to-three months to fully heal. If Jeff applied too much pressure, it would snap. This would be a very long and painful road. I started feeling the sadness and depression returning as I realized just how tough the next six months to a year would be. I longed to be back running with the kids again. I had just learned to slide into the wheelchair; how would I ever run again? Months of extremely painful therapy to break apart the scar tissue lie ahead and I wasn't even sure it would work. I hadn't even started yet on my shoulder and elbows. How much pain would that take? I just didn't know if I could do it.

Again, I asked God for the strength to keep going and got no answer. I had heard His voice before but not now. I would just have to *believe* He was listening. I would have to have *faith*.

# Chapter 25

## ∞ Rocky Road Ahead ∞

Everyone has their own mountain to climb. Mine was a 100-foot ramp connecting the rehab floor with the main hospital. I was spending time in my wheelchair every day but was still very weak in spite of doing rehab twice a day – once with Jeff and a second time with an occupational therapist who worked on me while in bed. The rest of the day I either slept or watched TV. I couldn't read since I was still on a lot of drugs and concentrating was impossible. With all the exposure to inane television programming, my brain would need some rehab too once I was off all the drugs.

One night I decided to take a spin in the wheelchair since my arms needed the work. I got into the chair and headed down the hall, advising the nurses as I wheeled by that I would be right back (like I could go anywhere). I headed for the ramp.

From the bottom I rested as I gazed up at it: one-hundred or so feet with a gradual climb, *no big deal*. I started up with confidence but within ten feet, my arms gave out and I could go no further. Already in a sweat, I locked the wheels and rested. After a minute I tried again. This time I only made it about five feet and had to stop; the ramp was too long. I turned and headed back down. At the bottom I turned back around in the direction of my room. This ramp would be my mountain: if I climbed it every day I could judge if I was getting stronger. Tomorrow I would try again.

Week after week, Jeff and I continued to work. Through forgiveness for Jacobs and faith that God wanted me to go through this, I had beaten back depression and anger; I would still cry but only about every third night instead of every night. I did not hold back – if I needed to cry, I cried. This wasn't a lack of faith in God's plan or a show of weakness but justifiable sadness over the predicament I found myself in. As long as I didn't allow it to consume me and push me off my path, the path God had chosen for me, I would be fine. Unwavering faith that I was following *His* path now, not my own, gave me the strength to keep going It allowed me to accept the pain and the boredom of being in bed for 23 hours a day; it made me accept the reality of being far away from my family and my job. Knowing that there was an intended purpose, that He was making me stronger for another reason, enabled me to accept what had happened as my mental and spiritual workout – one designed to make me better and stronger than I had ever been. I needed spiritual rehab as well as physical.

I was also learning how to fend for myself in a wheelchair, developing a decent ability to move from the bed to the chair and back again. Soon, I could do it on my own without a board to slide on.

Again, they moved me to the bathroom to take a sponge bath. Thanks to my sister Kim, I didn't have to wash my hair. A nurse at the hospital with access to all the toys they could employ for their patients, Kim had brought in a self-contained hair-washing machine since I could not shower or hang my head over a sink. This contraption – designed to wash a patient's hair in bed – was basically a plastic bag with a hose to bring water and shampoo in, with another to suck it back out. It washed the hair but kept the bed dry; a great invention.

Now I rolled over to the sink to clean up everything else. Every time I took my shirt off, I confronted the complete loss of muscle. As I removed my pants, I noticed my legs were just knobby knees crisscrossed with long scars. Frankly the scars did not bother me; as I mentioned before, being a guy, scars were a badge of courage. What bothered me was the muscle loss. I had expected some loss but this was amazing: I literally had no muscle left on my body. Yes, I knew the muscle was still there because it doesn't disappear; it just shrinks from lack of use. Because I had been down so long, there was literally no muscle left on my frame.

However, this time as I looked in the mirror, I laughed (I was learning to do that again). This was just my starting point and I would work the muscle back from here. It helped that I had seen this in animals that had been starved. They'd come in with no muscle and protruding bones but with some exercise and good food, these animals would rebuild their muscle mass; within six months they'd be healthy and vibrant – forgetting the past and wagging their tails in their joy to simply be alive. I would learn from them. This time I thanked God for being with me and smiled: at some point I would be wagging my tail too.

The sponge bath felt great. I experienced that clean and cool feeling that comes after washing up. Within moments though, that cool feeling became a *cold* feeling, necessitating a return to bed to snuggle under the covers, my teeth chattering. Soon, I learned to ask a nurse to preheat the bathroom in preparation for bathing and have my clothes ready the second I came out. My clothes were all modified with Velcro sides so I could put them on myself but the minute it took to dry off and dress left me exhausted and shivering under the bed linens and blankets. Being thin may be a good look for supermodels, but handling the cold requires fat and muscle. It would be a while before I had any of that.

# Chapter 26

## ∞ More Pain ∞

By now I was sick of hospitals: I had reached the point where all I wanted was to go home. I missed my kids, I missed Mona, and I missed my life. Yes, this hospital was located in the town in which I grew up; the same place where most of my family still lived but I had left 20 years earlier. This was no longer my hometown; I knew very few people anymore and it had changed greatly. Prior to the crash, I still liked to drive around during visits to Fond du Lac and pass by my high school and junior high. However, both the town and I had moved on. I needed to get back to the area that I now called home, the area where my own family was living. Lake Geneva was my new hometown.

But the hospital had a rule: they would not discharge me until I could function in a home environment. This meant being able to feed myself, clean myself and get to the toilet myself. I also had to prove I could get in and out of bed, up and down stairs, and in and out of a car. All these everyday tasks I'd been doing since I was four years-old had to be relearned with the reality of my new body.

Eating wasn't a problem since my right hand was working fine. My stomach was still terribly shrunken but even though I could not eat much it was getting better. I was so sick of ice cream after having it with every meal that I had to stop eating it entirely. I could still hear God laughing about that. My left arm was still pretty immobile with the broken elbow and shoulder but the right arm functioned near normally so I could do the first one.

The other tasks I needed to master would either require crutches or be made a lot easier with crutches. It was time to learn to use them.

The problem with crutches was that they require stable shoulders and arms. My arms were just starting to get there; I had been strengthening them in rehab and with my nightly trips to the ramp. Although they were definitely stronger, the thought of supporting all my weight on arms that were smashed just a month-and-a-half ago was pretty scary – especially when I knew I could not allow myself to fall down.

But I also knew that the crutches were my ticket home: I had to learn to use them and get out of the wheelchair if I wanted to leave the hospital and get back home. That day I asked Jeff to teach me.

My PT was ready with a set of crutches waiting. He didn't even have to measure me; he had done this so long he could determine the size I needed simply by looking at me (this guy was good!).

He placed a belt around my waist to help lift me and had me sit up on the edge of the bed. "On three," he announced before counting. On the count of three, he pulled as I pushed up, trying to get the crutches into my armpits. Jeff did not want to help too much; I needed to do this mostly on my own. Like riding a bike, there was a certain amount of "feel" to it. Since I didn't have it, I fell backward onto the bed.

"Try again?" he asked.

"You bet," I replied, getting excited about the prospect of being on my feet. We counted again; this time I got up and almost fell forward onto my face. The adrenaline rushed through me as I envisioned doing a face-plant onto the linoleum floor and re-breaking my arms and nose. Jeff caught me and pulled me back onto the bed again.

"Not quite so fast," he said. "On three."

This time I got it. I had never been on crutches before and this was all new but soon I was starting to get the hang of it. I took a few minutes to get my balance and then, tentatively, I started to take little baby steps forward. The thought of falling still terrified me and I made sure Jeff was continuing to hold my belt.

"Don't let go," I reminded him.

"I don't let my patients fall," he answered as I started to wonder if I should apologize for doubting him.

My shoulders and armpits were aching almost immediately. Even though the crutches were well padded, the muscles and tendons were screaming in protest at having to carry my weight. At this time I probably only weighed 150 pounds – 20 pounds less than my normal weight, but it was more than my muscles could handle. I ignored the pain (the Oxycodone I'd taken prior to rehab didn't hurt) and started moving forward. This was freedom from the bed, freedom from the chair, and the first time I'd been off my butt since the crash. I had expected some discomfort as the muscles got used to their new task but this involved so much more. This was screaming pain from joints and bones that had been stretched and shattered now protesting at having to hold together. The shoulders and elbows I was using to bear the weight had been dislocated and broken just about a month ago; they reminded me that my recovery would entail a significant amount of pain.

I'd become accustomed to the fact that nearly everything I did now had an element of pain associated with it but I'd had worse. Still, pain is still never easy. After I was back in the room and the staff was gone, I broke down again. Not only was this pain unbearable, it was inescapable. Every move was a struggle; every task now involved planning how to do it. Rolling over in bed required thinking about exactly what arm or leg to move first, then next, to accomplish the task and minimize the pain. With every task I debated whether it was worth the effort. Often, I decided it was not and reach for the OxyCodone that made it go away. I knew I was walking a dangerous line with this stuff but after all the pain that I had been through and the long road ahead, I just needed a break. I popped a few more pills and closed my eyes for a rest.

Day after day, we kept working on the crutches. I no longer wanted the wheelchair; I knew that using the crutches would eventually be a lot easier and would get me home. They just hurt...a lot.

I still used the chair to go around the hospital. It was a great workout for the arms and chest and didn't put the strain on my joints like the crutches did. Yet I knew that the crutches would provide more freedom, which was now my main focus.

After a week, I was getting pretty confident on them and using them more and more without any help. One night I got up to use the bathroom and grabbed my crutches. About five feet from the bed, I make a mistake by moving a little too fast. I felt my weight shift from forward to back as I started to lose my balance and fall. With so many broken bones, falling had been my absolute worst fear: it could re-break them and hurt like hell. Now I knew I was going to hit the floor and there was nothing I could do about it. I let out a yell hoping a nurse would happen to be near but no such luck.

As my weight shifted backward, I tried to minimize the damage. I would be landing on my butt with its broken pelvis, catching myself with my arms – and their broken elbows – jarring all my weight onto a shoulder that had popped out not too long ago. I rolled a bit to the right to use my best arm to cushion the fall, the one that had broken at the elbow but had *not* dislocated at the shoulder. Even that was not a great option but it was the best one I had.

I needed to get the crutches out of the way; otherwise they'd catch me halfway down and put all the force into my armpits. They clattered across the floor as I threw them to the side. This noise, along with my yell, was enough to bring the nurses and a doctor running. I hit the ground with a thud and the pain shot through me. I took most of the fall on my right but primarily landed on my butt.

The nurses and doctor arrived a few seconds after I had hit the floor as I lay there feeling the full effects of the fall. My butt was throbbing and my right arm felt like it had been hit with a baseball bat. Reverting back to my veterinary training, I evaluated the situation. I had not re-broken anything to the best of my knowledge; I had not heard anything crack, nor did I feel anything shift. I would be OK; I would just hurt for a while, again.

The staff looked at me in horror. I could see the expressions on their faces, that "Oh, shit!" look when something goes wrong. In the medical profession, it is also the *"Oh shit, we are going to get sued!"* look. I tried to put their minds to rest. "I'm OK," I assured them. "This was my fault; I thought I was better at the crutches than I am. Just give me a second and then help me up."

I sat there for about 30 more seconds as the pain started to subside. This was why I'd feared falling: I was *really* hurt and *really* embarrassed for needing three people to pick me up. The nurses and doctor each grabbed something to pull on and, on three, lifted me back to the bed. I lay back down exhausted. They left the room and I reached for the Oxy again. I deserved some more; I had just hit the floor and my whole body now ached. As the meds kicked in, the pain stopped and I started to drift off to sleep again. I remembered that I had never made it to the bathroom but decided it wasn't worth the effort. I could pee in my sheets like a baby if necessary. It was just too painful to move.

The next day, I crutched down the hall for physical therapy, moving very slowly and concentrating on each step. I wanted to do it myself, the proverbial *getting back on the horse that just kicked you off* idea, but I was scared.

Jeff met me at the door with a big smile on his face. "How is your butt?" he asked with a grin.

"Pretty sore," I replied.

"I guess I had better teach you how to get up from the floor."

"I never thought about it but you are right, I can't get up like I used to and I may not have help around if I fall at home."

"Before you are released, we have to know you won't be stuck on the floor waiting for someone to come home and find you. Let me show you how you can get to your feet if this happens again."

The next hour was spent on and off a two-foot high mat working on ways to get up. They included using a chair, the crutch, and nothing. The biggest problem was my inability to bend my left leg. It was like trying to get your butt off the ground with a three foot stick attached to your hip. It was virtually impossible without something to grab onto. A heavy chair was the easiest since I could pull myself up to seat height, rest, and then use the crutch to get to my feet. Jeff taught me three or four ways to get off the floor depending on what was around me. Now I could do it: one more hurdle down. I was just very careful when I got to my feet that I didn't shift my weight backward again and end up on my can.

The second thing Jeff had to teach me was how to get into the car. They actually had a small car mock-up to practice getting in and out without going to the parking lot. It sounds easy but that long left leg made it near impossible to get my foot in and close the door. I could slide over on the seat but eventually I had to turn my body and get my foot in front of me. There simply was not enough room if I couldn't bend at the knee.

"We need to get your leg to bend before you can go home," Jeff declared.

"That sounds painful."

"You should be getting used to it by now."

"You seem to be really enjoying it. Do you like to kick puppies in your spare time?"

"No, just rehab patients."

I still had a long way to go before I could get my leg in the car; I was only bending at about 30 degrees and probably needed 40 degrees more before I could get in. Hopelessness washed over me again. There seemed to be no way to get that much bend out of this knee. Jeff pressing on it had nearly killed me. *How was I supposed to get this to stretch all the way to 70 so I could get in the car and go home? How would I ever get back to near normal at one-hundred degrees?* It just didn't seem possible. I couldn't wait to get back to the room and take more Oxycontin.

Later that night, I woke up and thought again about the long road ahead. The ramp that I once perceived as a challenge now seemed like nothing; I'd believed the worst pain was behind me and it would get better as time went on. Now I realized it was just beginning and that the rehab would get much worse before it got better. I had slept through the initial pain after the crash and then been on a morphine drip. Now all I had was the Oxy.

This sucked. I didn't do anything to deserve this. The drunk that hit us wasn't getting his leg bent until the muscles ripped. He had gotten a few bruises that were probably gone in a week. What an asshole.

The anger washed over me like a flood. I stewed for 20 minutes unable to sleep, getting more and more upset. I should be at home with my kids or at work fixing broken bones on dogs and cats, not waiting for my own bones to heal. I reached for the OxyContin, assuring myself that I needed it to sleep. There was no way I would be able to nod off with the pain – in my leg, in my arm, in my other arm – take your pick. The pain would keep me awake and prevent me from doing my rehab in the morning. I deserved more Oxy.

In reality, I wanted the Oxy because I was mad. Mad at where I was, mad at the man who put me here, mad that I would need to suffer everyday if I ever wanted to bend my knee again, mad that I would have to endure so much pain just to get back to anywhere near normal. Just a few weeks ago, I'd been normal; I just didn't deserve to go through this hardship.

Though I normally took 30 milligrams of Oxy, tonight I took 50. The nurse had advised me I could take up to 80 so 50 was not a big deal, right? At least it wasn't TWICE the amount I had taken before and 30 milligrams just wasn't cutting it at this point. Anyway, I was only taking 50 milligrams just this once; tomorrow I will cut back down to thirty.

I downed the pills as the anger boiled within. I had tried to do everything right: attended church whenever I could, tried to be nice to people, made an effort to do the right thing and *this* is what I get.
Again, I heard the words repeat inside my head, "It is not your plan."

"What does that mean?!" I shouted out. "Why do I need to go through all this? I just want to know why."

Silence.

"Figures," I retorted. "No answers, just more pain."

I had no idea how right I was.

# Chapter 27

## ∞ My Life is the Worst ∞

Jeff started physical therapy the next day with a lot of stretching and strength exercises. I had worked for almost an hour before he decided it was time to stretch the leg.

I was still pissed from the previous night, doubtful if I could go through all this pain. If I didn't have the guts to make the effort, I would have to quit my career as a vet. Yes, I could collect disability to keep us from going broke but we would have to sell the house and downsize. I also knew I would hate not working and be completely bored to death.

I knew I was wallowing in self-pity, as did Jeff, who noticed my distinct lack of enthusiasm. After our normal rehab routine, he set me on the chair to try to bend my knee, noting, "Like my dad used to say, 'this is going to hurt you more than it is going to hurt me.'"

I told myself to relax but tightened up as soon as he touched my leg. As he pressed, I fought to suppress a scream. Jeff counted down from ten, applying pressure to the foot with his shoulder in a downward motion. As he released, I tried to catch my breath. Before I could, he pressed again.

"Ten, nine, eight . . ." he counted down again.

After the third time, we were done. I laid flat on the mat waiting for the pain to subside. Jeff waited for my eyes to open and bent down to help me up. I got to my wheelchair; he had suggested I use it today knowing my leg would be killing me. He was right. There was no way I could use crutches after this latest grueling session.

"See you tomorrow and we will do it again."

I nodded but remained silent; the pain was still too fresh in my mind. I thought about having to go through this again: *Was it even worth it?* The pain had been excruciating and the thought of repeating this daily pattern of rehab was draining my will. This amount of pain was more than I thought I could stand. I got to bed and popped some more Oxy – 60 milligrams since my leg was killing me. *This is temporary,* I told myself. *Just until I get through this leg thing.* I drifted off to sleep, thoroughly unconvinced I could do this much longer.

The next day, Jeff met me with a smile. "Ready to go?" he asked.

"Sure" I replied half-heartedly, "I'm ready to scream again."

"I could go easy but your sister told me to push you hard. You must have really been an awful baby brother to her."

"Pay-back is a bitch," I said.

I smiled but was rapidly losing my drive. The pain was wearing me down and the drugs were sapping my willpower. Although I told myself I needed them to get through the day, they robbed me of my strength and clouded my mind. I had taken 80 milligrams of Oxy this morning knowing that this day was going to be hard, reasoning that without the drugs, I would not be able to do the therapy. In order to get flexibility back into my legs, 80 milligrams was necessary. It was temporary – just until the leg could stretch further and then I would drop it down.

On this particular day though, Jeff wanted to take me to the stairs because the ability to go up and down stairs was one of the skills I needed develop to get back home. Though our house was single story, navigating stairs was part of life and very scary. If falling onto the floor was painful, I couldn't imagine what falling down the stairs would be like, especially if I was half way up and fell backward. My right foot was no longer immobilized and they had taken the cast off my left foot, replacing it with a boot. The nurse had cut it off the day before while I slept. I didn't even remember them doing it; I was out cold on the Oxy.

"Let's first see what your ankle can do," Jeff announced as he pulled out another one of his exercise devices from his stash. It was a flat board with a half-ball on the bottom. "This will force you to use your ankle to keep balance," he explained as he brought me over to the parallel bars.

Using the bars for support and with Jeff holding my waist, I put my right foot onto the platform. Immediately the foot bent to the left and I was unable to straighten it because my ankle was too weak. I pushed my weight off that foot and tried again. This time my foot bent to the right; there was just no strength left in it after being in a cast for five weeks.

"Let's try this sitting down," Jeff suggested. We moved to a seat and tried again. This time I could at least start to keep my foot stable until I put some weight on it; then it would fall to one side or the other.

"Don't worry," Jeff encouraged, "it will take about a week for you to get some strength back."

"A week?! This looks like it will take a month."

"You'll be surprised."

After working on the ball-board for 20 minutes, we continued with more upper body stretching and exercises. At the end of the session, I knew it was time to try to bend my leg again. I got over to the chair and Jeff asked if I was ready.

"As ready as I'll ever be."

"Here we go" he said, while I braced. He pushed my shin and my knee started to bend. The pain ripped through my thigh again as he bore down, counting down from ten. I clenched my teeth and tried desperately to think about something other than the pain tearing through my leg.

"Three ... two ... one."

He let off my leg and the pain eased up – not entirely since the muscle still throbbed – but it did ease up.

Thirty seconds went by in what seemed like two. Jeff was ready again. "Here we go," he warned he pushed once more. Again the pain ripped through my leg for the ten seconds he kept it there. By now there were tears in my eyes.

He let off as I fought to keep myself from crying like a baby. Men were not supposed to bawl like that – especially not in front of other men.

"I know this is tough," he offered, "but it is the only way to get you home."

"I know, it just sucks," I replied, wiping away the tears and feeling ashamed for crying.

"One more time and we will check your angle."

"Okay, one more."

Jeff pushed and the pain hit me again. He counted back from ten for what seemed like an hour.

"Three . . . two . . . one." He let off and I collapsed back on the chair, my leg screaming at me.

"Let's measure," Jeff suggested as he grabbed his goniometer and carefully adjusted it to my leg. Once satisfied, he read the number, "30 degrees. That's better."

*Four degrees difference with all that agony!*

I would probably need another 30 to get in the car and over 60 before I got a functional knee. *How could I withstand this much pain for that long?*

Jeff read the disappointment on my face. "Four degrees is great," he assured me. "We only worked at it for a little over a week and it got better but I should warn you, it may not improve every time. You will have setbacks and days where it stays the same."

"Great," I retorted, "if I can't get a degree a day, this will take a hundred sessions, a hundred times having my leg scream at me. I just don't know if I can do this. Maybe I just need to go on disability forgetting about ever bending this leg again. I had a horrific injury. Most people would just go onto disability and collect a check, wouldn't they?"

"Your sister says you are not like most people. I've seen people like you before. You would be bored out of your mind in a month and wishing you had done the rehab right away. Now is the best time to get that leg functioning; it only gets harder if you wait."
I knew he was right. I had told myself that I would do whatever it takes. I should not have been surprised that it would not be easy.

"I just never expected it would be *this* hard," I confessed.

Too exhausted to crutch back to the room, Jeff called Renee to bring a wheelchair and she pushed me along the way. I was mentally and physically shot. She helped me into bed and I stared at the ceiling for a while contemplating whether this was worth it. Undecided, I took another 80 milligrams of Oxy. I still could not roll onto either side due to the boot on my left leg and the pain in my shoulder. I could roll about halfway to the right but it was so much work to stay in that position that I could not sleep. I was stuck on my back like a turtle for the foreseeable future.

My life was upside-down. The Oxy kicked in and I began to drift into sleep as the pain subsided. I thought about how life would be if I was on Oxy for the remainder of it. The Oxy sure made the pain better, so maybe I would just stay on it forever. People would understand. Anyway, I figured I could stop it at any time. Now I just needed it.

I was going through my personal hell – the of terrible pain, drugs, uncertainty, and fear. I had always been in control of my life and now I couldn't even roll over in bed. The Oxy had constipated me to the point that even going to the bathroom was an agonizing struggle. I was a shell of the man I had been before. I knew I couldn't work with my body like this and certainly not with my mind clouded with drugs. It seemed like my world had ended. I was lost.

I cried again, this time for a long time. I had never been so depressed and scared. It seemed like my hell would go on for eternity.

The next day, Jeff arrived an hour ahead of schedule. "Hope you don't mind, I wanted to do your session a little early."

"No problem, I didn't have any plans."

Jeff handed me the crutches.

"I think I need the chair today, my leg is too sore for the crutches."

"Okay, let's get you rolling." Jeff could sense the lack of energy in my voice. He could tell I had realized the length of the road ahead of me. I wasn't Superman who would be back to work in a month as if nothing had ever happened.

We rolled into therapy and I started to move to the chair to work on the ball-board. I needed to strengthen my ankle before I could do much else. As I started to work, the other therapist called Jeff over to help her.

"Be right back," he told me.

Since we had started early, there were a number of patients in the rehab room I had never seen before. Over by the other door was a younger man; just a kid really. He looked about eighteen, roughly half my age. He was a good looking kid but very thin like me. Although he was in a wheelchair, he did not have casts or bandages like mine. He smiled at the two nurses and the two physical therapists who were helping him. I noticed a slight tick as his head moved back and forth between the two nurses, who started to place his feet into position on the floor as he gazed at them. With his feet set, they pulled him out of his chair. Jeff and the other therapist stood on either side behind him bearing most of his weight. His knees buckled and his hips swayed hard to the left. Jeff caught him and pushed his hips back under him. He continued to smile and look back and forth at the nurses.

"OK, take a step," a nurse told him. He gazed at her with a smile but his foot didn't move.

"Come on, Jimmy, take a step," she repeated.

He smiled.

She pulled his foot forward and placed it about six inches in front of him. The physical therapists and nurses moved him forward placing his feet and congratulating him on his progress the whole time. Jimmy just smiled as his eyes moved back and forth. They repeated this for about five feet and moved the chair back behind him. They lowered him into it and again congratulated him on a great job. Jimmy smiled.

By now it was obvious that this young man had a severe brain injury. He was not comprehending much; just *how much* was anybody's guess. His body was thin and atrophied; obviously he had been in a bed for a prolonged period of time. His mind was atrophied too.

Jeff returned and began to move me over to start my next exercise. As I got up, I noticed a face in the hallway window. She was about my age or maybe a little older. She smiled at the nurses and therapists as they waved and gave her a thumbs up. She nodded weakly but her smile was noticeably forced now. I could only assume that this woman was Jimmy's mother. As she started to move to the doorway I could see she had a tear running down her face. She walked over to Jimmy who was smiling at her – the exact smile he'd offered the nurses. He just continually grinned like that with his head swaying back and forth. His mother was just another face to him; he didn't recognize her.

"Jeff, what happened to him," I asked.

"I can't tell you due to confidentiality issues but let me just say that if you ride a motorcycle, wear a helmet. Now let's get to your therapy."

We spent the next hour stretching, doing weights, walking with crutches, and starting to walk without them at the parallel bars. The entire time, Jeff supported me to keep me from falling. At the end of the session, I sat on the chair and he pushed on my leg, trying to get it to flex. Once again, the pain was intense and I had tears in my eyes when he was done.

"Let's measure the angle," I said.

"It probably won't change every day," he warned.

"I know. Let's measure it anyway. I want to keep track."

He grabbed the goniometer and measured again.

"This can vary day to day and I will try to measure it the same each time but this is not exact."

"I understand but I want to see anyway."

He lined up one leg of the goniometer down my thigh and the other leg down my shin.

"Try to flex your knee as much as possible," Jeff suggested. "We will measure it the same way each time so try to flex it as much as you can on your own."

I bore down and flexed the knee. I could tell the knee didn't move much. The foot still stuck out almost straight.

"Thirty-six degrees," Jeff announced.

"By the end of the week, I break forty," I said.

"You can't expect progress every day, there will be ups and downs."

"Then I guess I will just get a new therapist."

"I'm more worried about your sister than you."

"I don't blame you. I have been afraid of her as long as I can remember. She used to beat the snot out of me," I said. "Thanks for bringing me in early. I was feeling sorry for myself."

"Look, I see bad injuries every day. Yours are extreme and you have a lot of work to do, but you have a shot at getting back to close to where you were. Many of my patients don't. Therapy may help but we won't get Jimmy anywhere close to where he was before his accident, you *can*."

As he got me in the chair and started to roll me out into the hall, I told him I would make it myself. I had gotten the hint and was sick of being sad and depressed. It was time to be thankful that I had a chance. I didn't know how close to normal I could get but my brain was intact. When I came in after the crash, I did not even have a pulse. I had nearly bled out and should have lost oxygen to the brain. In fact, I was sure I had. But I hadn't lost brain function, at least as far as I could tell. Not to mention the fact that my brain had been whipped forward as the cars hit and then spun violently in a circle. Any of these should have killed parts or all of my brain leaving me smiling in a wheelchair with my head swaying back and forth for the rest of my life. I still had a long road in front of me but long roads had never stopped me before. College and vet school was seven years of hard work. It would have been easier to get B's and not work so hard but I had labored to get A's. I was not always the smartest but I had outworked almost everyone and therefor had succeeded. That struggle had prepared me for this. I was looking at six months of really hard work to see how good I could get. What was I complaining about? Six months was nothing; college had been seven years. We had been building a business for eight. Nothing I had ever done that was worth anything had happened quickly. This would be no different and I shouldn't expect it to be.

Jimmy did not seem to fully contemplate his surroundings, thankfully for him. Knowing what he had been before and comparing it to what he was now would be the worst part – at least for me anyway. He did not have to deal with his "old" reality; that life he had forgotten.

He was living in the new one. Good for him that he didn't know what he had lost.

Of course his mom knew.

I knew what my life had *been*; now I had to get it back. I knew that my chance was now. The longer the scars had to form and mature, the harder it would be to stretch them out. It was now or never. My brain had been spared and that was the most important to me. I was fighting the daze of the Oxycodone but I realized that I was in a pretty good place. My doctors had saved me and my limbs. I knew the bones would heal. The muscle of my leg could be stretched if I could handle the pain but I did not have much choice; the leg was pretty much useless as it was. All in all, I had a good chance to get back close to normal. Jimmy, I figured, would never be close to what he had been, I could see that. My mother had hope, Jimmy's mom did not. I had a path out of my own hell – Jimmy, or I should say, Jimmy's mom – had no easy way out of hers. It was time to quit whining and be thankful.

That day I prayed for my newest angel, Jimmy.

# Chapter 28

## ∞ One Hurdle at a Time ∞

Renee entered my room one morning with her perpetual smile and asked, "Do you want to try the shower this morning?"

They had taught me to take a sponge bath but if I wanted to go home, I had to learn to shower since baths were not an option for me with two broken arms. Unlike the hospital, I did not have a wheelchair accessible shower at home so I had to develop the ability to move myself in and out. Fortunately the home shower did have a bench, enabling me to sit down once inside; however, the doorway into it had a raised lip that the chair could not cross. I would have to crutch in and out.

You bet," I replied as I started to sit up in the bed. The casts were all off but I still sported a walking boot and a brace on my left arm. The bones were healing but I was not ready to trust it yet. Because I had broken my elbow where the muscle attaches, bearing weight would put a huge amount of strain on the fracture. At this time, there was still a good chance that bone might be unable to handle it and come apart. This was especially true if I fell backward and tried to catch myself with my left arm. For these reasons, it was splinted to keep it in position but both the splint and the walking boot were attached with Velcro to make it easy to remove them before showering. Renee slid the chair over to the bed and gestured her assistance in getting me in.

"That's OK," I countered. "I can do this myself."

I struggled to get in position at the side of the bed and had to grab the far arm of the chair to slide my butt into the seat. As I did, the chair started to roll away from the bed, inciting a huge adrenaline rush as I envisioned the chair rolling out from under me. Although I caught myself, the adrenaline made me nauseous. Renee gave me that "wife look," indicating I had screwed up.

"You always want to make sure the wheels are locked before you try to get in or you will end up on the floor."

"Do you do that to everyone or did I do something to you growing up that made you want to scare the crap out of me?"

"No, I do this to everyone. Don't worry; my foot was an inch behind the wheel in case you didn't stop in time. I wanted you to learn your lesson. You will never make that mistake again."

I knew Renee had been doing this a while; she told me that most falls occur during the process of getting in and out of the wheelchair – usually because the wheels are not properly locked. This valuable lesson may have saved me from a lot of future hurt. I thanked her and tried again.

This time after locking the wheels, I slid into the chair with little effort. In fact, I was getting good at it and as a result, my arms were getting stronger every day. Of course, it didn't hurt that I was still 20 pounds lighter than before the crash. God was probably still laughing at me for my inability to gorge myself on all the fatty, high calorie foods I was now permitted to eat, thanks to my shrunken stomach and newly developed hatred for ice-cream.

We rolled to the shower with Renee carrying my crutches. It was much like the one at home with the exception that there was no lip going in and the chair could roll right up to the bench. I locked the wheels and slid onto my perch.

"Next time, we will work on getting over a lip but today you can just get the shower done."

With that, Renee stepped out and pulled the curtain closed. "Just hand me your clothes when you are ready," she stated.

I was not wearing the usual hospital garb. Another couple of angels had taken care of that; the wife and the mother-in-law of one of my best friends had made me three sets of hospital clothes. These were made of a thick flannel to keep me warm. She had split them down the outside seams and stitched in strips of Velcro. This allowed me to fully open the pants down the outside of each leg. I could get them on and off by simply sliding them out from under my butt instead of pulling them off over my feet. Without the seams split like this, there would be no way to get them on and off by myself with a leg that didn't bend. She had also made matching shirts that split down the seam under the arm allowing me to take it on and off with one hand like a poncho.

Having been a nurse herself who had witnessed the struggles of patients with my type of injury, she knew this would help greatly. I had only met this woman once at a baptism for my friend's child but she, in a great act of kindness, had spent hours making these special garments for me. Just being able to get out of hospital clothes with their thin material and terrible fit had done me a world of good. It created a little bit of normalcy to be in pajamas instead of the hospital gowns. And they felt great. I thanked God for sending yet another pair of angels.

As I sat on the bench, I tore the Velcro seams open on my shirt and pants and slipped them off. Now I remembered why they were made out of flannel; it was freezing in here. I was still very thin and had no body fat or muscle to keep me warm. I handed Renee the clothes from behind the curtain as fast as I could and cranked the shower on hot. It seemed like forever until the water warmed up. I just let it run onto the floor for a while to heat up the shower stall. I had it so hot I could not be under the water myself; I just sat in the steam and waited for the shivering to stop. I made a mental note to heat up the bathroom and let the shower run before I stripped down next time.

This was the first shower I had been able to take for five weeks. Never one to take long showers because I regarded them as utilitarian – a quick method of cleaning up before moving on to more important things – today I took a long one. Yes, it took me much longer to get everything washed with one working hand and being forced to sit down, but I was really enjoying the process of cleansing my body. Sponge bathes are OK but not the same as a good, hot shower. For the first time in years, I simply sat under the spray and allowed the water to wash over me. I was starting to feel human again. This was a major step toward going home and I was fully enjoying it.

"Everything OK?"

I had forgotten about Renee waiting outside the curtain.

"Just finishing up," I yelled, somewhat embarrassed. I grabbed the razor in the shower and quickly removed a few days of stubble. Previously, my sisters had been shaving me, which prevented a beard, but now I could perform the task myself.

I turned off the shower and Renee handed me the towel. I got a blast of cold air as the curtain open up a few inches and immediately began to shiver. I quickly toweled off and asked for my clothes, dressing as fast as I could and going "commando" since it was too hard to get underwear over my feet. The Velcro pajamas would be just fine. Renee pushed in the chair and I moved myself into it, this time checking to make sure the wheels were locked.

"You remembered," she enthused with a wise smile on her face.

"The feeling of that chair starting to roll as I tried to get in it had scared the shit out of me. I hadn't felt that since the time I fell at the other hospital and I remember how much that one hurt."

"You were always pretty fast learner, even as a kid," she replied.

"Pain is a pretty good teacher."

Showering was just one requirement before earning the right to go home and now I could check it off the list. Only two tasks remained: doing stairs and getting into the car. Those I would work on next.

At rehab, I asked Jeff to try getting into the car.

"Maybe next week. You're not quite there yet."

"I think I can do it. Let me try," I insisted, pushing him just a little past where he thought I should be.

"You are not going to stop pestering me until I let you try so let's give it a whirl."

We went over to the car cab mock-up that they had brought in for practice. It was the cab of a car complete with a door and steering wheel. They kept it very realistic in order to determine a patient's readiness and ability to truly get in and out on their own.

We rolled over to the car and Jeff stepped back. I opened the door with some difficulty as I tried to swing it open while in a wheelchair. The door hit the wheels twice before I figured out how to pull it open with one hand and turn the wheelchair out of the way with the other. I could use my leg in the boot to push the door open all the way. Jeff just laughed at my use of my broken leg to move a thirty pound door.

Having accomplished this, I sat and stared at the car seat. "Now what?" I asked looking over my shoulder at Jeff.

"The trick here is to shift your butt in first and then swing in the legs."

"Okay, I'll give it a shot," I replied.

Getting into a car would seem to be a very simple task: we all do it multiple times a day, though not with weak, injured arms and an unbendable leg. I tried to rotate in but soon realized my foot could not even get past the door, much less get into the body of the car. I tried to bend my knee and move my left foot – still encased in a walking boot – past the door. Unable to bend it, I tried to slide further into the car. But sliding was painful and difficult due to the weakness of my arms. Instead I had to "walk" my butt back across the car seat shifting side to side, using my arms to lift some of the weight. I got my body almost half way across the bench seat before trying to swing my feet into the car. My right leg could bend so this one was not a problem. The left leg could now swing past the door but it soon became apparent that there was no way it could get inside the car body. I tried to slide further into the car and swing again but again the leg wouldn't fit; it was just too straight to fit under the dash. My heart sank. I was exhausted from the effort and sweating.

I knew I would not be able to go home until I could get in the car and for that I needed at least another 20 degrees of bend. Now I could appreciate just how critical the ability to bend the knee would be – and how important it was to get this ability back. A knee that does not bend would render the whole leg useless and nothing more than an obstacle. Of course, the only way to bend it more would be to continue Jeff's incredibly painful, daily torture sessions; there was simply no way around that. The next few months would be very painful, but also critical. If I did not get good range of motion now, the scarring would mature and get worse. Eventually, it would be impossible to stretch it no matter how hard Jeff pushed. The leg would stop improving and I would be stuck.

I looked at Jeff and he smiled. "Ready to get back to work? We will get you in there eventually."

I knew I'd been expecting too much; no matter how much I wanted to go home, I just wasn't physically ready. I'd made good progress over the few weeks I'd been at the rehab hospital but I still had a long way to go. I was disappointed but not really surprised; I just hadn't anticipated these kinds of hurdles. Like most people, I had never dreamed that the ability to get into a car would be lost after a crash; now this was the one thing preventing me from going home. I got back into the chair, again checking to make sure the wheels were locked, and rolled back into the physical therapy section.

After doing the stretching exercises, Jeff told me to grab my crutches and follow him. Now I was getting pretty good with them as my upper body, though still weak, was getting stronger and stronger. I followed him as we crossed the rehab unit expecting him to stop any second at one of the therapy contraptions that were scattered everywhere. Jeff just kept walking. Finally, I saw where he was headed: the far end had a door with a word that literally scared the out of me "STAIRS."

*"Shit!"* I thought.

It made perfect sense that I would have to learn how to do stairs but the thought of navigating them on crutches with a foot in a boot and non-bending elbows brought back memories of falling backwards in the hospital. Falling this time would be much, much worse. I envisioned getting my weight too far back and tumbling down eight or ten stairs at a time; I still did not trust my broken leg. Though I knew it was healing, it wasn't healed. There was still a gap in the bone where I had lost the piece, and a fall would re-break it. Jeff opened the door as my anxiety level shot up again. These were concrete steps – no padding whatsoever.

Jeff saw my thoughts reflected in my facial expression.

"Still don't trust me not to drop you?"

I sighed, "Yeah, I trust. If you drop me I will kick your ass."

"Julie never told you I have a black belt did she."

"In that case, if you drop me I will give you a really nasty look."

"I am not going to drop you so it is not a problem. Now let me tell you how to do this."

As I was learning, there's a trick to everything when you have a disability: nothing is done normally. Here, I had to get up or down the stairs with both crutches under one arm and the other holding onto the stair rail. Jeff had me put the two crutches under my left arm (the one with the bad elbow and shoulder) which freed my right arm to use the handrail. With Jeff holding me, I moved the crutches down a step and stopped.

"Now just lower yourself down," Jeff instructed.

I was frozen. Taking a single step like that while I looked at the next five concrete steps was akin to jumping off a cliff. I did not trust my leg to hold, I didn't know that my arms would not give out, I feared the crutch would slip on the concrete. Jeff waited a few seconds and encouraged, "I got you, go ahead."

I literally closed my eyes and stepped off my six-inch cliff. Everything was OK, no pain, everything held. I prepared for the next step and took the leap. OK again. With each step I gained confidence; only the first one was hard. Soon I had it; I could go all the way down the flight with Jeff letting go on the final two steps. I turned around and repeated the procedure on the way up, with Jeff behind me but no longer holding my belt. Check this one off the list: I had the stair thing down.

"Good job, now when we get you in the car, you may be able to get home."

"Well, I guess it's time to stretch the leg."

"Sorry, but this is the only way to get it to bend."

"I know. This is what will get me home and get me closer to normal, so go ahead and torture me."

We went over to the dreaded chair and did the same routine. Three times Jeff pushed on my foot trying to flex my knee as far as he could. He would hold it there for ten seconds as I tried not to scream in pain. The pain was not getting better. I figured it wouldn't. Scar tissue is full of nerves and doesn't really "stretch;" the fibers have to "tear." And that hurts – there's just no way around it. It just really sucked.

Back in bed after the therapy session, I wondered if there was a better way. Maybe, I thought, Lang could just cut the scar tissue and "free it up." Trouble was, Lang wasn't here but in the Madison Hospital. I wouldn't be able to ask him until I saw him again in a few months.

Then I tried a different tack. Maybe a surgeon here could do it! Since I had an "in" with my sister, I waited for her to stop by. She usually did after work and I figured she would come in tonight. Either Kim or Julie typically dropped by at some point during the day and brought me a meal from some fast food place so I didn't have to always be eating hospital food. Even though the food here was decent, there were only about five choices on the menu and they were getting pretty old. They had also delivered some Gatorade that the nurses kept in a fridge on the floor. The hospital had soda, milk and juices but I was tired of them, too. Hopefully, Kim or Julie would bring in some lunch.

I was exhausted from therapy and needed to sleep but I held off on the Oxy, waiting to see if my sisters would visit.

I got lucky. Kim walked in with a sub.

"I got you an Italian with the works, hope that's OK."

"Sounds great. Who is your best surgeon around here?" I asked as I unwrapped the sub and sank my teeth into the greatest tasting sandwich in the world (I had been eating hospital food for a long time).

"Now what do you want to get cut?"

I want a surgeon to cut free some scar tissue on my leg so I can bend my knee."

"I'll ask but nobody around here wants to touch you. You are too much of a mess."

"Yeah, I know but do you think you can ask?"

"Sure, I'll ask Dr. Robbins. He is a good guy. I'll see if he can come up and check you."

That afternoon, Dr. Robbins walked in the door. He was about thirty-five, good-looking and athletic, just what surgeons always look like on TV.

"Your sister is Kim, right?" he began.

"Yep, and thank you for stopping in. I just need an opinion on this leg. I have a compound femoral fracture fixed with a locking plate. The outside of the quad muscle was torn and now is all scarred up. It is keeping me from bending my leg and I was wondering if the scar tissue could be cut to free it up again."

"Let me take a look," he replied. I pulled off the covers and undid the Velcro on the side of my pajamas. "I like the pants," Dr. Robbins complimented, noticing my custom-made pajamas. He felt the side of my leg and lifted the knee. My leg stuck straight out. He tried to bend it and saw it was frozen.

"Kim told me you are a glutton for punishment but I don't think surgery will be very helpful. First, the bone won't be healed enough yet to risk opening this up. There is too much risk that we will re-break the bone trying to free up the muscle. We also run the risk of getting the bone infected, which would be a huge mess and may cost you your leg. Most importantly, I don't think it will help in the long-term. If I cut this, it is half your quad muscle. There is a high risk that your kneecap would be pulled toward the inside by the intact part of the muscle and start to dislocate. You would not be able to do the stretching exercises for weeks due to the pain so the scar tissue will reform and you will be back to where you started or worse. You have to also remember that your good muscle has not stretched to full length for over a month and will have shortened. Pulling on it could tear it and then you'd have scarring on the whole quad, not just the outer half. Sorry, but even as a surgeon who thinks I can fix almost anything by cutting it, I wouldn't touch this one."

"I figured this was what you were going to say."

"Jeff will keep working on it in PT. It will keep getting better if you really push it but don't wait. The longer you wait, the less range you will get."

"Jeff is stretching it now but the pain is intense. I was hoping to get around it."

"Sorry, nothing I can do."

"Thanks for coming up and looking at it."

"Looks like you are pretty lucky to still be around. I read your chart."

"God must still want me around for some reason. I'm just not sure why yet."

With that he nodded dismissively and walked out the door. I could tell he thought I had just been lucky. I laid my head back and sighed. There was no way to get around the daily torture sessions of stretching this leg. The scar tissue would have to be slowly broken down and it was just going to inflict a world of hurt. I felt my spirits sink again as I contemplated the daily agony awaiting me for months. I prayed, "God just help me get through this. I don't know what you have in store for me yet but I know you have a reason for this. I see now that the plan is yours and I am just along for the ride. That's OK since I realized I was never really in control anyway. I just ask for the strength to endure it and that it works. I really want to play with the kids again and not be the dad just sitting on the sidelines. But, God, if that is the best I can do then I will accept it. Just please help me get through this."

I was hoping again for some voice answering my prayers but heard nothing. Discouraged, I reached for some more Oxy. I didn't really hurt now but I figured it would make me feel better – just a few more pills.

Scot Hodkiewicz

# Chapter 29

## ∞ Time to Give Thanks ∞

Thanksgiving was coming. This was the day the kids would finally come in and see me. We had kept them away until I was in better shape to protect them from the sight of me laying there with feeding tubes and IV's running in and out of my body. By now, the bruising in my face had mostly healed and the only remaining casts were on one foot and one arm. My foot still had a big, nasty, open wound that was still healing but invisible to the kids since it was under wraps. At last I was somewhat presentable and no longer at risk of giving them too many nightmares based on my appearance. It was a good time for a reunion.

My sisters came also – including Bonnie, my middle sister who lived with her husband and daughter down in Chicago. Bonnie had felt bad since she could not really help with my care due to geographical distance, but now she had a few days off and drove up for the holiday. They all came in with loads of food – something my Polish family never skimped on. Just for me, they had made the traditional Thanksgiving turkey dinner. I had been looking forward to this for a week, dreaming about the turkey and stuffing I loved.

Mona and the kids were the last to arrive. Uncertain, the kids nervously hung out against the far wall, obviously unsure if they could touch me, lest I just fall apart. "It's OK," I soothed, "They have me pretty well back together so you can hug me now."

With that, they all ran over. They didn't know quite how to do it since I was all bandaged on my left side and could barely lift my right arm, but we managed. It was one of the best hugs I had ever received. Mona came over next and gave me a kiss on the cheek. It had been now about five weeks since I had seen the kids and about two weeks since I had seen Mona. When they inquired as to how I was doing, I told them everything was going well, neglecting to inform them about the grueling physical therapy – my daily torture session. I figured they didn't need to know everything.

My mother, in her infinite optimism, kept repeating how well I was doing and how I would be home in no time, blissfully unaware that I was now getting by on 80 mg of Oxycodone three times a day to control my pain, both physical and otherwise.

Shannon, my niece, asked if they could all sign my cast, "Sure," I agreed with a smile.

One of the nurses tracked down a Sharpie, gave it to Shannon's twin, Erin, and all the kids gathered around to sign the cast on my leg.

Erin bent down and started signing.

"Oooowwww!" I cried, prompting all the kids to jump back in horror.

"Just kidding," I teased breaking out into laughter. After a one-second delay, everyone else started laughing too. The tension was finally broken; people could see I wasn't depressed anymore and could be touched without something breaking,

Erin did not think it was so funny though, "You jerk!" she cried as she threw the pen at me. I laughed again. "Now I'm not signing it," she announced as she turned away.

"I'll sign it. I don't care if it hurts him," Shannon piped up.

The rest of the kids followed her example, including Chase. He was still a little confused about my condition and had been asking for weeks if I was going to be OK. Now he pulled mom aside and whispered in her ear, "I thought Dad would look like a mummy?"
Mona laughed at the sweet innocence of our four year-old. He had naturally assumed that with all my injuries I would be bandaged from head to toe like what he had seen on cartoons. He actually thought I looked pretty good!

We then headed down to a larger break room the nurses had set up for our use. They had also rolled in a TV and DVD player at my father's request.

"I have a DVD of the news report out of Madison. Thought you may want to see it," he said.

"Sounds great. I haven't seen any pictures or anything yet."

He started the DVD and the reporter began the story.

"Six people, including three children, were injured in a two-car accident on Highway 94 today," the camera showed our wrecked minivan with exploded airbags and the doors pried off by the Jaws of Life.

"The victims were identified as Doctors Scot and Mona Hodkiewicz, veterinarians from the Lake Geneva area and their three children. They were all taken to the University of Wisconsin Hospital and both parents are listed in critical condition with severe, life-threatening injuries. Also injured was the driver of the other vehicle, identified as Mike Jacobs, who currently has seven drunken driving arrests on his record. Police report that Mr. Jacobs fled the scene and was arrested a short time later. He was taken to the hospital and released to the police with minor injuries. He is currently in jail on suspicion of his eighth drunken driving charge."

As the report continued, I could feel the emotions welling up inside of me. I fought back tears but soon was sobbing. My father ran to stop the recording and apologized for showing it but I told him to continue. I needed to see this for my own wellbeing; I needed to see the truth of what had happened – the shattered vehicle, the caved in front-end, and the collapsed dashboard that had shattered my leg. This was all part of the healing process – confronting what had happened – so I could appreciate the miracle that we were all still alive.

As I looked at the devastated car and contemplated the force of the impact, it became very apparent that I never should have made it. The forces put on Mona's and my bodies simply should have killed me and paralyzed her – there was no logical reason that they had not. Again I thought, "There is just no reason for any of us to have survived this."

Then I heard the words again in my mind, *"It is not your plan."* It was the first time I had heard them in weeks.

The report continued, "Two of the family's pet dogs were in the car also. On is at the Emergency Veterinary Hospital while the other is missing." The reporter made no attempt to hide the disgust in her voice as she ended with, "Police report Mr. Jacobs had registered 0.22 on the breathalyzer, nearly three times the legal limit."

By now I was actively sobbing. Mona had her arm around me and her face pressed down against the top of my shoulder. I could feel her body brace under her clothes. Everyone was quiet as there was an awkward silence in the room. I wasn't crying in anger; it wasn't that I was sad that something bad had happened to us since I was sure there was a purpose for it. They were mostly tears of relief and gratitude: I could not believe anyone had survived this crash much less that *everyone* survived, even the dogs. God had protected us, though he had allowed some pain into our lives. I thought about the twelve disciples who had followed Jesus, most of whom died in all sorts of terrible ways. I remembered the words of my pastor, "God never promised our lives would be *free of pain*, just that He would be *with us* as we went through it."

I wiped away the tears and regained my composure, more convinced than ever that God had more for me to do, that I just wasn't seeing the whole picture yet. The crash photos and the devastated vehicle convinced me that I had beaten incredible odds to be alive; there must be some reason for it. I also was convinced that it was not anything I had done. It was not that I was Superman or had more will than other people. I was very average in this. It was not that I had been such a great person that God knew the world could not go on without me; I was way too flawed for that. I had survived simply because God had wanted me to survive, nothing else.

I also realized that He had not miraculously prevented me from being injured. He had let me feel the pain because this was part of the lesson. It was so terrible I'd never forget it. I would remember the hard work of the tortuous rehab. And that was the point: I was getting stronger *because* it wasn't easy.

I was convinced the pain was necessary in order for me to change; to refocus on what was right. Just like the workout mantra, *"No pain, no gain,"* changing my "perfectly planned" life was the same. The pain was transforming me, both physically and spiritually, teaching me forgiveness and how to deal with real adversity – lessons I had never *had* to learn in almost 40 years.

I would not have changed on my own. *Why would I?* I thought I was doing everything *right*. But now I knew I could do better.

Still, change is hard and won't just happen on its own. I needed to have a reason to change my life. It is like a drug addict who must hit rock bottom before they can face their addiction: if they do not hit rock bottom, they rarely kick it. I had certainly hit rock bottom and was learning from the experience. I was going through but it had changed me for the better. I was beginning to see that all this hardship might be worth it.

I remembered a card one of my clients had sent with a bible verse. I could never remember bible verses or recite them chapter and verse like some others but this one had stuck in my head.

*"Consider it pure joy, my brothers and sisters, when you face trials of many kinds, because you know that the testing of your faith develops perseverance. And let perseverance have its full effect, that you may be perfect and complete, lacking nothing."*

I was being tested and as a result, I was developing great perseverance. I was getting stronger than I had ever been spiritually and mentally at a time when I was at my weakest physically.

I looked at my family surrounding me with all their love and support and knew I would be better. Maybe not perfect but better than this. I was convinced that there was just more to this whole thing than I knew – I was just blind to what it was and where it might lead. All I knew was that it was leading somewhere and I would know when it happened. Somewhere, sometime, somehow, it would all make sense. I still had my family. With time I would be, maybe not physically, but spiritually perfect and complete, lacking nothing.

"Alright," I announced, "let's eat."

That night I wanted to try getting up the ramp. The nurses had gotten to know my schedule though I never mentioned the ramp to them. After dinner and a rest, I would get in the chair and wheel myself down the hall. The halls were empty of visitors and most patients were asleep. I would roll myself over to my mountain – my hundred-foot ramp. I would try to get up it, fail and turn back toward my room. I would then take three then four then five laps around the hallway pushing my arms to get stronger.

I thought, "Today is the day. I'm getting to the top of that ramp."

I had been close before but had always had to stop. I psyched myself up and started to push. As I reached 75 feet, I was sweating and puffing; my arms ached but I felt great. A few weeks ago I had stopped at ten feet, now I was at seventy-five. I was getting stronger and the sweat and the pain told me that this work was starting to pay off. A few more last pushes and I crested the top. I yelled in triumph dropping my aching arms to my side, feeling like Rocky. I would have shadowboxed if I could have.

Behind me I heard more shouts and applause. I had not known it but the entire nursing staff had been following me out for the last week, secretly watching to see if I would make it. Now they were jumping up and down and whopping like high school cheerleaders.

For a moment I was embarrassed but that feeling was fleeting and soon replaced by a flood of joy. I realized my triumph was their triumph. Their work changing my bandages (as well as my dirty sheets), bringing me food, and getting me in and out of bed had gotten me to the top of the ramp – the top of my mountain – and we all rejoiced. I turned and headed back down at full speed. The nurses lined up for high fives as I sped past, slapping their hands as they cheered. Today was a good day.

## Chapter 30

## ∞ One Step Forward and Two Steps Back ∞

Another month of rehab and I was getting close to going home. At one time a healthy, physically fit, and energetic husband and father, in an instant I was fighting for my life with a horribly broken body. During the last two months of rehab, I had progressed from barely alive, to struggling to sit up, to a wheelchair, to now walking on crutches. By now I was even pretty good at the whole crutch thing and could get around very well.

I still lacked stamina; therefore, simple rehab workouts would exhaust me for the rest of the day, but I was getting stronger. At first I had been unable to brush my teeth or take care of any personal hygiene but now I was able to shower (though I had to sit), and mostly care for myself. I had gained back about 20 of the 35 pounds I had lost and was now able to eat small meals (my stomach still did not allow me to eat a lot at one time). My broken bones had had two months to heal and were getting stronger every day.

At last I was getting ready to go home. I thought I could do it, though I conceded I'd need some help from Mona and the kids. No matter, I wanted to get out. Because I was still working on the ability to simply get into a car, I would definitely not be driving for a while. But I didn't think I would be a huge burden either.

Mentally, I had forgiven Jacobs and moved forward. I would still cry over what had happened and I no longer cared. I figured I deserved to bawl a little every now and then, no longer embarrassed by it. Like most men, I was brought up to believe crying wasn't "manly," that you were expected to hold unpleasant emotions in, but was anyone going to question my toughness *now* after what I had been through? If they did, I didn't give a shit.

Deluding myself that I was ready to be home was just wishful thinking. In truth, I still needed a lot of assistance. Yes, I could get out of bed but it was a huge effort. It was also an enormous risk; one fall could set me back a month so I was actively avoiding getting in and out of bed. I called for a nurse to get my food or drink and limited my trips to the bathroom. If I went home, I wouldn't be able to help with laundry or dishes, nor would I be able to drive or make a meal. I couldn't even do anything with the kids.

I wasn't thinking this through but was somehow convinced I was ready; I just needed to get my leg in the car. This was progressing with Jeff pushing on it to bend every day. It still just about killed me every time he did it but it was working. I was getting about two or three degrees of additional bend every day or two. Now it was just a matter of time until that foot could make it into the car: time and pain.

At least I had the Oxy. I still needed about 80 milligrams three times a day. By now, I had developed a tolerance, which meant I needed a whopping high dose. I told myself that the Oxy was just a vehicle to enable me to do my physical therapy and get home. If I took some extra medicine for the purpose of getting home quicker, then it was all good.

The reality? I was addicted because it made me feel good.
Mona didn't think I was anywhere close to being ready to live at home again. She was still in the back brace but had started to return to work. Owning the business, we relied entirely on its income for our paychecks. If the business didn't make a profit, then we didn't get paid. Worse yet, if the business failed, everything we had worked for the last eight years would be gone.

The fear of losing the business pushed Mona to start back at work very quickly after breaking her back in three places. Alexa still had to help her bathe and dress in the morning but they managed. Due to the lingering effects of the concussion, she would still forget things and mix up words.

The staff did not let her lift any dogs and a technician was always with her in the room to prevent a dog from jumping on her or knocking her over. Still, even with the extra help, work was exhausting. A day for a vet may include seeing 20- to- 30 appointments in an eight- or- nine-hour period. There was usually little time for breaks since there was always another client waiting, another phone call to make, or another surgery to perform, especially being short one doctor. It included a six-day work week and emergency calls after hours. Mona also had to run the house and take care of three young kids, plus we owned three rental homes as a side business. She was dragging through every day. When she got home, she would feed the kids (luckily we still had meals being delivered every night from our church), help them finish homework, and then collapse.

I was oblivious to all this – exclusively focused on getting home to the point where I didn't see the added stress my presence would cause. I'd be just one more thing for Mona to deal with and worry about. My wife may have said she wanted me back in the house but she didn't think my homecoming would take place anytime soon. She had been told I would be in the hospital for four-to-six months; we were only two months out. Although Mona could easily tell I wasn't close to being independent, I couldn't. She kept dropping not-so-subtle hints I should not rush my return and take advantage of the care I had here.

Every male knows (and women eventually learn) that *"subtle"* hints go right over a guy's head. We have no concept of *subtle* so her inferences did not register with me. I was in mission mode to get back: all I could see was that if I just got my leg to bend some more, I could get in a car and head back to Lake Geneva.

Finally, about two months after the crash and a week before Christmas, I succeeded. It was an arduous struggle and bending my leg sufficiently to enter a car hurt like hell, but I got it in. Jeff congratulated me and advised if I could do it every day for three days, he would sign off on the release. Subsequently, I did it with no problem. I was going home.

I had a great idea (again, I was oblivious): I asked my dad to drive me home so I could surprise Mona. *And surprise her I did!* She looked absolutely shocked to see me as the kids ran out screaming with glee that their dad was home. Later, Mona told me she wasn't shocked but highly pissed that I had left the hospital, fully expecting I would stay for at least another month or two. By then, she would have healed a little more and I would need less nursing care. At this point in time, she just didn't need one more thing to deal with.

She kept her feelings to herself though, and hugged me. My father helped get me into the house. A friend, another angel, had stopped by the day before to install a wheelchair ramp he had made. He had also installed a new showerhead for me and some grab-bars around the toilet. The house was ready but now I had to learn how to do these things on my own.

I stopped my father as he motioned to wheel me up the ramp into the house. "No dad, let me do this." I knew his intentions were good but I was sick of everyone helping me so I pushed myself up the ramp. This was steeper than the ramp at the hospital but I wanted to show everyone, including myself, that I could do it. I pushed and struggled, getting up the steeper incline and reaching the top; out of breath but smiling. I was home. It would be a hardship for a while yet, but I was healing and knew I just needed time.

I had set up in the living room on my favorite recliner. Mona always hated this chair since it didn't match anything else in the house but it was the most comfortable and I really didn't care what it looked like. I could get in and out relatively easily and would spend a lot of time in that spot.

The Wisconsin winter had settled in. I had come in from the cold but it took a good half-hour under a blanket to warm up, which I'd attributed to the fact I'd lost a lot of weight and had very little fat left on my body. Once the excitement of being home started to wear off, I got I very tired. Then the doorbell rang and my aunt and uncle came in for a visit from out of town; I could not sleep yet. Mona had made me some food, which I was just finishing up as the visitors arrived. I would not be able to sleep for the next six hours as I recounted to my relatives all that I could remember about the last eight weeks. I had told the story many times now and could recite it well. I kept quiet about hearing God's voice and His lesson to me about "His Plan," because I still wasn't quite sure about how people would react. If I'm honest about it, I couldn't even be sure I hadn't made the whole thing up so I kept it to myself while I wrapped my head around what had happened, in an attempt to discover a "why" in all our pain. I had become convinced that good would emerge from the experience but still had no idea what it would be. I had learned not to guess; it was out of my hands and I would not have been right anyway.

Still, I wondered if there was some greater good I had not seen yet. My best guess was that God wanted me to work on changing the drunk driving laws in a state that sorely needed it. Wisconsin had some of the most lax laws in the country. First-time drunk driving wasn't even a crime, it was a traffic violation. Since this had to change, I figured that was the purpose behind the accident.

As I conversed with my visitors, I remained cold in spite of wearing a sweatshirt and pants and huddling under a thick blanket. I simply could not warm up. Winter in Wisconsin was tough but I was chilled to the bone. My joints ached and I needed to take a higher dose of OxyContin to control the pain, especially in my left elbow which was now starting to throb.

The move was tougher than I had anticipated but I was thrilled to be back home again. I had closed the door on the hospital phase of my recovery. I had found a great physical therapist in town that a client had recommended and, starting in a few days, I would go to see him. I was mentally ready to hit it hard and heal. Yes, once again I had a great plan.

By the next day, I wasn't feeling too well: I could not stay warm and would shiver for 20 minutes anytime I got out from under the covers. I figured it was just from my weight loss and the previous day's drive. I just needed time.

I made the not-so-wise decision to go to church that Sunday. Mona told me I should stay home but I loved my church and wanted to show people that I was back in town and on the mend. After bundling up in full Wisconsin winter garb, I made my way out to the van. Mona and the kids had to help me get in and put my wheelchair in the back. Mona was still wearing a back brace so Alexa helped her get the chair in the car.

We made it to church where I was mobbed by well-wishers. My pastors came over and hugged Mona and me. Everyone was thrilled to see us after almost two months away. The pastors addressed the rest of the congregation and everyone cheered as it was announced that we were there. I basked in the glory of all the attention, exactly what I should *not* have been doing in God's house. Again, I needed to be reminded that it was His plan and His glory, not mine.

When I got home I was freezing. It was about five-below outside and the trip home had left me shivering with my teeth chattering. The car had been warmed up before I got in but it didn't make a difference. Mona helped me change into sweats and get into bed. After an hour, my teeth were still chattering. Something was wrong. I felt weak and simply could not get warm. My left elbow was pounding in pain and swollen. Mona saw it when she helped me change and immediately noticed a problem. "Was your elbow always this big?" she asked. I looked down and noticed it also.

"No, I guess not."

"I'm getting a thermometer," she announced.

She soon returned and stuck the thermometer under my tongue. When she touched my elbow, I winced: it was much more painful than yesterday. I knew before she checked the thermometer what she would say.

"One-hundred and three, I'm taking you in."

With that, she quickly got on the phone to call a neighbor to watch the kids while she drove me to the local hospital's emergency room. As soon as she rolled me in, the staff took one look and rushed over: I was bundled up in layers of clothing – white as a sheet – with eyes barely open and body shivering. Mona tried to explain the situation and her suspicions about an infection in my elbow.

We were now scared. Mona explained to the attending nurse, "There is a plate in that elbow. If it gets infected, they will have to take it all out. It's not healed yet and removing the plate could let the whole thing fall apart. He could lose his arm."

A nurse took my temperature: 103.5 degrees and getting worse. They called for a doctor as they changed me into a hospital gown and got me into a room. Mona started to explain everything that was broken or injured. The nurse looked at her in disbelief, "Seventy miles an hour, head–on and you all survived? I have never heard of that. People just don't survive that kind of collision."

"Yeah," she replied, knowing the nurse was right, "We were really blessed."

I looked and her and smiled. A broken back and major head injury, kids scared and injured, a husband in a wheelchair with a fever and "we were really blessed." We sure weren't looking blessed right then!

When the doctor came in to evaluate me we told him we were both vets so that he could speak to us in medical, not lay person's terms. He confirmed what we already suspected. "I think you have an infected elbow. We are going to X-ray it to see if anything is out of place. Then we will stick a needle in it to get a sample of the pus and culture to see what is growing. In the meantime, we will set an IV and start antibiotics. Tomorrow, you are getting sent back to Madison. You should be back there with your history. In fact, I am a little surprised you were back home already."

Mona gave me the "wife look," agreeing with the doctor's statement.

"You don't want me to stay here? I'm offended." I protested with a smile.

"I don't want to even touch you," he replied. "The doctors that put the plate in can deal with you now. If you were in better shape, I would send you tonight. Let's get the antibiotics started immediately and I will send you when the fever is a little better. Right now, you look like crap – no offense."

"I figured I did."

The X-rays showed that nothing had moved or let loose. A nurse prepped my elbow and the doctor stuck a long need into it. I clenched my teeth as the needle slid in. He pulled back on the syringe and removed some thick, yellow pus.

"We will see what grows," he declared, "and start the antibiotics. Get some sleep and we are sending you to Madison as soon as we can."

By now, I just wanted to sleep. I was exhausted and still freezing. I had gotten "toxic" from the infection in my elbow. I was absorbing all the bad chemicals formed by the bacteria and it had caused my temperature to spike and my blood pressure to drop. This had given me "the chills" that I could not shake. If it didn't respond to medication, my blood pressure would drop further and I could go into shock. My organs may not get perfused and suffer damage. I was again at risk of systemic infection, organ failure, and death. The bacteria from my elbow could spread infection to other areas, including any or all of the other five fracture sites and any of the hardware, the screws, and plates. All I wanted to do was sleep but I knew I was in trouble; bacteria on the loose in the bloodstream can quickly be fatal.

The next few hours were critical and I knew it. I was so tired I knew I would have to fall asleep; I couldn't fight this forever. I stopped and prayed, asking God to help me one more time. I kicked myself for going out to church that morning, not because of the weather, but because of my reasons: I had gone as much for the attention, the words of encouragement, and the praise for being such a strong fighter. I had gone into the Lord's house for selfish reasons and now I knew I had screwed up. I asked God for forgiveness. I understood that church and prayer was not about me; it was about talking with Him. I was almost 40 years-old and had gone to church my entire life but was only now learning what prayer and God was really about.

I asked that He help me through this infection and that I keep my arm. In the past, I would have bartered with Him stating that in exchange for His help I would do something in return. I would be nicer, never miss church, read the Bible from start to finish, any of those favors that I had tried to trade with Him in the past and promptly forgotten as soon as the crisis ended. This time I didn't barter. I knew He would do His will whether I did my "horse-trading" or not. It wasn't my decision and God did not need me to "trade" something for His will. I just prayed for His help healing but I would accept His plan no matter what.

With this, the tears began to flow. Mona had left to get back to the kids so she never saw me crying but I knew the next 24 hours could change my life again. I was helpless and my life was out of my hands – another lesson about who was really in control.

Now I thought it was truly getting through my thick skull as I once again went through hell. Winston Churchill's words came to me, "If you're going through hell, keep on going." I really had no other choice.

The nurse came in with the antibiotic. "This may sting." she informed me as she injected it into my IV. She was right; it stung all the way up my arm. Antibiotics can be very irritating to the veins. Repeated dosing would likely cause my vein to collapse and the IV to stop working but this was a battle for another day. I would worry about that tomorrow. The fever burned hotter and hotter as I shivered under the blankets. Even though I was drenched with sweat I could not get warm. I knew I was in trouble: this infection was serious.

Now I wasn't concerned about losing my arm, I was concerned about losing my life. The fever, the chills, the sweats, the swelling and pain in the elbow – I knew what they meant. This infection was spreading and releasing toxins into my body. No different than after the crash, the body responds the same way. It doesn't care if the toxins originate from infection or from tissue damage after severe injury, it reacts in the same way. My arteries and veins had dilated and my blood pressure had dropped, resulting in the chills. Too many toxins in the bloodstream leads to the blood clotting uncontrollably, along with D.I.C., the bleeding syndrome that had almost killed me once already. They had saved me before with the Factor VIII shot but I knew the chances of survival were one in a hundred. I had beaten the odds once but the odds of beating them twice was one in ten-thousand; I would not be that lucky again. Since they didn't even have the Factor VIII shot in this little hospital, it didn't really matter anyway.

If the infection didn't respond to the medicine, I would likely lose my arm (or at least the ability to move it at the elbow) and my career as a veterinarian. I also knew I had no control over any of this. It was God's plan, not mine and I accepted that. I had given control of my life over to Him. In the face of all that was going on, I felt strangely calm. There was simply nothing I could do to change my fate. All the doctors could do tonight was administer the antibiotics; all I could do was pray.

I asked for help. "God, I pray that I heal and can keep use of my arm. I accept your plan may not be what I want, but I will accept whatever you give me. If I die, I pray then for Mona and the kids; that they heal and are happy. If I live, then I pray that I can continue to do my job since that is what I love to do and I feel I can help a lot of your creatures. I pray for your help to get me through tonight."

Simply, this was all I could do, knowing the outcome was out of my hands now. I may live, I may die. I may lose my arm or the joint may be forever trashed and only partially usable. Whatever happened was just my fate. Knowing I had done all I could and resolved to stop worrying about things I couldn't control, I felt peace.

I was so tired I knew that staying awake while alone in a hospital room was not going to happen. So I gave myself up to God and fell into a wonderfully deep sleep – the deepest, most peaceful sleep I had in months, possibly years. All my cares were gone even though the stakes were high.

The morning came quickly. I had slept through the night but had a quick flash of panic as I checked to see that my arm was still there. I had to make sure they hadn't amputated it. With a sigh of relief, I reached over and felt my hand. Whew!

I could feel that the fever was gone. I felt warm under the blanket, no more chills. I knew the infection was responding. I would survive. I realized I could still lose my arm if the plates or joint got infected and that the inflammation could create so much scar tissue that I may not ever bend it again, but I could still work with an immobile elbow. To do my work, I needed two good hands, not a good elbow. Surgery on my patients generally occurs in no more than one square foot, often much less. An elbow that doesn't bend would make work difficult but certainly not impossible. Now the worst case scenario just wasn't that bad. Not great but not terrible; it could be managed. My elbow still throbbed but not as much as the previous night. It was still swollen, red, and nasty. The infection was not systemic but was still there.

Once Mona arrived we headed for Madison. The hospital had called ahead and they were waiting for us. Once admitted, Doctor Lang came in and inquired as to how I was doing. "Better than last night," I replied.

He then asked to see the arm. As he checked it over, he frowned, "How is your IV doing?"

"Terrible."

It hadn't been running and the vein was red and sore. The IV antibiotics were so irritating to the vein it had collapsed. A new one would have to be placed but I was running out of good spots. Most of my veins had been hit so many times that they just didn't stand up anymore.

"Don't worry," Dr. Lang announced, "We are placing a PIC line in an hour.

"What is a PIC line?"

"I suppose you don't do those much in your profession."

"Never heard of one."

"The PIC stands for "Percutaneously Introduced Catheter." We are going to feed a catheter from a big vein in your arm up and into the first chamber of your heart. This can stay in for six months, provided you take care of it and it doesn't get infected. We connect it to a pump that will infuse the antibiotics continually for the next month or two."

"The antibiotics won't collapse it or hurt my heart?"

"No, we can infuse virtually anything through a line like this since it is dropping into a huge vessel with a ton of blood running through it. We could infuse gasoline and it wouldn't cause the vein to collapse."

"The gas would probably kill the bacteria in my elbow," I said.

"Yeah, that problem would be solved wouldn't it but why don't we try the antibiotics first? If they don't work, I may consider the gasoline option."

They placed the PIC line that morning. An ultra-sonographer localized the vein in my arm where the line was to be placed. Normally veins are seen or felt just under the skin so a catheter can be fed into them. This vein is much larger and deeper on the inside of the upper arm. It cannot be felt or seen so they use the ultrasound to find it.

"You're a vet right?" the ultra-sonographer asked.

"Yeah, I also am the one that does most of the ultrasounds in the practice," I told him. I wasn't bragging. I just wanted him to know how to speak to me, that I would understand him if he spoke in medical terms. This is more a courtesy than anything since then the doctor knows what he has to explain and what he doesn't.

"See this?" he asked as he pointed to a large, dark, pulsating tube on the screen.

"Yeah," I said, "That looks like a big artery."

"Don't want to hit that one. The arteries are pumping blood out to the limbs so are high pressure, the veins are returning it to the heart so are low pressure. Putting the PIC line in an artery would have blood spurting all over the room. It would be nearly impossible to get anything back through the line. Yeah, don't want to put it there."

"I assume there is a vein around there somewhere," I noted.

"Right there," he answered as he showed me a similar black tube without the pulsing. The veins don't have the pressure so they don't pulsate with the beating heart. The blood flows much more passively than in the arteries.

Next he grabbed the longest catheter I had ever seen. It was probably a foot-and-a-half in length. For comparison, the catheters they had put in my hand were an inch and a half. A nurse began scrubbing the site with iodine and alcohol. She grabbed a needle and shot some lidocaine into the spot where the ultra-sonographer pointed. She rescrubbed it as I could feel the local starting to work. The guide needle was inserted through the skin and we all watched on the screen as a bright white line pressed against the vein. The vein depressed slightly until the needle broke through and appeared in the dark tube. He was in.

He fed the catheter over the needle and up toward my heart. The ultrasound could not follow it the entire way so he shifted to a view of the heart itself. He isolated the Anterior Vena Cava, the large vein heading into the heart and returning blood from my arm. Soon a white double line appeared in the vein: it was the catheter, the PIC line was in place. The nurse placed a few layer of tape to hold it and we were done.

Shortly thereafter I was back up in the room, exhausted from the procedure. I had not done more than move from bed to wheelchair and back again but it felt like I had run a marathon. The combination of being so completely out of shape from laying on my back 20 hours a day for the last two months, and the toll the infection had taken on me had wiped me out. A nurse came in with the pump that I would now carry in a pouch around my waist. I would sleep with it next to me, trying not to roll onto it. It would be my constant companion for the next month, disconnected only when I showered. Not comfortable or convenient to have but I was used to inconvenience by now.

I spent the next week in the hospital to ensure that the infection was under control. They had stopped my physical therapy and would not restart it until I was home. I was disappointed that I was not working at it since I knew how quickly the gains I had made in stamina and strength would disappear if I just laid there. Anyone who is working out trying to get stronger knows that a week off will set you back. I was still too weak to handle any strenuous work but I was also too anxious to not do anything. I began pushing myself in the wheelchair again to get some use of my arms. This hospital did not have a ramp to scale but I was able to cruise the halls for long periods of time. Mainly, I just wanted to get home and start my real physical therapy; I had had enough of the lying around.

The day before I left for home again, Dr. Lang came in, dragging a third-year resident by the arm. He said, "See, see this is the one I told you about. This is the one that survived a Factor VIII shot." Looking at me he added, "Dr. Johansen doesn't believe anyone survives a Factor VIII injection. I had to have him meet you so he could see that someone did."

"Everyone I had ever seen given the shot died within an hour," Dr. Johansen explained. "Obviously, they were all in terrible shape to begin with but I had never seen it work before."

I was a bit shocked but laughed. "Dr. Lang did a lot right that day. Stick with him and do what he does and you will be OK."

Again, I thanked God for saving me by working through all the angels that had made it possible. This conversation reminded me how close I was to being dead.

A week later I was back home. The infection was under control but I would have the PIC line in for the next month, attached to a pump that fed antibiotics continuously. If the infection was not cleared in a month, then I would stay on the pump for another month until it was gone. I prayed that it would not take that long.

By now I was starting to see that it would take me another four or five months to get back to work and I was starting to get antsy. I had never been away from work that long and did not know how to handle it. Though I was starting to receive disability payments, I wanted to be back to seeing patients again. Our business relied on me doing the more complicated surgeries. If I was not there, we had to refer these patients elsewhere. It was inconvenient for the owners and delayed care for the patient. If an animal had a broken leg and I wasn't there to fix it, we had to move them 30 or 40 miles to a hospital that could handle them. This was painful and stressful for both the animal and the owner. I needed to get back so we could treat those animals here.

In the past, part of my drive to do these procedures was financial: these were expensive surgeries that brought in thousands of dollars – much of which went directly into my pocket. Every time we sent a patient to another hospital, we lost the money.

After what I had been through, my drive to make money had changed: it was no longer about making money for *me*. If I was not there, forcing the practice to send patients to a specialist, the cost to the client would be double what we charge, putting many procedures out of reach. A good portion of these patients would simply be euthanized instead. I could save them, but only if I was there.

Second, lower income for the business puts employees at risk of lay-offs. Those major procedures required a large support staff. If the procedures were not getting scheduled due to my absence, I would not need as much staff. These employees were like my family and darn good at what they did so I did not want them to lose their jobs.

Making money was no longer just about me but also about them. I figured God was telling me – no, forcing me – to wake up and put my priorities back in order. I had started my career as an idealistic young doctor who did not care about the business side of veterinary medicine. Over time, that had transitioned into concern about *me* not *them*. I had begun to use the gifts He had given me to better my life and to acquire more stuff, not help animals. This was going to change.

I remembered the story of Jesus turning over the tables of the money changers in the temple. He had become enraged that *business* was taking over a house of worship. I had done the same; my business had taken over my life.

The crash, that one in a million chance that Mike Jacobs would cross the median and hit us, was my wake-up call. It was like Jesus turning over my money changing table and scattering what I thought was important all over the ground. I had told myself I would change my priorities. I would make God, family, and patients my reason for doing my job. I would make the money I needed by doing this but it was no longer the driving factor. Now I wanted to get back to work because veterinary medicine was my calling; it was the gift God had given me and I needed to use this gift in the right way. Maybe that was why He put us in the crash; maybe He needed me to refocus.

At last, I had it all figured out – I had a plan for my life and knew where it was going.

I should have known that I didn't know squat.

# Chapter 31

## ∞ She Had Seen It Coming ∞

A few weeks later, Mona had a recheck back at Madison, per her doctors' recommendation. As a necessary step on her journey to full recovery, they needed to examine her back, head, and elbow to determine if they'd healed as anticipated. Thankfully she hadn't had much pain recently, other than the usual soreness that comes with being in a brace for so long. By now, Mona hated it and was in a hurry to get it off; she just needed the OK from her doctors. This checkup would confirm that everything was back to normal and she could close this angst-filled chapter over the state of her health. Her medical team treated this check-up as an afterthought too, completely confident that all would be well. I was not worried either and stayed home.

Mona's doctor had given her the option of doing the CT or regular X-rays since there were pluses and minuses to both. They could simply X-ray the spine, but that test could be less sensitive than a CT and not show things as well. In cases like Mona's, often fracture lines become blurred and overlapping at this point in the treatment process; therefore X-rays may not detect whether or not the bones had completely healed. If the bones were not healed, getting out of the brace could allow them to shift and cause paralysis. The CT scans the bones and surrounding tissues in much greater detail and can detect subtle changes in the fracture; it would also peruse the abdomen where she had bruised her pancreas and suffered internal bleeding. A bruise would certainly be gone by now and the internal bleeding long since resolved. The downside of the CT was that it was much more radiation, equivalent to hundreds of X-rays rather than just two spinal radiographs. They expected everything to be healed so they did not push strongly for the CT: Mona could choose.

She considered having the X-rays instead of the CT because of the increased exposure to radiation. Radiation, and the cancer it can produce, had always scared her. She got more radiation exposure than most people because of all the x-rays we took in our profession. Unlike people, dogs and cats usually have to be held in place for an x-ray and so we are in the room as the radiation is employed. We wear lead aprons and gloves but we are not covered everywhere. Worse yet, Mona had started out working for a vet as a teenager who had used an ancient X-ray system that scattered radiation everywhere. The vet had insisted Mona wear full lead apron and gloves and would even shield her with his own body when he could but she had been exposed to much more than would now be acceptable. In addition, we had both gotten loads of radiation from all the CT's and X-rays we'd endured over the past two months. For these reasons, she understandably didn't want a ton more radiation and told the doctors to just do the plain X-rays. They would shoot her back and elbow to ensure they were both healed, then take off the brace. It was scheduled for the following week.

That night, Mona was uneasy and did not sleep well. We hadn't been sleeping the same bed since she had taken to sleeping in a chair with her back brace and I was stuck in bed or in my recliner. The next morning, I could see she was troubled even through my haze of OxyContin. She just seemed off, as if her mind was elsewhere. Figuring she was just tired, I did not push the subject; Mona went off to work as usual that day and I assumed all would be well by the time she returned.

However, her mood had not improved at all by evening and she seemed very distracted. In response, I did the "good husband" thing and assured her it was all "routine;" we both knew the fracture should be healed. Mona agreed that it "should be" but still something bothered her.

We both had learned in our profession that you always trust a gut feeling. I had also learned by now that a gut feeling is often God's voice and you had better listen up. We'd discussed changing the X-rays to a CT if it would make her feel better. I thought she was being a little paranoid but I also knew that the CT provided much better images. Again, I left it to her discretion but encouraged her to follow her "gut".

The next morning she had made her decision: she would risk the radiation of the CT and not do the spinal rads. Her gut just kept telling her that this was the right way to go and she would follow that.

By now, I felt the same way. There was a reason why she felt so uneasy about not doing the more sensitive test. Maybe, as we'd witnessed countless times before, these were God's messages to us to take one path or the other – one of those *forks in the road*. When we chose not to heed His voice, things generally went terribly wrong. How many times did we end up saying, "I had a feeling this would happen. I should have listened to my gut." Of course, this statement fails to credit true source of "gut feelings," but He is used to us turning a deaf ear to what He is trying to say and then forgetting to thank Him. It is just the way we all are.

Today, Mona would listen. When we called to reschedule for a CT, the nurse informed us it would be another week before Mona could get in. It didn't matter: my wife was now adamant – in spite of having to wear the hated brace for another week – that she would do the CT. That night she slept well for the first time in two days, finally at peace as if God had smiled on her. Mona knew she had made the right decision but still did not know why. After all, there was no reason to believe her back would not be completely healed.

The following week, I did not go with her to the CT because I wasn't worried about it. Besides, loading me into a car for an hour drive was a real project since I still needed the wheelchair instead of crutches, due to my infected elbow. I was also starting rehab that day and felt she was just being paranoid. So Mona drove herself to the hospital, knowing they would not sedate her. She was fully aware she would not get the results back for a week, yet she was strangely nervous about the CT. I knew her fractures were pretty stable and unlikely to have had any problems healing. Mona couldn't pinpoint the cause of her concern either, but we both attributed it to trepidation about returning to Madison and reliving the worst day of her life.

The CT came and went without a hitch. Afterward, they told her to expect a call in a week with the results. But as she waited for the valet to bring her car around her cellphone rang and displayed an unknown number from Madison. Her heart sank as she guessed it was the hospital: there was only one reason they would be calling so soon; they had found something wrong.

Mona answered to her doctor's urgent voice advising her to come back in immediately. Fear overwhelmed her. This could not be good news. Had the back not healed? Would she need to have surgery and have it plated? She turned around and headed back to the doctor's office careful how she walked, expecting some major problem with her back. By now, her adrenaline was pumping. She was scared but not surprised because she had seen it coming – that gut feeling to do the CT was about to be validated.

Once at the doctor's office, the receptionist escorted her into a room right away. Mona was no longer smiling or making small talk.

The nurses wore troubled expressions also; they looked at her as she came in, then quickly went back to what they were doing. *Something* was very wrong.

The doctor walked into the room after just a few minutes (an alarming sign since she was not kept waiting), accompanied by another older doctor (another bad sign) and his nurse. He sat down on his stool in front of Mona with a very serious look on his face.

"What is wrong," she asked, "did the vertebrae not heal?"

He shook his head. "No, your back is fine. You don't need the brace anymore. The radiologist looked at your CT as it was being processed. The problem isn't your back. That mass on your pancreas that was seen on the first CT is still there. We thought it was a bruise but it should have resolved by now. Mona, we no longer believe it's a bruise."

My wife felt like her world was collapsing again around her. She knew there were only a few other choices when there is a mass on the pancreas.

The doctor continued, "It is a mass of some sort. You will need some additional tests." His nurse began getting needles and tubes ready for a blood draw. "We can test for some of the pancreatic markers and repeat the previous blood work but I want you to have an ultrasound. This is Dr. Wilson; he is a specialist in pancreatic disease and surgery.""

Mona sat in disbelief. Though he'd been careful not to say the word "tumor," she knew "pancreatic markers" meant that was what they were looking for. "Markers" are proteins given off by specific tumors in the blood, an indication not only of the cancer but also the specific type.

Could this really be a pancreatic cancer? This was supposed to be a simple recheck to confirm that everything had healed and the worst was over – the day she was supposed to be allowed to get back to her life and put this nightmare behind her. She had been through already: now she was finding out that not only was she still traveling through it, it was about to get ten times worse. At this point, her very survival was in question. Pancreatic cancer can be fatal in weeks. *What if it had spread? How would she tell the kids she was dying?* The thought of months of chemo and radiation terrified her as she sat there stunned.

Dr. Wilson took over as he sat down in front of Mona and calmly explained the tests. They would draw blood today and set up an ultrasound to look at the spot more closely. If they suspected a tumor, she would need surgery to remove it.

She fought to catch her breath but couldn't; it was coming short and fast. *Could she die before her fortieth birthday? Could she miss her kids graduating from high school? Had she survived the wreck and all of this pain only to die a few months later of something completely unrelated?* She slowly formed the words to ask, "Is this pancreatic cancer?"

"I think it is going to be a pancreatic tumor of some type. I just don't know which one. The tests may help but it is very likely I will have to take it out. Set up the ultrasound as soon as possible and I will wait for the results."

"How likely is it that it is cancer?"

"I can't tell yet but I will say that over 90 percent are removed surgically whether they are cancerous or not. We rarely can leave them alone. Let me tell you, this is what I do. I am very good at it but pancreatic surgery is rarely easy. I see you are a veterinarian so you already know this. Let's get the tests done before we jump to any conclusions."

With that, he left the room and the nurse prepared to draw blood. Mona just sat there not knowing what to do, unable to move. The thought of "cancer" had stopped her in her tracks. There are few words in the English language that strike fear so quickly in people's hearts as the "C" word. Today she had heard it in connection to "pancreatic cancer," one of the most aggressive and deadly forms of this dreaded disease. The father of a good friend had died in his 50s of pancreatic cancer and we'd witnessed his rapid, terrible decline and inevitable death. Mona knew pancreatic cancer was one of the most aggressive forms and came with a terrible prognosis: people just do not survive it. But she also knew that there are multiple types of pancreatic cancer – the aggressive type that usually takes the patient in a matter of months and less aggressive types that are deadly but at least take years to end a life. There are also benign (non-cancerous) tumors that can be removed and cured but these are rare. The blood tests and ultrasound could help determine Mona's particular brand of pancreatic cancer and ultimately, whether she would live or die.

As the nurse moved forward for the blood draw, the room suddenly felt cold; Mona tried to hold back the feeling that her world was caving in. A few months ago, her world had been smashed to smithereens and was starting to slowly return to normal. Now she felt it happening again just as quickly as that Jeep crossed the median. Last time, she had been wheeled up to say goodbye to me before I died; now I may soon be doing the same for her. The nurse applied a tourniquet to her arm; Mona didn't move. The nurse tried to make small talk; Mona didn't hear a word. She put the needle into her arm; Mona didn't flinch. She was numb.

Doctor Wilson returned and briefly stuck his head in the door, oblivious to the ton of bricks now sitting on Mona's lap, "Set up the ultrasound at the desk and we will call in a few days with the lab results."

Then grasping the terror on Mona's face, he stepped in and placed a hand on her knee. "Don't panic," he said, "we don't know what it is yet."

While it's easy to say *"Don't panic"* it is simply impossible not to; the mere thought of a cancer diagnosis and impending death will naturally cause any human being to lose control of their emotions. It doesn't matter if you are thirty-eight or eighty. We have all seen the effects of cancer and most people have lost loved ones to this menace. But watching someone else deal with cancer is very different from having to cope with it yourself. Dazedly, Mona stopped at the front desk on the way out, where the receptionist put down what she was doing and inquired as to when Mona could come back. She responded by asking if she could do the ultrasound near home, much to the receptionist's surprise. Most patients facing this diagnosis opt for the ultrasound as soon as possible but Mona wanted to be close to home. The receptionist nodded and assured her that would be fine; the doctors here just needed the report.

Although still shaking, Mona knew exactly what she wanted to do. Dr. George Fueredi had been a client of ours for years, starting in the early days when we were just getting our practice going. He had three big Labs that were always getting into trouble so we had gotten to know each other well. Most human doctors get along well with veterinarians as there is a lot of mutual respect between the two professions.

Dr. Fueredi was an interventional radiologist. His job is to use ultrasound, CT, and radiology to diagnose and fix problems. I had called him once to help me find an abnormal liver vessel on a two-pound Yorkie I'd suspected was there but could not seem to locate. Dr. Fueredi found it within minutes. He excelled at his profession and would perform the ultrasound for Mona. As soon as she arrived home she'd call him – right now, she just needed to leave ASAP.

She walked out of the hospital without even noticing the world around her. Once the valet brought the car, she got in and held the steering wheel, unable to put it into drive. As she fought to summon the strength to move, she just held onto the wheel as she began to cry uncontrollably. The overwhelming fear of cancer flooded out in waves: her hands were shaking, her breathing was shallow, and she gasped in between sobs. Then the questions came hard and fast.

*"Why me? What did I do wrong? I don't deserve cancer; I didn't do anything to deserve this. How much pain am I going to go through? What about the kids? How will they deal with their mom having cancer? How will they deal with it if I die?"*

She didn't want to miss the rest of their lives and she didn't want to miss the rest of *her* life, either. Like any mom, Mona wanted to watch her kids grow into adulthood. Now there was a very real chance she might not live to see our oldest even *get* to high school, much less graduate. All she could think was, "This CAN'T be happening to ME."

After she let it all out, she started to gather herself with the admonition that she would fight with everything she had and that she needed to be strong. We all want to be strong and brave; no one wants to live in fear. But this wasn't going to happen today. Mona had just faced her mortality in a very palpable sense – not just this theoretical knowledge that we will all die *someday*. Ten minutes ago, the doctor told her she had a pancreatic mass. Although he didn't elaborate, declaring instead that more tests needed to be done, Mona knew. Pancreatic cancer can be one of the most aggressive and could very well kill her within a few months. True, there was a chance it was not cancer, but she now had to face the fact that cancer was a very likely outcome that could rob her of all the plans she had ever made. Mona would probably not be around to see her kids go to prom – much less graduate college, get married, or have her grandkids. Cancer would also steal her opportunity to grow old – something none of us wants to do until the opportunity is suddenly yanked away.

Throughout her battle, she'd also have to watch her children and husband cry every day as she endured chemo, surgery, and radiation. In spite of her characteristic strength and desire to remain brave and resolute, this prospect was simply terrifying. Mona had gone through for the past three months and was now supposed to be through the worst of it. Life was supposed to get back to normal. But in one instant, she realized her trip through had just begun. She started to pray asking God the questions we all ask *"Why me God?" "What did I do?"*

She waited for an answer that never came. *"God, aren't you listening?"*

Now she started to get angry, *"Damn it! Why don't You answer me? Tell me what I did wrong?"*

Of course, she was too scared to realize that God had been with her the entire time. That "bad feeling" she'd experienced when she was scheduled for a simple X-ray was His warning to get the CT. Listening to Him had enabled her to find the tumor and given her options that most don't get. Usually, pancreatic cancers aren't even detected until they have already spread – after it's too late to do anything to save the patient's life. In Mona's case, she was finding the cancer before it caused any symptoms. She was finding it *because* of the crash.

God had been with her during the accident and would be with her now also. We all think God should save us from pain and hardship but we were learning that was not His will. God is always with us *through* the pain but He never promised a life *without* pain. We all need trials and tribulations to teach us how to cope and to force us to reexamine ourselves. God is there to guide us through to the other side.

Mona's questions began to shift from *"Why?"* to *"Please help."* She knew this would be the hardest six months of her life; that she would endure more pain, more sickness, more trips to the hospital, and more doctors than ever before, even including the crash. Fear would be her constant companion as she went through all the treatment, with no guarantee she would even live in the end. Worse yet, she had absolutely no control over where her life was headed. The doctors would do the tests, the surgery, and any necessary chemo. She would have very little say in her course of treatment. Mona was fully aware the cancer is treated according to standard protocols; there is very little variation in treatment once the type of cancer is determined. Cancer therapy is very much a cookbook, using the latest study and drug combinations that offer the best chance of survival. You administer this much of one drug, wait this many days, expect these side effects this many days out, and follow with this other drug on another determined day – just like following a recipe. Mona had no control over her cancer recipe, nor did she know if it would do anything other than make her sicker before ultimately killing her.

All she could do was ask God for help. She told herself she should prepare for the fight; an easy thing to say. The first step was to just get home.

Scot Hodkiewicz

# Chapter 32

## ∞ Here We Go Again ∞

Mona hadn't called me to tell me the bad news. Instead, she drove home crying the whole way. Before walking into the house, she gathered herself so as not to scare the kids but I noticed her deep red eyes and shiny tear-stained face immediately. As she hung up her coat, the kids met her at the door while I rolled in on my wheelchair to inquire about her check-up. But the look on her face told me all I needed to know before I could even ask the question; now it was my turn to be shocked and confused. *This was just supposed to be a recheck.* I could see that her brace was off – why wasn't she happy? Instead of joy, her entire expression resonated utter devastation. Something was very wrong.

She quickly greeted the kids before we both headed to the bedroom for some privacy. The second the door closed behind us, I braced for the news, reaching for her hand as she sat down on the edge of the bed.

"They found a mass on my pancreas," she began, "They don't know what it is but they are checking for a pancreatic tumor." In spite of her best efforts, she burst out into tears. I just sat there in shock and fear as the tears began to stream down my face.

What could I say? *"Don't worry, it will be alright?"*

Give me a break! How could I possibly speak the words *"Don't worry"* when my wife was just hit with the news that she might have a pancreatic tumor? She had the absolute right to worry. There was no way I could tell her, *"It will be alright"* when she could die in a few months. Should I suggest, *"Maybe they are wrong and it is nothing?"*

Being doctors ourselves we viewed *normal* anatomy all the time; understanding human and animal bodies was a discipline we'd spent countless hours on through dissections in anatomy class, along with studies and lectures in other courses like biology. We had both diagnosed hundreds of animals with cancer and seen many, many tumors, fully aware that little else looks like a tumor – a round, solid mass that shouldn't be there. It is almost never just a normal structure that someone misinterpreted. Doctors see "normal" things every day; it was highly unlikely that they'd be wrong about this. In that moment, there was simply not much I could say or do. Stuck in my wheelchair, I couldn't even hold my wife so I just held her hands as we both sobbed.

After about ten minutes, the kids started knocking on the door. Even though they were young, they knew something was wrong. It was time to tell them. Our policy was to never lie to our kids and we weren't about to start now. Yet we were also uncertain as to what we were dealing with and wouldn't have confirmation for a while.
Mona walked over and opened the door.

"Dad and I were just talking," she began. They could all could tell we'd been crying and knew there was trouble.

Never shy about asking questions, Alexa spoke up first, "What's wrong, why are you both crying?"

"Mom will need some more tests from the doctor. She has something in her tummy that isn't supposed to be there." I hoped that would be the end of her questions but of course that wasn't the case.

"What's in your tummy? Did you eat something you weren't supposed to?" Chase asked in the typical innocence of a four-year old while the other two kids waited for the answer.

"No, it isn't anything I ate. We don't really know what it is yet. That is what the doctors will find out."

There was a brief pause during which I hoped this was the end of the conversation but Alexa was not one to give up easily. The next question was the one I feared the most.

"Mommy, are you going to die?"

*Now* what to say? We honestly didn't know if Mona was going to live or die: a pancreatic mass certainly could kill. I gazed over at my wife and noticed the tears beginning to flow again. Instantly, I felt my own eyes welling up once more as I struggled to speak without choking up. "Mom is going to have some more testing and the doctors will deal with it. This is what they are good at so we will have to trust them."

I didn't really answer the question but I didn't lie to them either. From the beginning, I always taught my kids to tell the truth; I surely was not going to lie to them about something as serious as this. Lying to them would also be dumb and counterproductive because they already knew something was up. The truth would emerge in the end anyway, and I didn't want to betray their trust. They were small, not stupid.

However, at their age they did not have the capacity to deal with the thought of their mom dying – especially after coming so close to losing both of us a few months ago. Telling them that we did not know *was* the truth and they deserved that.

Next, they ran in and hugged their mother; the only thing they knew for certain was that they wanted to be with their mom and dad. All five of us just stood there holding each other because it was what we all needed. I realized then just how much we had relied on each other since the crash; in the aftermath of this dire prognosis, we would need each other even more.

We all cried, fully consumed with dread and fear. The thought of Mona having pancreatic cancer was absolutely terrifying: surgery, chemo, radiation, vomiting, hair loss, diarrhea, and the knowledge she would probably die anyway was beyond anything we had been prepared to deal with. The crash had been horrific but I had no memory of it and because of her concussion, Mona had only foggy recollections. In those moments when we *could* comprehend it, we knew we were going to heal.

But now we had no idea if Mona could heal; if there would be a light at the end of this new tunnel. We fully understood the gravity of what could happen and felt the overwhelming horror. Even though we didn't yet know much about the mass, we did know it was not good and was going to be a real bitch to remove. As doctors, we were both aware that pancreatic surgery was one of the most difficult, fraught with problems. The pancreas did not like anything or anyone messing with it and got inflamed easily – a terribly painful problem with limited treatments. An inflamed or damaged pancreas would leak digestive enzymes out into the surrounding tissues. Since these enzymes are designed to digest our foods, they have no trouble digesting any surrounding tissue. In our profession, we'd both seen animals suffering incredible pain from inflammation of the pancreas, helpless to do much more than administer simple pain relief. Often, even our morphine drips were not enough to ease their discomfort. In Mona's case, because the surgeons would have to cut out the diseased pancreas and leave the rest, we both knew she had this coming. And that it would be indescribably awful.

As I sat there motionless in my wheelchair, anger flared inside of me, along with a thought most would have in this situation: *"God, why are we going through this? We can't handle anymore. Our family has been beaten and battered for months and I thought this was over. I thanked you every day for saving me and now we're getting kicked again, facing possible, no probable, cancer and quite possibly the death of my kids' mother and my wife. How much more can anyone face?"*

We were both exhausted from our ordeal and now we realized that the worst was yet to come. I wanted to face this with an upbeat and positive attitude but we had both hit a wall – emotionally and physically exhausted – which made it very easy to get angry. We needed rest and time together to heal from our injuries, but now we were about to start a new journey, one that none of us wanted to take. The best we could hope for was to get back to where we were now; the worst we could face was Mona dead in a month after being eaten away by pancreatic cancer. We really had nowhere to go but down. Fear and anger flooded me in waves, worse than I had ever felt before.

Just like the crash, I knew that we had no choice in the matter: we were going to go through this no matter what. There was no avoiding or ignoring it – the fight was going to be fought. Problem was, we were simply worn out from fighting. This was the low point of all this; the point where we just wanted to give up.

Loss of control was the scariest part. As a dad, I was expected to protect the family, both my wife and kids. Now I had no way to do this, no way to change the course of the next few months. Obviously, we could take control by choosing to do nothing but this would put our desire for control ahead of what was best for Mona. We had to face this head-on. This would mean more tests and probably more surgery.

As I looked up, the kids were still huddled around looking at us; they hadn't said another word. I gazed over at Mona, who looked tired and scared. Nobody really knew what to say anymore. The thought of my great plan for my life flashed through my head again. We would get married, raise the kids, and grow old together fixing dogs and cats and raising animals on our little farm. My son and daughters would be protected by living in a small, Midwestern city surrounded by a community where people treated each other well. That had been the plan and now it was all unraveling. Worse yet, I could not change the end result of this no matter what I did. I figured the mass would certainly need surgery and, if it was pancreatic cancer, it would kill her. Yes, I would continue to hope and pray it was all benign, that it would all turn out to be nothing but the chances of that were slim. Up until the crash, things had always worked out well for us but now our fate was completely out of our hands. I just didn't think we could do this.

"Yes, you can. You have done it before."

Was that God speaking to me again? I can't say for sure. Once again, there was no burning bush in the desert. Yet as I looked at our family, I knew one thing: we had been through once, we had the support structures of family and community in place, and we knew all about hospitals and recovery from major surgery. We were ready for this. Yes, we *could* do it again.

The only thing we could really control was our attitude and behavior; the way in which we faced this new challenge. We had a choice: we could remain paralyzed in fear and anger, or we could take it on, no matter how tired we were or how difficult the struggle. We were going to go through and I could not change that, but we could control *how* we went through it.

After two months of being cared for as the patient, of being a victim, it was now time for me to take charge again. I was still in a wheelchair and had a splint on my left arm – far from an imposing figure as I sat there covered with a blanket, still close to 20 pounds underweight. Due to the pain meds I was still taking, I could not even drive but I could set the tone. Mona was an incredibly strong woman who had kept it all together through what seemed to be the worst possible time we could imagine, but she was too close to this. It was far too personal for her to have to carry the kids and me anymore. It was time for me to lead.

I also knew that this was more than I could do by myself. We would have to support each other but we would need help again from our families and friends. Even though we'd asked so much from them already, we would have to ask again, knowing we could rely on our families, church, and community to help pull us through like they had done the first time. The crash had helped to get everything into place in time for us to deal with this next obstacle. It had been a practice run, a warm-up for the real struggle coming down the road.

I released the hug for a second and announced, "We are going to fight this. We have been through a lot already but that made us stronger for the fight we are now in. Getting through the last few months allowed us to put the people and faith in place to be strong enough to take this on. It will be tough but we are tough already. This family can do this, we have done it before."

While I talked a good game, I still didn't think our determination would be enough. I did not start this journey as a person who let God into his life very much. Like most people, I had only talked to God when I needed help; I wanted him to hear me when I needed something or to complain when I didn't get what I wanted. Rarely did I even stop to thank him when things went right.

Up until the crash, I really hadn't needed God's assistance for anything major in my life. I had prayed to get into veterinary school after I had applied but I had earned excellent grades and done all the things required for admittance. It had never really occurred to me that I would NOT get in; I was still in control. When I asked Mona to marry me, I had prayed she would say "yes" but because I was pretty sure she would, I had control there too (obviously, Mona had control also but I asked only when I was confident in the answer). I had prayed for healthy kids each time Mona was pregnant but most children are born healthy in this part of the world and our family histories had few medical problems. For most of my life, I had simply never thought I needed God's help with anything. Even in the aftermath of the crash, I was not able to ask God for help since I was unconscious. Our collision with Jacobs' Jeep was the first time I had not been in control of the major changes in my life, and as my recovery progressed I was expecting to get back in control very soon.

But once again, control had vanished. We would pray for help but acknowledge that it would be God's plan for the outcome, not ours. We would put ourselves completely into His hands, surrendering completely to Him and His will.

We could choose the doctors and the treatments and could search out the best specialists in the country but I knew as a veterinarian that the course of a disease often cannot be altered even by the greatest doctors. If this was the aggressive pancreatic cancer, there was simply no effective remedy. It would keep going and Mona would almost certainly die even with the best doctors and hospitals out there.

Even less aggressive forms of pancreatic diseases are notoriously difficult to treat. If it had not spread, she had a chance but would require a nasty, painful surgery and she would go through hell. Could it be benign and need no treatment? I doubted it and I knew of no way to tell without removing it.

She would almost certainly need surgery either way. We were looking for a way out but we were trapped; there was simply no good alternative here. Mona was going to endure this hardship with the rest of us along for the ride. There was nothing much we could do about it. The kids and I would have to face the thought of losing a mother and wife we loved dearly, the woman who ran and organized our lives for us; a mother who loved and cared for me and the kids, tending to all of the mundane details. She was the "snuggler" for the kids, curling up with them under a blanket when they needed that kind of comfort. I saw myself as the provider and protector, though I wasn't even sure I could do that anymore. Our roles in the family were very different but complemented each other well. Now I faced the fact that I may be raising these kids alone – possibly without any way to provide for them.

We hugged and cried and held each other for a long time. The kids did not really understand the threat of pancreatic cancer; they didn't need to know the details, which was fine with me because I had none to give them anyway. Either the tumor was benign with no cause for worry, or their mother could be dead in months. As we consoled each other in silence, there was simply no way to know.

## Chapter 33

### ∞ Good Things Happen to Good People ∞

The first step was to call Dr. Fueredi to get an ultrasound. Mona had the CT images on a disk in her hand but she was too shaken to speak to him. I had his number on my cell and dialed him as soon as I felt I could get through the call.

When he answered I identified myself, prompting him to cheerfully inquire as to my wellbeing. I told him I was getting better but we had a problem with Mona and I needed his help.

"Anything you need. Shoot."

I filled him in on her latest news, requesting that he please take a look at the CT and offer his opinion.

"Do you have the images?" he asked. "I could get access through the network but that may take a while."

"I have the CD in my hand."

George replied, "I am on my way over. Should I meet you at the clinic or your house?"

"We are at the house right now and I am in no condition to drive so could you come over here?"

"I will be there in a half-hour."

Although veterinarians and physicians share a professional courtesy, this was above and beyond the call of duty. Due to similar training, physicians and vets have great respect for each other; they also understand the busyness of our professions, thus will only call for favors when absolutely necessary.

George had brought in his hunting dogs to our practice a few times on emergency – usually needing stitches. But he had also nursed them through the night a few times to avoid having to call after-hours. Of course, I surely would have seen his dogs at any time but he understood the hardships of getting called out at night so he avoided it unless absolutely necessary. Nonetheless, he had three big Labs I'd examined more than once in the middle of the night. I had given him my cell number so that he could call me anytime and not have to take his dogs to someone he did not know.

Now he was returning the favor. He could have stopped by on his way home from work but that would have left us hanging for hours.

Understanding the stress we were under, he dropped everything with the intention of arriving on our doorstep as soon as possible.

Within 20 minutes, Dr. Fueredi was knocking at our front entrance, where I met him in my wheelchair, welcomed him into our home, and led him to the computer. Although I'd already loaded the images, I had not looked at them. Doing CT's on dogs and cats was very new when I was in vet school and I had not been trained to read them; I had no idea what I was looking at. While I could have guessed, that would have confirmed nothing and at this point, I needed expert advice. George began scrolling through.

I could see the liver as he slowly moved through it. The gall bladder was easily identified and I knew the pancreas sat just below it. I could start to make out the stomach and first part of the intestine. The pancreas sits right below these structures on the right hand side. The mass should be right in this area.

George scrolled more slowly now, studying every inch of every image.

"There it is," he said, pointing to the screen.

As he continued to scroll down, the mass was clear. It was about the size of a quarter, round and solid. I could see large vessels all around it. I knew it would be in a really tough spot to remove. If I had found this in a dog, it would have been non-resectible. This was not good.

George continued, "Let me show this to a colleague and get the blood work. They probably checked some tumor markers and I want to see the results. I should be able to get the results today; I will put my assistant on it as soon as I get back to the hospital. I have a friend I'd like to take a look at this but I may not get the opinion until tomorrow. I will have him check it out right away. Regardless, she will need an ultrasound. We will do it as soon as I seen the blood results."

"Thanks George," I replied gratefully. "I really appreciate your help and getting over here so quickly."

"No problem. You both have met me more than once with my boys. I'm glad you called."

With that he left, CD in hand. I returned to Mona and announced we'd have another opinion by tomorrow.

"I just can't believe I have cancer," she sighed, tears flowing and voice cracking. "I never felt sick; I just don't know why this is happening to me. What did I do wrong?"

These were the same questions I'd asked during my recovery. "Why me? What did I do wrong?" The questions everyone asks when they are embarking on a trip through hell.

"Mona," I began, "I can't believe it either. We have been through a lot already but we learned in the crash that we do not see the big picture, His big plan for us. We were both angry that we had gotten into the crash and that it wasn't fair but the crash enabled us to find this thing on your pancreas. Maybe God put us in the crash that day just for that purpose. Maybe *that* was the reason all along. Maybe He put us in Jacobs's path to *save* us, not to hurt us. Now that we found it, we can deal with it. This is another hurdle to get over. We will face it the same way we faced the others. We will bear down and do it together. We have done it before so we can do it again."

With that we both just cried together for a long time, knowing that the next few months would be the hardest yet. Medical confirmation about the mass and the degree of difficulty involved in removing it would determine her future. An aggressive cancer would mean surgery, chemo, and ultimately death. Some are less aggressive and grow more slowly, but are still fatal. Yes, a few are benign but we'd be really lucky to receive that sort of diagnosis – and our luck hadn't been so good lately.

There was nothing more we could do tonight, except try to sleep though neither of us would sleep very well. Due to my injuries, I still mostly slept on my back, which wasn't real comfortable. Mona was out of the body brace and had started the day expecting her best night's sleep in months; of course now she'd spend the entire night too scared to sleep for more than an hour at a time.

# Chapter 34

## ∞ A Glimmer of Hope ∞

The next day Mona drove me to rehab as usual, where I spent over an hour working on my body while my mind focused exclusively on her. Pancreatic cancer: I still couldn't believe it. More bad news, more struggles. Now I could lose my wife in the next six months. Could I raise the kids on my own? It was a struggle before the crash to balance work and the kids with both of us healthy. How could I do it with just me, especially when I was nowhere close to the physical condition I enjoyed before the crash? My youngest was just about to turn five – big enough to get himself dressed and into the car seat but he still needed a father who could keep up with him, playing and roughhousing. I still needed to carry groceries and do yard work. Various things around the house would still need fixing but crawling under a sink was impossible with arms and legs that still did not bend.

*What if I could no longer work?* I had some disability insurance but not enough to maintain the lifestyle we had had before the crash, especially if I was the sole parent. Mona had some life insurance but we had never taken out a huge amount since we were both relatively young and healthy. Most likely, we would have to sell the house and downsize. I had never been emotionally attached to any house, including this one, but I also hated moving with a passion and the kids had never lived in town. This would be all new when what they needed now was normalcy.

John, my new physical therapist, could tell my mind was racing. He didn't ask any questions, however, knowing that I would tell him if I wanted to. At this point, I was nowhere near ready to talk about it. Any mention of Mona's pancreatic cancer incited immediate tears. Since I could not drive on my own, John's assistant gave me a ride per his instructions. This was a wonderful service he offered to clients who were unable to operate a vehicle. Mona, in an amazing show of toughness, went into work that day. We were still dependent on the business to generate our income so she put in a full day at the office. The staff did not even know anything was wrong.

About two o'clock, my cell phone rang. It was George.

"Scot, I tried to call Mona but she didn't answer."

"Yeah, she is at work."

"Really? Wow. Anyway, I showed the CT to Dr. Jackson. He is a leading specialist in arteriovenous fistulas. He thinks this may be one, not a tumor."

I couldn't believe it. An arteriovenous fistula is an abnormal connection between an artery and a vein. Arteries carry oxygenated blood into the tissues and veins carry the deoxygenated blood back to the heart. The blood then goes back through the arteries and the process starts all over again.

An arteriovenous fistula (called an AV fistula) is an abnormal connection directly connecting an artery and a vein. It bypasses the tissues and allows arterial blood, under high pressure, to flow directly into the vein which is under very low pressure. This subjects the vein to the high arterial blood pressure which it was never designed to handle, making its thin walls bulge and give the appearance of a mass. In this scenario, a vein wall often ruptures, leading to a potentially fatal hemorrhage.

These AV fistulas often develop after injury when the artery and vein are torn and fuse together during the healing process. This obviously fit with what had happened to Mona during the crash when they suspected internal bleeding and a "bruise" (i.e. a torn blood vessel) on her pancreas. It was a dangerous thing and it would have to be fixed but it wasn't cancer.

"Can Mona come in tomorrow at seven? She can meet with Dr. Jackson and I will do the ultrasound. If it shows what we expect, maybe I can try to fix this thing tomorrow afternoon. I already cleared my schedule so I will have time to do it. I can feed a catheter up from her groin and place some metal coils or inject some glue into the vessels feeding it. We will try to cut off the blood supply to this area and keep it from rupturing. It should not involve major surgery but I want to get on it before it tears. Mona may even go home that night if it goes well."

I was thrilled: this was great news! *Not cancer – just an AV fistula that a friend can cure without major surgery?* That was the best news in the world. God was smiling on us again. All those good things we had done in our lives were paying off.

"George, I can't thank you enough. We will be there at seven. No food and water in the morning I assume."

"Right, she won't have surgery until the afternoon so the water is OK but no food. I will be going into her groin, just so she is aware."

"I will let her know but I am sure she won't be embarrassed, we both got used to very little dignity when we were in the hospital before. Thanks again George."

"No problem, see you tomorrow."

I hung up and called Mona right away. My hands were shaking with excitement. Things had always worked out for us in the past and now I thought the luck, good karma, whatever you want to call it, was returning. We had dodged a bullet and were not going to have to deal with cancer after all.

Of course, I forgot to thank God.

"Hello," Mona answered.

"Mona, I just got off the phone with George; that buddy of his looked at the CT. He thinks the mass is an AV fistula, not a tumor. They want to try to fix it tomorrow. This is great news."

There was a pause. I expected her to be jumping and screaming with joy but there was nothing on the other end of the line but silence.

"Did you hear me?"

"Yeah, I did. I am not going to get too excited."

"Not too excited? They don't think this is cancer anymore."

"They don't know for sure. I have to hope they are right but I will not be convinced until they are sure. I have an appointment waiting."

I hung up the phone a bit deflated. She was right in that they did not know for sure what this was and they would be unlikely to find out for sure tomorrow, even after the procedure. They would guide a catheter up from her groin and feed it into the vessels surrounding the mass using fluoroscopy (basically taking another few hundred x-rays to see where they are going). Once in the right vessel, they would deposit a "coil," basically a small spring that expands once released that wedges itself into the vessel. This foreign substance quickly becomes covered with a blood clot that fills the vessel, cutting off the blood supply. Eventually, if the inflow to the AV fistula is cut off, the whole thing scars up and is gone forever. In very small vessels they can inject "glue," basically modified superglue that does the same thing. Large vessels will wash the glue away before it becomes hardened, which is why glue is only used on vessels that are too small to coil.

Mona decided to inform Dr. Wilson and left a message explaining Dr. Jackson's diagnosis and her impending procedure the next day. In less than an hour, he called back.

"Hi Mona. I had the radiologist look again at the CT. They still think it is a mass."

"I know Dr. Wilson and I hate to second guess you but Dr. Jackson disagrees."

"I would love to be wrong but I have been doing this for 40 years now and I think it is clearly a mass."

"If I have this done and it ends up being a tumor, would that change the surgery if you end up having to do it later?"

"Maybe. The coils may change the blood supply and I may have to adapt. I hope I can but it complicates an already complicated surgery."

This was not very consoling; Mona could hear some irritation in Dr. Wilson's voice as much as he was trying to hide it.

Dr. Wilson was convinced she had a tumor that needed to be removed immediately. Nobody likes to be told they are wrong, especially doctors, but it was Mona's call and this was the decision she had made.

"Good luck tomorrow. Let me know how it turns out."

She hung up with the thought that she had ticked off the man she may ask to save her life down the road.

We showed up for her procedure the next day. While I beamed with excitement that this would cure her, she remained cautious.

"Mona, things have always gone well for us. This will also," I stated confidently. We were good people and I was positive God would look after us.

When we met with Dr. Jackson, he painstakingly went through the CT, pointing out what he saw and his findings. When he was done he asked if we had any questions,

"Dr. Wilson in Milwaukee thinks this is a tumor. He said that this is what he does and this should come out."

"I understand but this is what *I* do and *I* think it is an AV fistula. We should be able to coil this without major surgery."

"When will we know if it worked?" Mona asked.

"In about a month we will recheck a CT to see if the mass is gone. If it is, we are done. If not, we will re-evaluate."

*Re-evaluate?*

I thought such an event would mean it was really a tumor and that we'd lost valuable time by waiting an extra month to have it removed. It was a risk but it just made better sense that this was anything but a tumor. Mona was only thirty-eight; she could not really have cancer. It just couldn't be; enough bad things had happened to us and we were not bad people. We deserved this to be something other than cancer. Unlike the procedure Dr. Wilson suggested, this one was minimally invasive. It just HAD to work.

After Mona shook her head to indicate she had no more questions, Dr. Jackson left. That's when I gripped her hand and assured her, "This is the right thing. They will find out that this is just an AV fistula from the crash and we will go home tonight cured. Dr. Wilson was a good doctor but he was wrong here. He saw every mass as a tumor, not something like this. He also didn't really know us; our families did not get cancer."

Sure, some of our family members had dealt with cancer but all had been at least 60 years-old and/or smokers. By contrast, we were still young, had never smoked, and had kept ourselves in pretty good shape by being active and eating relatively healthy. Cancer did not happen to people like us; it happened to bad people or smokers or people who did not take care of themselves. "We had always been lucky. Today we get lucky again."

Mona smiled and nodded. Still, there was doubt and fear in her eyes. I was a little offended that she didn't see the simple logic that this was an AV fistula from vessels tearing during the crash because it just made perfect sense. Nevertheless, she remained very cautious.

"We will see what happens," she replied.

In about an hour the nurse came in and administered some morphine to sedate her. "Take this and we will call you when she is done," the nurse informed me, handing me a pager similar to the ones they use in restaurants. In a few minutes, the morphine kicked in and they wheeled her into the prep room. I kissed her goodbye and told her that we just had to clear this one hurdle and we would both be through the worst.

She nodded but, again, did not look very confident. "We will see," she muttered, half dazed from the sedative.

Two hours went by before they paged us that the procedure was done. I'd spent most of that time in her room watching TV by myself. Our families were not present since all this had happened so quickly.

Time seemed to drag on forever; I'd seen most of the uninteresting televisions shows before and couldn't wait for Mona to be finished.

When the pager went off to inform me that Mona was in recovery, I was crutching around the hospital floor trying to work my muscles. In response, I crutched over to her room to see her, still heavily sedated with her head back and her mouth slightly open. She turned to me slightly as I said her name.

"Did they get it?" she asked.

"I haven't spoken to anyone yet," I answered. Mona did not smile; she just turned her head.

A few minutes later, Dr. Jackson walked in. "How did it go?" I blurted out.

"The procedure went fine," he answered. "It was more vascular than we had hoped but we coiled and injected everything we could see."

"Great," I replied, "when can she go home?"

"Tomorrow. I want to watch her incision tonight in case there are any problems."

"OK, thank you for all you have done. This was much better than the Whipple procedure Dr. Wilson wanted to do."

"I will order a CT in a month and see how everything looks. We can't tell much before then."

With that, Dr. Jackson left and I turned to Mona. "The procedure went well, they said they got it. You are over the last hurdle."

"He said the procedure went well but he didn't say they cured it. They got all the vessels they could see but he did not say he was sure it was an AV fistula."

Even through the haze of morphine, Mona had heard every word. She was right; the doctor did not say she was cured. It could still be a tumor, we had to wait and see. I had heard what I wanted to hear, what I had *expected* to hear. An AV fistula would fit perfectly into my perceptions of how this should go as well as my new plan for our lives but the doctor had not definitively stated one way or another what we were truly confronting.

The next day, Mona left the hospital. She was sore in her groin where they had made the incision and located her femoral artery but was otherwise doing well. She was only sent home on ibuprofen for pain and some OxyContin if needed. She took the Oxy the first day and slept but was off of it by the second. While she felt good physically, emotionally she was on pins and needles. It would be a month before she would know if we'd made the right decision. Dr. Wilson – the pancreatic specialist – had been adamant that this was a tumor and not an AV fistula. On the other hand, Dr. Jackson – the specialist on AV fistulas – had been adamant about his diagnosis. In a month, we would find out who was right. In the meantime, Mona's life hung in the balance.

The fact was, in medicine this happens all the time. Most diagnoses are an educated guess based on formal training (book smarts) and real life experience. Nothing is one-hundred percent accurate and all doctors – no matter how brilliant – will be wrong at times. The problem is that a doctor's "wrong" analysis has the potential to end your life. *If Dr. Jackson was wrong and this really was a tumor, would a month's delay make a difference? Would the coils he put in make removing the tumor more difficult?* We didn't know but it could spell the difference between life and death.

Now we were expected to go back to our lives as if nothing was happening while we waited for confirmation yet I remained optimistic that Mona had avoided a life-threatening surgery. We had always avoided major bumps in the road; I expected this to be no different.

I was reformulating the *plan* for the rest of our lives. Sure, the first plan had been changed when the crash happened, but now we were back on course and I figured that I could see the road ahead. Mona would heal up and get good news in a month; the AV fistula would be gone. I would continue rehab and my body would heal. I had a long road yet but was making progress and was not going to die from my injuries. I could see that I would be back to work in a few months. While I still needed a lot of OxyContin to get through the day's activities – especially rehab – that was OK. It wasn't like I was addicted. The Oxy was necessary with the injuries I had. I could stop it anytime once the pain was gone.

The next month was spent trying to get better. Mona took three days off after surgery and went back to work. She couldn't lift anything but the staff hadn't let her lift anything since the crash. She put on the happy face telling each client who asked that I was healing well and she was fine. This was getting a little old since she repeated the story about twenty times a day.

Still, being on her feet all day was very hard. The clinic has a tile floor which holds up great against dogs but is incredibly hard on your feet. Now she was asked to stand on it all day with a sore back and groin. With her characteristic toughness, Mona made it through but at the end of the day, she was completely exhausted. Thankfully, we were still getting food delivered from the church, which was what we all lived on for the next month. Each delivery was like manna from heaven for Moses in the desert.

I figured we had beaten the odds. Here we were facing cancer and potentially Mona's death, but instead had found out it was all a big mistake. There really was no cancer, just an image on the CT. Mona would be declared healthy and we would all fully recover. I was more and more upbeat as I thanked God for helping us through this latest scare. Mona was much less optimistic, saying she would believe it when she saw the next CT.

I was confident that things had worked out for us again. We had been basically good people and helped countless animals and owners with our skills. We would be rewarded for our good works by avoiding cancer. It all made perfect sense. My view of how God worked would be confirmed: good things happen to good people. That was what I expected. That was my new plan.

# Chapter 35

## ∞ Now I Get It ∞

A month after surgery, Mona returned to the hospital for another CT. I didn't go along since I was still extremely immobile and the results would not be read for a few days. She scheduled a meeting with Dr. Jackson for two days later to discuss the findings.

The delay was terrible: two days of pure stress and anxiety while waiting to find out if you've been cured and can close an awful chapter in your life, or if you have cancer, and will need major surgery – yet still die, regardless of your medical team's best efforts.

In this kind of scenario, there's very little you can do to ease your mind and live life normally. Mona tried to go back to work but her every thought focused upon her upcoming meeting about her test results. Putting on a brave face, she went through the motions of her life – working, tending to my needs, taking care of the kids, sharing my latest health updates with every client (most clients assumed she was all better since she was back at work) – all while coping with overwhelming anxiety. Two days seemed like a year.

The morning of the second day, her phone rang while she was at work. It was Dr. Fueredi. Her heart seemed to stop beating as she picked it up, knowing she would finally have her answer one way or another.

"Hi George," she answered as she sprinted to get to the break room and away from everyone.

Dispensing with the formalities, he got right to it. "Hi Mona, I have your results." His voice was clinical; he was speaking as a doctor, not as a friend.

"Mona, the mass is still there."

Immediately, she knew what that meant. This was a tumor, not an AV fistula like we had hoped, but more like what *she* had expected: her lingering pessimism had been accurate.

The doctor continued, "I spoke with Dr. Jackson and he agrees, you need to have this removed surgically. We could try the procedure again but I don't think it is an AV fistula."

Her hands were shaking as she collapsed onto a couch.

"Thank you for the call, George. I guess I will call Dr. Wilson and beg him to take me on again."

"Dr. Wilson is a good man and you are in the best of hands. Good luck. Mona, I am truly sorry that we were wrong here."

"We both know medicine is not an exact science, George. I will call Dr. Wilson. Tell Dr. Jackson I appreciate his efforts."

With that, she hung up the phone. A flood of fear washed over her as she sat there alone in the break room. Meanwhile, the busy practice was humming along while her next appointments awaited her. My wife had to process the news of her having pancreatic cancer without her family around – all alone in an employee lounge. A wave of nausea compelled her to run for the bathroom while she broke out in a sweat, her heart racing. Then the tears came – an unstoppable torrent of sobs. Her world had crashed yet again.

After a few minutes, our office manager and good friend Karen knocked on the door.

"Mona, are you alright?"

When she opened the door, Karen immediately knew what had happened.

"Did the doctor call?"

Mona nodded.

That was all it took. Mona and Karen had always been very close, in part because Karen had been our first employee when we'd purchased the practice eight years prior. She knew immediately that it had been confirmed by the doctor that Mona now had pancreatic cancer. Karen encircled Mona in her arms as she cried along with her, without another word spoken. These two had been through a lot over the years but this was entirely different; this was life and death, not an irate client or someone wanting to return half-used medicine. It was Mona's mortality and it was downright terrifying.

After a few minutes of holding her close, Karen pulled away and told her, "I will cancel your appointments, Chris and Kay can handle the rest of today. Give me a minute and I will drive you home."

When Mona arrived, I was in bed resting from my physical therapy session. She made a bee-line for the closet as she walked into our bedroom yet I didn't really notice in my Oxycodone-induced stupor. "You are home early," I observed, oblivious to anything being wrong. There was no answer.

A minute later, she emerged from the closet dressed in pajamas in an effort to just get comfortable. By now, I saw her face and noticed she had been crying.

"Did you get the results?"

"George called," she replied, and immediately I knew what it was. "It's still there?"

"Yeah, I knew it was a tumor," she declared.

"I will call Dr. Wilson."

"I don't know if he will see me after doubting him."

"Of course he will see you. I can't see him putting his pride in front of your health. We have had enough people going and getting a second opinion and then coming back to us that we know how it is. You don't turn them away, if anything you welcome them back since now they trust you completely. It is the same for us; we believe him now and will trust what he says. If he turns you away then he was not the man we thought he was and we don't want him as our doctor anyway."

I realized that this was another lesson from our first stay in the hospital: we'd gotten good at picking the right doctors for us. Having to pick and choose among various physicians throughout our ordeal taught us what to look for: confidence but not arrogance. We wanted someone we could talk to, who would spend the time answering our questions; someone who could put our needs ahead of their wounded pride and ego. We wanted a doctor whom the nurses liked and recommended. I had found it with Dr. Lang and thought I knew Dr. Wilson well enough to expect the same qualities in him. I did not think he would let us down. Choosing the appropriate doctor was another lesson we'd learned in our first round of hardship following the accident, one that would assist us in this new trial. Yet another way in which the crash – the incident we'd thought would be the hardest struggle of our lives – had prepared us for an even bigger challenge to come. It was God's spiritual workout for us, getting us in shape for what was coming around the bend.

With that, Mona's eyes filled with tears, as did mine. We knew about the different types of pancreatic cancer – the most aggressive that took its victims within months and the slower-growing kind that could be "cured" or managed for long periods of time. At this point, we had no idea which one she would be facing. Only the biopsy would give us a concrete answer but we could only get a biopsy with a risky and complicated procedure. That surgery was necessary was no longer in doubt; there was also no doubt that it would be grueling. Mona would end up with a large scar – not that it really mattered – but she certainly wasn't looking forward to sporting one from her ribs to her pelvis. What terrified her the most however, was the thought that she had cancer. The pain and scars she could handle but facing the fact she could have a fatal disease consumed her with fear and dread.

Now it was crystal clear. Again, there was no booming voice and no burning bush in the desert but I knew God was telling me something loud and clear: Neither I, nor Mona was going to be in charge. The only one in control of any of this was God. He had saved us during the crash; He had protected the kids; He had allowed Mona to break her back in three places but protected her spinal cord so she wouldn't be paralyzed. In the end, it was all part of a larger plan. It could not have been more perfect: the breaks in her back were the first and second lumbar vertebrae (the mid-back just below the last rib) and just "happened" to be directly over the pancreas. Of all the places and bones that could have been broken, she broke the ones inches away from a potentially silent-but-deadly tumor. The radiologists HAD to focus on this area and would no doubt see it. This was more than a coincidence; I could not believe this was just plain luck. This was God's plan, it was Him in control. This was the reason for all we had endured in the last few months. The crash, my survival, and Mona's injuries were all about getting her a CT of her pancreas; the whole ordeal was about finding her tumor. I had been looking for the reason God had put *me* through this when it really had nothing to do with *me* at all.

I also realized once again that I was not, nor had I ever been, in control of anything. My life had been directed for me and the crash was just part of His plan. I thought back about the day at the cabin. My last memory had been of going to check the door to make sure it was locked. I remember sitting in the car ready to head out and *needing* to recheck. I walked up knowing I had locked the door and uncertain as to why I was checking it again. I had just had this feeling to do it and had learned to trust that gut feeling when I got it. I remember walking back to the car muttering to myself about wasting time checking something I already knew was OK. That half-minute delay had ultimately put us in line with Jacobs. Had I not obeyed my gut feeling, we would have been a half-mile ahead and evaded the crash. In that case, we would not have found the mass. That voice in my head was God's, telling me to do as He said; it had nothing to do with a locked door.

I also thought about the other warning I had been given the night before the crash as I was preparing for bed, the one that told me "if a car comes across the median, your job is to protect the kids in back." There had been something about it that forced me to pay attention. Somehow it had seemed a very important thought though I did not understand why. But there had been no mention of protecting Mona, even though she was my wife and I therefore had an obligation to protect her as well. I had just assumed she was included among the people I was told to safeguard. But the voice had only mentioned the kids. He did not want me to protect Mona, just the kids. Mona *needed* to break her back if we were going to find the tumor that was inside of her. That night in the cabin before all of this had started, I hadn't fully understood the meaning of this apparently random thought, but now it stopped me in my tracks. I had not seen the entire picture and could not possibly foresee where our lives were heading but now I did. Nearly six months later, it finally made sense.

Now I understood that Mona HAD to break her back to ensure they found the tumor. God was telling me He would take care of *us* not just *me*; just do *exactly* as He says. Don't ask why. This is true faith, not asking why, not understanding why, but trusting Him nonetheless.

I thought about my survival with the clotting problem that should have killed me, the one-in-a-hundred chance that the Factor VIII shot would save my life. I thought about how Dr. Lang had kept me alive with his quick thinking and superior skills. I thought about how he wasn't supposed to even be there that day, how he had changed his schedule due to coaching his son's football game, which placed him at the scene that Sunday instead of Saturday. How he was supposed to be gone at noon but was stuck filling out paperwork after his shift when the call came that we were on our way. His subsequent decision to help rather than go home. How the man who would make all the right decisions in his effort to preserve my life had not even been scheduled to work a shift at the hospital that day.

No, too many things had gone right; too many things had fallen into place to attribute it to just random luck. We had survived the crash mostly intact and found a potentially deadly tumor that would otherwise not have been discovered until it was too late – and we'd found it only because of the crash, only because I had heard and heeded the inner voice urging me to check a door I knew had already been locked. That same voice had later told me not to swerve but to use the mass of the car hitting head-on to protect the kids in back. I'd been solely focused on our dire circumstances in the aftermath of the accident, but our collision with Jacobs on the highway had proven to be the only way to find Mona's tumor and the only chance to remove it before it spread. As I sat there and pondered everything, I was amazed that a collision that had nearly killed us had ultimately saved us.

I now knew that this was out of our hands; that I didn't know, nor would I ever know His plan. Though I could not tell for sure, I simply couldn't believe God would take us through this horrific ordeal, only to lose Mona in the end. It just could NOT be. We had become a very close and strong family, tempered by pain and fear. We were now focused on what was right, not money or business or popularity, but on being better people. We had grown spiritually and emotionally. We were better in so many ways that it couldn't end with Mona dying. *It just couldn't.* Still, I knew that only God was the final decision-maker and I could easily lose her.

The more I thought about it, the more I realized this crash had never been about me. It was all about Mona, getting her a CT, and finding the tumor. That is why I survived. There was nothing special about me; I'd just been in the car along with her. The reason I didn't die was because He didn't want me to die. God wanted Mona to find this cancer and remove it.

However, He also wanted us to change into the people He wanted us to be and was using the crash and now the cancer to get us there, to refocus our priorities because we had drifted away from Him. He had arranged it all to allow us to work through the fear and trepidation that comes with cancer to force us to change, to make us better people.

At this point in our journey, I also knew our fate was out of our control. In truth, I really did not know the details of His plan but I had to believe that the discovery of this tumor represented the good that comes from the bad. Some refer to it as the silver lining; I call it our spiritual workout. Like one of those intense 90-day programs advertised on infomercials, the crash was an intense training program that pushed us to our limits and made us stronger than we ever thought we could be. As with the physical workouts, it takes great drive, dedication, and discipline to achieve the desired results. There were many times when we wanted to just quit but we had kept going. Now we saw the benefits. We had a long way to go physically, but mentally and spiritually we'd changed for the better; we were in as good a shape as we could possibly be in order to face this new challenge. It had been arduous work to get to this point – a long, hard slog – but we were truly ready to confront this next challenge.

Our spiritual and emotional workout had prepared us to go the distance. In my profession, if I want to learn something like a new surgery, I must put in a ton of effort learning the anatomy and the steps of the procedure – often visiting a specialist to observe the operation or attending a course. I usually pay to attend weekend workshops to learn the more complicated procedures; I invest time and money to do something new, all with the idea that it will ultimately make me a better veterinarian. It is not easy and requires a ton of work.

Likewise for the pain and struggle we were now enduring. It was intense – the hardest thing we had ever done – but the end result was strength. There was no easy way; we had to put in the work if we wanted to be fortified beyond anything we'd experienced before.

In the end, it forced me to reexamine who I was as a person and my relationship with God. Before the crash, I had thought I could handle anything; now I knew I could not. My spiritual growth had been achieved as I worked through my pain and fear of what lay ahead. Yes, I had definitely needed to become a better person, but before I could, I had to invest the time and energy. Otherwise, I would revert right back to the arrogant S.O.B. I was before the crash. I would receive nothing in return for all of this pain and work and be just like the person who faithfully does the workout for three months, gets in great shape, and then goes back to their old, unhealthy lifestyle – the one they sought to change in the first place.

However, I was ready to change permanently, having understood the extent to which my life was beyond my control and how God wanted me to take a different course. We humans are naturally resistant to change; it usually takes a major cuff upside the head (figuratively speaking, or in my case, a literal whack of my face against the airbag) for a person to realize they are doing something wrong. Of course in my case, if all had continued to go well, with no pain in my life, I would not have had a reason to change. And that is why God had to give us a wake-up call to get our attention and force a spiritual transformation: we hadn't been listening.

In this matter I had no choice; my life had been changed for me. As I spent countless hours in my hospital bed, I'd been given plenty of time for self-reflection. The process of recovery – during which I couldn't even do the most basic things for myself – had forced me to realize I controlled nothing. It is hard to be cocky and self-assured when you can't even use a bedpan and therefore must urinate and defecate in your sheets. It was impossible to convince myself I was in control when I had to call a nurse for a suppository because the morphine constipated me to the point where I couldn't empty my bowels without one. It was hard to be cocky when I would then have to call her again later because the suppository had worked and my sheets and my ass were soiled. Nope, under those humiliating circumstances, arrogance and self-assuredness had pretty much vanished.

I remembered something I had once been told, "People only change when the pain of what they are doing is greater than the pain of change." That is why drug addicts or alcoholics can only stop using and become sober *after* they finally hit rock bottom. They will change when the pain of their addiction is greater than the pain of quitting. Now I was forced to see that the crash had changed me; it just wasn't an easy realization.

Previously, I'd thought we were pretty good people who went to church on Sunday – at least most Sundays – and that was good enough. Now I knew God thought I could do better. Therefore, like many other fathers when their son steps out of line and isn't paying attention, He gave me a good whack in order to wake me up: first the crash and now Mona's tumor.

*Yes God, you have my attention now.*

Strangely, I felt a real peace, a peace that came from knowing He was in control and we were just along for the ride wherever it took us. We had been through once; we could do it again.

Our family had made it through hospitals and recovery, learning countless lessons about how to cope with tough times. Now, we would have to confront another hardship but this time around we were seasoned veterans, not rookies; all the pieces were in place to support us. Our families were together and strong. They knew their roles and what to do to really help us; they would take care of the kids while Mona had surgery, they would transport us to and from the hospital, and they would feed the animals and keep the house clean.

Once the community found out about this latest health scare, it would rally around us. The church would deliver meals and keep prayer chains going. Our pastors would visit the hospital but not until a few days after surgery so Mona could rest and regroup. Our partner and employees could run the business until we returned, with no bickering or complaints.

This struggle would be a terrible one – maybe not harder physically but much more difficult emotionally – but we had confidence going in that at least we could handle it. We were simply better prepared for dealing with this than we had been just a few months back: we were ready.

In a grander sense (though I hesitate to equate our personal struggle with the hell of war), we had a similar experience to the men and women of "The Greatest Generation," those who'd fought in World War II. These people were not forged in the war but in the years leading up to it – the terrible years of the Great Depression of the 1930's prepared them for the unspeakable Hell of war in the 1940's. By the time they entered the war theater, they'd already been well acquainted with sacrifice, with doing without creature comforts, with surviving with whatever they had, no matter how meager. They knew about relying on each other and teamwork. Consequently, they'd win the war because of what they had learned already during the Great Depression. Dealing with the hardships of the decade of the 1930's had forged these kids into the men and women who would win the war a few years later.

I was still terrified by the cancer and the prospect of losing Mona. We'd been married for fourteen years, with three small kids who relied on us. The thought of our young son and daughters having to witness their mother wasting away to her ultimate death was unbearable. Yet there was also hope that we could remove the tumor and cure her. At the very least, there was hope – all because we had found the cancer early, thanks to an eight-time drunk driver named Mike Jacobs.

# Chapter 36

## ∞ This Ain't Going to be Easy ∞

We called Dr. Wilson immediately. While I don't know if he's a Christian, he certainly acted like one: he was kind, gracious and forgiving. Alleviating our fears, he never held a grudge against us for doubting his judgment the first time; instead he scheduled Mona for surgery a week later. She would have a Whipple procedure to remove a large part of her pancreas. They would also remove dozens of lymph nodes to look for evidence of spread.

This surgery is very risky – one of the most technically difficult performed on a routine basis. There are several valid reasons why. First, unlike some other organs such as the spleen, the pancreas cannot be fully removed when riddled with cancer because it functions to make the digestive enzymes that break down the various foods we eat into the smaller building blocks that make them up.

The body can only absorb these nutrients after they are divided into smaller parts and in this process, the pancreas does the majority of the work. Loss of the entire pancreas would eliminate most of the digestive enzymes, making it nearly impossible to digest food. Without the ability to break down food, it would fail to nourish the body because food would simply pass through and be excreted as waste.

As vets we often see a similar disease in dogs called pancreatic insufficiency, meaning that these dogs have a nonfunctioning pancreas. They can eat all they want but cannot digest the food to absorb it. As a result, they're always acting as if they are starving (which they are) because anything they consume passes through undigested and unused. All of the undigested food causes them to make tons of stool, and if left untreated, they will waste away and die. The treatment consists of giving them the enzymes they need (in a powder made from cow or pig pancreas) for their entire lifetime. While this approach keeps them alive, it is far from ideal because the powder is just not as good as the real thing. Consequently, these dogs constantly battle weight loss and diarrhea.

For Mona, removing the whole pancreas would also create a second problem: diabetes. In essence, diabetes is a lack of insulin – the hormone required to move sugar from the bloodstream and into the cells where it can be used. Since insulin is made entirely in the pancreas, taking it out would eliminate Mona's body's ability to make insulin, rendering her a terrible diabetic (most diabetics still make *some* insulin, making them more manageable). Her diabetes would be extreme, demanding multiple insulin injections every day – compounded by a lack of enzymes to digest her food. Diabetes creates all sorts of problems such as weight loss, nerve degeneration (leading to numbness in the feet and hands), cataracts (leading to blindness), and poor healing (leading to amputations).

Third, the pancreas is simply in a bad spot to try and remove. It is very close to the stomach and first part of the intestine and shares a blood supply. Complete removal would require removal of a large part of the stomach and intestine. The bile duct that drains the liver also travels through it and has to be saved. It was simply too difficult and complicated to take out the entire pancreas.

Dr. Wilson would have to cut out the section with the tumor and leave the rest. While this might sound easy, it is in fact fraught with potentially deadly problems.

Primarily, because Mona's tumor was smack in the middle of the pancreas, Dr. Wilson would have to cut on each side of it, creating two separate cuts into the organ. These cuts would then release enzymes every time Mona ate anything. These enzymes normally travel down the pancreatic duct and into the small intestine where they belong. However, with damage to the pancreas, they leak into the surrounding tissue and do just what they are designed to do – digest any tissue they touch. This "self-digestion" inflicts widespread damage and inflammation in the tissues surrounding the pancreas.

First, the enzymes break down the tissues into their components. Then as the body tries to repair the damage, the tissues break down even more, resulting in swelling, accumulation of pus (possibly from infection but more likely from all the dead and damaged tissue that needs to be removed) and formation of scar tissue. In reaction, the nerves in the area scream out, creating horrific pain, while the stomach outflow (sitting right near the pancreas) spasms shut, causing vomiting. This painful condition is called pancreatitis (inflammation of the pancreas) – one of the most deadly complications a person undergoing a Whipple procedure can endure. All patients get it to some degree, but in Mona's case, they just couldn't predict its severity. There is no magic drug to stop it: the treatment is to simply abstain from eating to prevent the release of digestive enzymes while waiting for the inflammation to subside. The hope was that the cut ends of the pancreas, sewn together by Dr. Wilson, would heal – a process that could require days or weeks of pain and vomiting before Mona could even attempt to eat again. In the meantime, the hospital staff tending to her would fight dehydration and muscle degeneration, holding onto hope that Mona's body could endure.

Ignorance would have been bliss going into this procedure but Mona, being a veterinarian, understood all the ramifications. She'd witnessed many dogs with the same condition die a horrible death, notwithstanding the medical care and attention she'd given them. She knew the recovery from this surgery would be tough and involve the administration of morphine for several days to ease excruciating pain. From her past experience, she knew the morphine would also make her nauseous, constipated, and paranoid but she'd have no choice but to take it.

She would spend days to weeks wanting to vomit at the sight or smell of food. Of course, vomiting with a fresh, long abdominal incision just compounded her fears. She knew this would be hell.

The incision itself would run from her ribs to below her belly button. There was no minimally invasive way to do a Whipple; she would inevitably be left with a huge scar. Aside from the obvious pain, no woman wants a large abdominal scar, no matter her age. Mona was a beautiful woman; the vain part of her abhorred the idea of sporting a hideous mark on her great body. Yet for her it wasn't so much the aesthetics of the scar, but the fact that it would be a constant reminder of her battle with cancer. Such a visible sign on her body would oppose her natural tendency to eliminate bad memories by suppressing them. The constant presence of this scar would ensure that she'd never forget.

There are also many technical concerns about the Whipple procedure within the medical community. Of course, the mere fact that she even needed the Whipple in the first place was our biggest concern because it signified the doctors' belief that she had pancreatic cancer. As one of the most technically demanding procedures for both doctor and patient, the Whipple carries a very high complication rate. Basically, there's a nearly endless list of things that can go wrong – and many of them will kill you.

To ensure a good blood supply and removal of the entire tumor, the middle of the pancreas, the end of the stomach, and the first part of the intestine must all come out together in one piece. Everything left is then reconnected in a completely new way. The pancreatic duct that drains the pancreas and the bile duct that drains the liver are also rerouted because the disruption in the normal pathway. Leakage from any of the connections or blockage of any of the ducts is deadly.

The pancreas itself is friable and does not hold sutures well. It tends to just tear through so it is likely to fall apart after surgery. Dr. Wilson would put some suture in place but the two remaining ends of the pancreas are basically held together for a while to try to get a clot to form between the ends. This acts like glue to hold the ends in place and then the whole thing is wrapped with some loose abdominal fat. The fat serves as a bandage around the damaged pancreas, helping to contain the enzymes leaking out. Long-term, it is the fat "bandage" that helps heal the pancreas supplying blood and a structure around it. Patients are warned that there is *always* some leakage in the first few days or longer until the pancreas can hopefully seal back over. Mona would not be allowed anything orally for at least three days to keep the pancreas from releasing its enzymes with that hope that it would then be strong enough to seal off any leakage when she tried to eat again. It was just a matter of her pancreas healing just enough to prevent the leakage from killing her.

Yet another risk surrounds the cutting and rerouting of the intestine and stomach. After the stomach and intestine are cut and sections removed, they must be reattached to restore the continuous path for the food. Usually there are two or three different spots where the stomach or parts of the intestine are re-attached to each other. Surgeons take great care in the reconnections but they are suturing tissues together in completely unnatural ways. A single suture that is placed incorrectly or doesn't hold will leak and release bacteria. This phenomenon, known as peritonitis (infection in the abdomen), is incredibly painful and likely fatal. As I mentioned, the sheer complexity of the surgery and high risk of seemingly endless complications renders the Whipple procedure one of the most difficult and potentially deadly surgeries performed. Any one of its multiple, complicated steps can go wrong and ultimately kill the patient. Unfortunately, "the patient" in this case was the woman I loved, the one my kids called "Mom."

While most pancreatic cancers are very aggressive Dr. Wilson suspected Mona's was less so, a neuroendocrine tumor. There are many different types of neuroendocrine tumors but all we cared about was the one affecting her. Mona's tumor's characteristics and the extent of its spread within her body would determine whether she lived or died. The Whipple, with all its risks, was our only option. Chemo, radiation, and even holistic treatments were all options, yet not the best ones. Most pancreatic masses do not respond well to chemo; radiation would blast the tumor trying to kill it but would not arrest or contain any spread. We needed a diagnosis – an actual a piece of it, to tell for sure what it was.

Holistic sounds good but rarely works, Steve Jobs, founder of Apple, had a similar pancreatic tumor that could have been removed with a Whipple. He thought the surgery was too invasive and tried holistic treatment. He died five years later, about when he would have died if he had done nothing. His holistic treatment allowed the cancer to spread and, ultimately, kill him.

Herbs weren't going to stop this one for Mona, either. The only course of action was to get this thing out for further examination and diagnosis. Only then could the doctors determine if they could successfully treat it and preserve her life. After consulting with Dr. Wilson again, I humbly asked him to save her.

God had taught us another lesson: humility.

While elated that Dr. Wilson would do the surgery, we were also very aware that we were headed right back into hell.

## Chapter 37

### ∞ A Fork in the Road ∞

The days leading up to surgery were characterized by pure, relentless stress as we attempted to live as if nothing was wrong. It was completely insane. *How could we go back to our old routine when in a matter of days, Mona would find out she had a cancer that could kill her in a few months, a few years, or never?*

As her husband, I wasn't much help because I was still pretty immobile and dealing with my own never-ending pain. Due to the drugs, driving was forbidden, and I could only walk with the aid of crutches. No matter how much I wanted to, I couldn't console her or assure her everything would be alright since she knew that things may not be.

*Do I tell her not to worry about the kids because as their father, I would see to it they were taken care of?* She already had to face the heartbreaking fact that she might not be around to watch them grow into adults, with all of the life milestones that journey entails. She could very well miss out on most of their lives: graduations, careers, weddings, and grandchildren. Confronted with that cruel reality, there simply isn't much anyone can say.

In preparation for her possible death, Mona wrote letters to all the kids and me to be opened if and when God called her home. She wanted each of us to know the exact nature and scope of her immense pride and love for us all, focusing only on the positive – not on the fact that if we were reading her letters, she would be gone.

Ultimately, we decided that all we could do was pray. And pray we did – alone, together, and with our pastors. Our church set up another prayer chain that enlisted hundreds, if not thousands, to pray for her much like they had done for us after the crash. We had to rely on our faith now more than ever. Even after everything we'd been through, it was still incredibly difficult to face the fact that the outcome of this new challenge was completely out of our hands. We longed to have control of our lives back.

One night, I awoke to the sound of Mona sobbing in another room because she was just so incredibly scared. She told me the thought of the pain that comes with aggressive pancreatic cancer was terrifying her more than the thought of death itself. We had both seen what cancer can do to animals and the torture it inflicts upon them. As veterinarians, we could end their suffering with a shot. A few times a week, animals would come into our practice clearly in need of euthanasia; invariably, we'd experience great relief as we ended their pain. Now Mona faced the fact there was a strong chance she would have aggressive pancreatic cancer – an agonizing form of this awful disease that would her subject her to indescribable misery over the next few months before robbing her of her life. Since there was no way to humanely euthanize people, humans were left to suffer in excruciating pain for days or weeks – much longer than we would ever allow an animal to go on.

Mona and I both had great reservations about doctor-assisted suicide but when you are the one facing this terrible possibility, those reservations go out the window. Having been raised Catholic, she was worried she would go to hell if she took her own life, but the thought of a slow death from pancreatic cancer frightened her even more. For now, she prayed that if God was to take her, He would not allow her to suffer too much. Privately, she hid a shot of euthanasia solution she could use if the pain got too bad. She had a syringe full of euthanasia solution that she used on dogs, an IV set up that she could place if she needed to kill herself. Yes, at 39 years-old, my wife had to plan how to end her life if circumstances demanded it.

Amazingly she continued to go to work, trying to act concerned about a dog's itchy ear or a cat's diarrhea. Mona confessed that being at the practice made time go faster and took her mind off of her upcoming date with destiny while the kids were in school and I was lying in bed. But the thought of her having cancer never left our minds. It is easy to say, "We are all going to die someday" but when that day could be a few days or months away it is in a whole new realm. Logically, we may accept that we are all going to die but we assume that we have plenty of time. When that time is short, when it has a definite endpoint, the thought of death reverberates through your head every three seconds. It is nearly impossible to think of anything else. Life just kind of stops.

Day after day, we kept going in a daze. Nothing could really progress until we had a full understanding and knowledge of the cancer. Time dragged on as we both counted the hours. We should have been doing all the fun and crazy things we had always dreamed of, but we were simply too scared. *Should Mona jump out of an airplane when the possibility of cancer would steal the joy from what would normally be an exhilarating adventure?* Awareness that impending death was the only reason for skydiving at this time in our lives would kind of take the thrill out of it.

Mona knew she would soon discover the truth about her mortality and understandably, she just wanted the wait to be over. Life had stopped anyway so there would be no more joy until we found out what was going on.

The only good thing that transpired that week was due to the fact that Mona needed to gain some weight. She had always eaten well and kept herself in good shape but Doctor Wilson had suggested she use the upcoming week to put on some extra pounds. He told her he expected ten- to- fifteen pounds of weight loss after surgery. Post-op, she would not be allowed any food or even water for a minimum of three days – possibly longer. The last thing Dr. Wilson wanted was a bunch of food pushing through the new stomach and intestine attachments a day after surgery. For three days, nothing would be given orally. On day four, provided all went well, she would start on some soup. Normally, patients lose about seven percent of their body weight after the procedure. Mona weighed about 135 pounds so we expected about ten pounds of weight loss in the week after surgery. She spent that week at McDonald's eating burgers, fries, and shakes. Any other time, this would have been a welcome treat to finally be able to eat whatever she wanted, guilt-free. Instead, she felt like a steer getting fattened up for slaughter.

On the day of the surgery, we arrived at the hospital at five o'clock in the morning. We could have arrived at 2 a.m. since neither one of us slept that night anyway. They wanted her there early so she could be ready for surgery at any time. Mona walked and I was on crutches as we approached the check-in desk, where after looking us both up and down, the receptionist asked what *I* was having done that day. I then explained that my wife was the patient, not me, and that she was here for a Whipple.

A bit embarrassed by the mistake, the receptionist apologized; I also noticed a change in her expression when we mentioned the words "Whipple procedure." First, surprise that a young woman needed this risky surgery, followed by a noticeable sadness as she helped us fill out the necessary forms. Although she made a gallant effort to stay upbeat and positive, we both sensed the change. This woman appeared to be the same age as Mona and no doubt knew that this procedure was only done for pancreatic cancers, which seldom turn out well.

Next we went up to the third floor surgery ward, already bustling with the day's activity. Nurses walked quickly back and forth in the halls setting IV's, filling out forms, and going through checklists to ensure each patient was identified and could recite which surgery they were having done. Mona was told to change into a surgery gown they had laid out on the bed. Luckily, the new gowns had a second layer that covered the opening in the back – no more walking down the hall holding the gown closed over your butt.

When a nurse came in to set the IV, it really hit home that our lives were going to change radically in the next few hours. The gravity of what was happening was in full force and we spoke very little. All I could think to tell her was that this was another step closer to being healed. We had taken step after step after step down this very long road since the crash and this was just another one of those steps, another difficult ascent up the mountain we were set to climb. I was convinced this was all part of God's plan from the start, to put us in the crash to find the tumor. I believed He wanted her to have it out, that He wanted her to heal. Yet Mona remained unconvinced, preferring to wait and see what happened, not getting too high or too low. She had been through too many ups and downs already.

Before the surgery, Dr. Wilson came in to check on her. Although he was always upbeat, he was also realistic. He would not tell her everything was going to be fine because he had seen too many patients found to have inoperable cancer that had been undetected until surgery. In fact, only about 20 percent of pancreatic cancer patients actually undergo the Whipple procedure since 80 percent have inoperable cancer due to spread at the time of discovery. Dr. Wilson was optimistic about Mona's chances but refused to give odds on the outcome. When asked, he would smile gently and say he would find out more when he got in there.

Now we waited. She was ready to go physically and holding up emotionally. I was amazed she wasn't crying and shaking but Mona had resigned herself to the fact that there was simply not much she could do at this point other than have the surgery and await the outcome. That is what we both did – wait.

About an hour later they came in to administer a sedative with some valium in the IV line. Mona watched it go in. Valium is thicker than the IV fluid and a little yellow so we could see it going into her vein. Her eyes started to glaze over as the drug kicked in. I worked myself over to her bed, struggling to get close. Finally, I arrived at her bedside and lowered myself to kiss her forehead. A few weeks ago, my arms would have been too weak to do this but those trips up the ramp in the rehab unit had paid off. Mona was already out of it and it hit me that this may be the last time I saw her as she'd always been. After the surgery, she may never be the same.

The nurses came in and started to wheel her out: Dr. Wilson was ready and the time had come. Life was at one of those forks in the road. We were either going to cure her or find out she was going to die soon. There wasn't much in between.

The hospital had given me a pager to allow me travel around the hospital while waiting for word. Mona's parents had arrived with her sister Carla. The wait was excruciating. *What would I do if she only had six months to live? How would I raise the kids and run the business without her?* I thought about all the nights and weekends that we had spent on call seeing animals instead of spending time as a family, all the times one of us left a birthday party because of an emergency or missed a school play due to work. Our plan had been to work hard when the kids were young so Mona could go part-time and be home when the kids were teenagers. Now she may be dead before our oldest was even ten.

It didn't seem fair that we were facing this: cancer was for older people who had lived a long life and smokers who had made their bad choices not us. All we had been through since the crash – the pain, the surgeries, the hospital stays, the rehab – all were a cakewalk compared to the agony of sitting there waiting to hear if your wife was going to live or die.

While serious, the crash injuries were temporary; we knew they would all heal eventually. Pancreatic cancer, on the other hand, had the power to kill her and destroy everything we'd worked so hard to build. Professionally, we could hire another vet but nobody had the bedside manner of Mona. The clients absolutely loved her. She also kept track of all the paperwork of a million-dollar business – taxes, payroll, staff benefits – all were her areas of expertise and things I had never done. We had a bookkeeper to fill out the forms, but Mona kept track of it all.

She also dealt with all the staff issues, and I couldn't possibly replace that. Chris or I would have to take that over if she couldn't do it anymore but I knew that neither of us would be any good at it. Additionally, our profession required concentration and attention to detail. *How could I concentrate on a dog that is peeing in the house when my wife is puking her guts out from chemotherapy that we knew would likely not work anyway?*

More importantly than the business, how would these kids handle the death of their mother? She was the "snuggler," the one they went to when they needed ten minutes of cuddle time. I was never their go-to parent for this; I was more about just dealing with whatever came up and not getting real emotional. I was the rational one, the fixer. The crash and the cancer had changed this some; the kids had seen me cry a lot and were getting used to my "sensitive" side, but they still needed their mother. Alexa and Victoria were going to be teenagers soon. They would want to go shopping, pick out clothes, and discuss boyfriends. I hated shopping and had no idea about the clothing styles they should wear anyway. *Who would teach them how to apply make-up or talk to them about boys?* Chase would be easier for me to raise but at just four years of age, he still loved to lay down with his mom. He would crawl into bed before school to be with her "just for ten minutes" before we all got going in the morning. They both always loved this time. I was usually already out of bed and "getting something done" but those two would just lay together and talk for a while before starting their day.

It terrified me to think about the kids watching their mother die. Pancreatic cancer could be so aggressive. It meant months of watching a strong, beautiful woman waste away to nothing. She may recover from the Whipple in about two weeks but then start chemotherapy or radiation and basically spend the next six months- to-a-year visiting hospitals and going to doctors' appointments – all the while getting thinner and weaker. In the end, she would be reduced to a shell of former herself, fed through tubes and suffering with excruciating pain. We would have to keep her on morphine which would put her in a fog, unable to interact with the people who loved her until her body finally succumbed to the cancer.

We would try to enjoy life, to do all those things that were on her "bucket list," but she would not take much pleasure in them. She hated traveling; it was always stressful with three little kids. She wasn't one to be jumping out of airplanes or riding a bull. She would likely want to just go home and be with her family and horses. But I couldn't imagine enjoying anything knowing that you were going to die an agonizing death in a few months. Fully savoring her remaining days on earth knowing they were few would be impossible. A diagnosis of cancer is something that just doesn't leave your head. Every thought is interrupted by "I have cancer and I will die soon."

Then, a bit selfishly, I thought about myself. If I lost Mona I would have to start dating again. I did not want to be alone all my life but bringing a new "mom" into my kid's lives was something I had never thought about. At four, eight, and ten, they were at a bad age for this. I could not think of a worse time in a person's life to watch your mother waste away and die and then your dad start to "replace her" with someone else. They would need a mother in their lives but this would be occurring as Alexa and Victoria hit the young teen years, a time when girls were very emotional anyway. The natural resentment the girls would feel at that age would be compounded by witnessing their dad dating. It would just be another devastating blow.

The thought of getting back into the dating scene again scared me also. Dating was fun in college, but I tended to have a few long relationships so I never played the dating game much. *How do I even ask a woman to go on a date? The women I met were clients or employees; when the date goes bad or the relationship doesn't work, how do I see them around town? What if women don't find me attractive anymore? What if I don't find any of them attractive?* I would be constantly comparing them to Mona, which was unfair. *What if they didn't like horses or dogs in the house?*

The horses were another dilemma. I was never a horse guy. They were fun to have around but I didn't *love* horses. These were Mona's and *she* loved them. I couldn't sell them because I would be selling something that was part of her. The kids could help with their care but the horses would become a constant reminder of losing their mom.

My head swam with all the *"what-if's"* but I kept repeating the words I had heard so often after the crash: "It is not your plan." I remembered what I had learned, that we couldn't control our future; only play the cards we were dealt. If Mona was to die in four hours, four months, or 40 years was simply not up to me. If the kids had to deal with the loss of their mother, it would be that spiritual work-out that would make them stronger than ever before. The loss would be terrible but it would bring us closer together and force all of us to grow from it in some way. God had a plan, I needed to accept that.

My tension level started to drop as I stopped trying to plan out the rest of my life. Mona, the kids, and I would just have to accept what God brought and deal with it. I had learned in the last few months that although the plan is always there, we only see a little sliver of it. We don't see the whole picture until much later, if ever. At the time of the crash, we didn't see that it would show us the real problem hiding underneath: Mona's cancer. Now as we faced the disease, I didn't know what the end result would be but I prayed that this was all about CURING the cancer, not just finding it. I prayed that God's plan was to have her here for a long time and that was why He put us in the path of a drunk driver careening across the interstate.

I prayed that this was the case but ended it with "your will be done," the phrase form the Lord's Prayer that I had repeated almost every Sunday since I was three years-old. After almost 40 years of hearing that phrase, it finally hit home. His will WILL be done and there is nothing I could do about it. It was what my faith had taught me; it was only now that I accepted it was true. That acceptance brought me some peace as I walked through this just like prayer is supposed to do. *"As I walk through the valley of death, I will fear no evil."*

It was about three hours later that the pager went off. I was in the hospital cafeteria trying to eat a late breakfast but I was really just playing with my food. I raced back up to the assigned waiting area, where we were told that Mona was in recovery, the surgery had gone well and Dr. Wilson was coming in to speak to us shortly. The surgery "going well" only meant that there had been no major complications. It told us nothing about the cancer or whether she would live or die. *Did she have pancreatic cancer or not? Did they get it all? Would it come back?*

A half-hour never seemed so long as Mona's fate hung in the balance. We would soon learn if our fears would be validated or if she would live. We sat in silence as we waited for the news. Nobody spoke. Nobody even moved. We all just waited.

Finally, there was a knock on the door and all four of us answered "come in," in unison. Dr. Wilson entered and sat down without smiling. He began to speak in a very matter-of-fact tone, reiterating that the surgery had gone as expected. My heart racing with sweat pouring out of me, I asked if the mass was cancer.

He replied, "Yes, it was what I had thought, a pancreatic tumor."

"Do you know the type?" I pursued, knowing that adenocarcinoma would kill her in a few months.

"It was a neuroendocrine tumor just like I thought it would be," he answered. He was not smug or condescending but he had been right the whole time and he knew it.

I was somewhat relieved since that meant it was not the terribly aggressive adenocarcinoma type of pancreatic cancer that is almost always deadly. However, it was still cancer, albeit one that grows more slowly. Now life or death would be determined by if it had spread.

Dr. Wilson continued, "It was in one lymph node." My heart sank as I realized it was not confined to the pancreas. "But we took out over 40 lymph nodes and it was only in one. I normally do not take this many nodes out but Mona is young and I wanted to get as many as possible, just in case."

"So it has spread already." My voice cracked as I imagined what would happen next. I knew that average life expectancy with a neuroendocrine tumor that had spread was just five years. They were considered slow growers but five years would put Alexa in the second or third year of high school, Victoria in middle school, and Chase in about fifth grade when their mother died, a terrible age to lose that guiding force in a young kid's life.

Dr. Wilson continued. "Well, it was only in one node and we usually only check ten or so. We are going to have to recheck her every six months for the next five years. If it doesn't resurface after five years it probably won't.

"And if it does?" I asked, knowing the answer.

"If it does, I go in and take it out."

"But it will just come back again."

"Yes, if we did not get it all, it will be back but these are slow growers and we will delay it as long as possible."

"There is no other treatment she needs?"

"No, as we talked about earlier, there is no chemo or radiation that works. These grow too slow for any of that to be effective. We just have to monitor and see if anything pops up."

Dr. Wilson sounded nonchalant about it but I knew he wasn't. If something "popped up" in the next five years, it would mean that the cancer was back. Taking out the spread would be a temporary fix until it popped up again. Eventually, it would be unresectible and kill her.

If she was cancer-free after five years then we could relax and say she had beaten it – though it could still come back at any time. Five years was the benchmark where it was just unlikely that she would die from it in the next 20 years. We would not know for that long.

I really wasn't prepared for this outcome. I had prepared myself for the aggressive carcinoma and losing her quickly. I had prepared, and prayed, for this being benign and the surgery curing it. I had even prepared myself for this being the neuroendocrine tumor Dr. Wilson had expected, finding a major spread inside, and losing her in four or five years. I hadn't prepared myself for not knowing the outcome. At this point we knew it was cancer but were not sure what that really meant. I didn't know if I should be happy or sad. It would take years to find out and the whole time Mona would be waiting for the ax to fall. She would have to live with the fact that her next checkup could start the clock ticking again toward her death. She would have to learn to live with the fear.

At that point, I knew our lives had changed. We always expected to live until well past retirement. Now we didn't know how many years we had left together and there was a real chance Mona would die early. We had already cheated death once when Jacobs' Jeep hit ours. Could Mona do it again? Nobody could be sure.

Yet I now knew that Mona and I did not get to determine the outcome. Even with all our schooling and enough money to pay for proper medical care, we could not control this ending. I had realized that my wife and I, with all our planning, never had control of much in our lives anyway, especially the timing of our respective deaths. We had to worry about the cancer returning yet it might not be the cancer that determines our fate – a drunk driver heading the wrong way on an interstate could just as easily end our lives. Our fate is in God's hands, according to His plan. We can't change it anyway. This realization brought me peace. It was out of my hands; I just had no control over it.

That, of course, was much easier for me to say than Mona. I wasn't the one dealing with the thought of cancer coming back in a few years. Our lack of control over our fate may be the truth, but the thought of cancer coming back would be Mona's cross to bear, not mine.

"You can go up to recovery. She is waking up," Dr. Wilson announced.

"Dr. Wilson, I can't thank you enough for what you did. We owe you her life."

"You were fortunate. Now she has to get through the recovery."

I noticed he used the word "fortunate," not "lucky." He also knew that there was no such thing as luck. Either you have good fortune or bad fortune, all according to His plan. Dr. Wilson's faith in God led him to take Mona back in for surgery but also told him that there was only so much he could do. He understood God's plan also.

Mona's mother, Anne, her sister Carla and I left for the room. Mona's dad, Joe, wanted to wait so there were not too many visitors, something we had learned from the crash. He also couldn't face seeing his daughter in this condition yet. Joe, like the rest of us, was still struggling with the fact that she even had cancer.

We walked in to find her heavily sedated though her breathing tube was out. We waited there for about five minutes, not wanting to wake her. We had also learned from the crash to let people sleep as long as possible after surgery because they will be in pain once they wake up. Every minute spent sleeping is one less minute in pain. It was another way the crash had prepared us for this.

Mona slowly opened her eyes and turned her head. The first thing she asked was, "Did they get it all?"

I had not prepared myself for that question though I should have. I looked at her and could see she was in pain already. At that point, I made a stupid mistake. I did not want to stress her any further, so I lied that they were still waiting on the final lab results. Technically, this was the truth since the pathologist needed to confirm the findings from surgery and I wanted to do some research into the prognosis of this tumor if it was in a lymph node. I justified my lie with my need with to find out more before I told her that they had found it outside the pancreas. I wasn't ready to tell her the truth even though she deserved to know. I chickened out just when she needed me to be strong, just when she needed me to be honest. I failed her miserably.

Mona asked for more pain meds and Anne went to get the nurse while I held her hand and told her how well she had done. The nurse quickly arrived to administer more morphine in the IV and soon after, Mona drifted off to sleep.

Anne and I left the room. Since this was a teaching hospital with a medical library on-site, I decided to go there to research the prognosis. Problem was, I did not have internet access and was still on crutches. The library was a quarter-mile away on the other side of the campus. I went anyway.

I searched the literature and found very little information. It was almost unheard of to find this cancer before it had spread to the liver. Mona's had spread to a lymph node and was not in the liver so the information was incomplete. This cancer was deadly in five years once in the liver and curative if removed when just in the pancreas. I just could not find anything about it being in a single node. Also, Dr. Wilson had said that he took out twice as many nodes as he usually does, due to Mona's relatively young age. He had also told us of patients who lived a long life with very high "tumor markers" in their blood but never developed cancer after surgery. Mona's tumor markers were normal before surgery so would be of little benefit after. Did these people have it in a lymph node and never developed more? There was no way to know. How many people were called cancer free because they had low "tumor markers" like Mona but still had it in a lymph node and went on to live normal lives? How many of those developed cancer in five years and died? There was just no data I could find that matched her situation.

I had no idea of the prognosis but I knew that cancer spreading into a lymph node was not good. If just in that one node the surgery would be curative, but if it was in a node somewhere else, it would come back. One cancerous cell left somewhere inside her would kill her.

There was no way to be certain: I wanted to give Mona a firm set of facts and I had none. I left the library not knowing what to tell her. I did not know what being in a lymph node really meant, though I knew the cancer had spread outside the pancreas, which meant a.) it was likely elsewhere, and b.) she was not cured. If I knew it, she would know it too. Still, I searched diligently for a way to make it not so – no matter how futile the attempt. I wanted to find something that said she was fully cured of cancer, including the spread to the one node, even though I knew it had escaped.

I also wondered if the delay we had imposed on this surgery in the vain hope of finding an aneurism and not a tumor had allowed the cancer just enough time to escape. *What if we would have had this done a month earlier when Dr. Wilson had suggested it?* We had not been ready to believe that cancer could happen in our lives: we were too healthy to contract cancer. Truly, we were too arrogant to believe that this could happen to us. We were good people so good things should happen to us. Bad things should happen to bad people. We already had learned just how wrong we were. Being good may make life more enjoyable but doesn't insulate you from undergoing difficult trials. Living an honorable life doesn't save you from hardship; it just provides the support and prayers of others so you don't have to go through it alone. That support had been invaluable to us but it hadn't changed the fact that bad things were happening in our lives.

These thoughts swirled around in my head as I went back to Mona's room, knowing she'd wake up about every hour as the morphine wore off. As expected, the pain was intense. It would increase exponentially as she waited for her next allotted dose of pain meds. Watching her obvious agony as the minutes went by, counting down to the time her pump would allow me to press the button on the morphine drip to give her some relief was heartbreaking. The drip was calculated to prevent a patient from receiving more than was allotted by the doctor but it was not enough. By the time I could administer more, Mona would be moaning and crying from the pain. This was not right. As a veterinarian, I would never let an animal endure such torture; surely my wife deserved the same treatment. Since she needed better pain control, I rang for the nurse.

An operating nurse named Jaime entered the room, where I explained the problem. I'd soon discover she was yet another angel. At that point, Mona had just received another dose and was sleeping soundly; however, knowing the intensity of the pain involved, Jaime called for the anesthesiologist. Unfortunately, he was not so quick to arrive, taking over 30 minutes. By then, Mona had been through the cycle three more times. The morphine would wear off after about five minutes but administration was restricted to every ten minutes. Therefore, Mona would cope with pain for two minutes, followed by pure agony during the last three.

For most of us, three minutes does not seem like a long time, but in Mona's case the pain was so incredibly intense she wanted to die: three minutes felt like a lifetime. We would count down and watch the clock until more morphine could be given, then push the magic button. As a result, she'd drift off to sleep for five minutes before waking up in agony again. When the anesthesiologist finally arrived, he appeared to be about 16 years-old. Of course, he was much older than that but he didn't look it. Just before he'd walked into the room, Mona had received a dose and drifted off again. He looked at her for two seconds and announced to Jaime she did not need anything more. Even after we explained that the morphine schedule wasn't adequate for Mona, the anesthesiologist brusquely dismissed our concerns and turned to leave.

Now Jaime and I were both pissed. I tried to wheel out after him but she beat me to it.

"I need to speak to you in the hallway," she stated. Her tone of voice left no doubt she was about to tear into this arrogant prick.

Although she shut the door, I could hear every word. "I am invoking my patient's right to adequate pain relief. Her pain is not being controlled for the ten minutes between allocated morphine doses and it is clear that she requires more. Either give her something else or up the dose of morphine and do it before she wakes up again!"

"She appears adequately controlled so she gets nothing more," came his cold reply.

I was at the door ready to bust out to the hallway when I heard our angel's voice.

"You have not evaluated this patient properly and seen the pain she is in when the morphine wears off. You can either stay in here until then or take my word for it but either way, she will need more. If you don't do your job here, I will be calling Dr. Wilson."

"Dr. Wilson is already in surgery."

"I will go in the surgery room myself and tell him his patient's pain is not being managed by you and I either need him to scrub out or I need someone else to do your job. You decide."

We both knew Dr. Wilson would be on fire if this happened. He would be mad for getting interrupted during surgery, even angrier that an extra person was coming into his operating room and increasing the patient's risk of infection, and really pissed that his patient, another doctor (though a veterinarian) whom he respected and regarded as a colleague, was not being treated properly. Dr. Wilson would not accept inadequate pain control and the anesthesiologist knew it. Dr. Wilson was also much more respected in the hospital and held great power as a senior surgeon; this young doctor did not want to ignite his ire.

"Fine, I will add some ketamine and lidocaine to her drip with the morphine. She will sleep for the day."

With that, I heard him quickly turn and stomp down the hall. His pride had obviously taken a beating from Jaime, who came back in the room to update me.

"Don't worry, I heard it all. Thanks for standing up for her; she really needed someone right now."

"I have been here for 12 years – about eleven-and-a-half longer than him, and have given birth to three kids. I know what pain is. My patients don't go through recoveries like this. We have drugs to stop it, there is just no reason not to use them."

"Thank you again. You are an angel."

Because of Jaime, two additional drugs were added to Mona's "cocktail" and she slept for the next six hours. I left to get some sleep also, while Anne stayed in the room with her. The pain would come back every now and then but was soon controlled with an effective drug cocktail of morphine, lidocaine, and ketamine. She would push the button and drift off to sleep again.

However, every time she woke up she would inquire about the lab results. Because she didn't want to be the bearer of bad news, Anne played dumb. I had placed my mother-in-law in a terrible position: I knew Mona wanted the truth – in fact *deserved* the truth – but seeing her in so much pain, I just didn't have the heart to tell her. Fact was, I was avoiding it because I was too weak. God would teach me to do better.

This continued for the rest of the day as Anne and I took shifts in the room with her. Mona's dad made it up to see her briefly but had to leave. He was a tough man but seeing his daughter in this terrible condition was incredibly tough for him. It would not help her if he started to sob. After all, he was still her dad and the rock that had always anchored her family.

The next day I awoke to my phone ringing. It was Mona. I had slept the night in a guest room that the hospital provides one floor below. I answered and asked how she was feeling. She replied flatly, "I need to talk to you."

I knew immediately she had found out; someone else had told her about the cancer spreading to a node. Immediately, I headed upstairs to her room and as I crutched in, she refused to even look at me; she was much too hurt.

"Why did you lie to me about them finding the cancer in a lymph node?"

"You were in so much pain coming out of surgery I didn't want to tell you. I needed to find out what it meant before I did."

"Scot, we both know what it means. It has spread."

"All the literature talks about is spread to the liver, not a single lymph node. Spread to the liver is much more advanced. I could not find a case like yours. Dr. Wilson said he took out twice as many nodes as he usually does and so did not know what to make of it being in a single one. He said we just have to monitor it."

"Look, whatever happens, I need you to be completely honest with at all times. I need to trust what you say no matter what. I can't be wondering if you are holding something back when I am going through this. I can understand you not wanting me to be stressed after surgery but not being able to trust you is much worse. I need you now more than ever"

"I understand. It won't happen again. I promise, I will tell you the truth no matter what."

She'd received the news of her mass being a neuroendocrine tumor that had spread by a first-year resident who'd come to in to her room to check on her. I was pissed at this young student for telling her but knew that I should have never allowed it to happen: it was my fault for not being honest with Mona in the first place. Again, I had learned.

My wife began to cry. The fact that the cancer had spread was sinking in. Initially, her anger at me had cushioned the blow; now that she knew the truth she was forced to deal with it. I tried in vain to console her but because she was still very angry at me, I simply held her hand as we both cried.

Finally, I spoke. "Mona, I still believe that this was the reason for the crash. I think God wanted you to find the cancer and get it out. I think he has other plans for us and that is why we didn't die that day. He is with you in this and wants you to live."

Mona nodded but wasn't convinced. She was still in a ton of pain and the stress had worn her out emotionally. She would need some time to deal with this and my withholding of the truth had just added to her problems. Unintentionally, I'd made things worse and had learned a valuable lesson. I vowed it would not happen again.

At this point there was really nothing more I could do or say. Words couldn't change the fact that Mona now had to cope with cancer in her life. She was incredibly scared. *Would the kids watch her waste away and die? Would she live to see them graduate high school? Would she miss out on all the things she was looking forward to as they grew up: volleyball or football games; boyfriends and girlfriends; dances and proms; and every other milestone a parent wants to experience?*

Physically, what about the pain that cancer invariably causes? She had already decided she did not want chemo since there was no evidence it would help. Once again, Mona had to face the fact that life had not worked out like we'd planned.

## Chapter 38

### ∞ A Lesson in Humility ∞

Mona spent the next two days drifting in and out consciousness on the morphine, not really saying much. She was still in a lot of pain and nauseous from the surgery. She was not allowed to eat for another two days while the intestinal tract healed. The cancer was on her mind with every thought; there is just not much else you can think about when dealing with such a grim diagnosis.

Joe and I drove home that night to check in with the kids, where Mona's sister, Denise was staying with them, ensuring they were going to school. Having received a wake-up call, I decided it was time to get off the OxyContin. I'd been taking up to 80 milligrams during the day and another 80 milligrams at night "for pain" but knew that my current level of pain didn't justify such a high dosage. Oxy just made me feel good. I was using it more than I needed. I was addicted.

Like most addicts, I was functioning pretty well on that huge dose. I had even started to drive with it in my system, though not the full 80 milligrams. Here, we had all been almost killed by an impaired driver and yet I was getting behind the wheel after taking OxyContin; I was no better than Jacobs.

It was another lesson. I could now understand how Jacobs had arrived at such a low point in his life: he had been self-medicating too, in an attempt to kill the pain. It would be revealed at his trial that he had been sexually abused by his own brother as a small boy. This horrific crime had understandably made him terribly angry. I had struggled with hating him as a grown adult but he had to deal with hating his own big brother as a child. It was no surprise his life had spiraled out of control.

He had lied to his parents and withheld the truth just like I had withheld the truth from Mona. He had started to self-medicate with drugs and alcohol just like I was now self-medicating with OxyContin. We were more similar than I had ever thought. Now he was in jail for the rest of his life and I was on the same path. What if *I* ran into someone as I drove around on my drug of choice? I would be facing prison just like him. This had to stop.

Being a veterinarian, I had heard all the stories of vets getting hooked on the pain meds that sat on the shelf of their hospital. For me, it was a slippery slope that was all too easy to slide down, especially with a DEA license that enabled me to order any drug I wanted. Drug abuse as a veterinarian will get your license to practice revoked and can lead to prison time. I could lose everything, including the business we had worked so hard to build. I would lose my ability to earn a living as well as the respect of my kids and the community that had supported us through all of this mess; I would lose it all and take Mona down with me.

I had already experienced a few instances indicative of my burgeoning addiction. Once, I had forgotten my drugs at my parents' house after a visit and immediately called them in a panic because I needed another dose of my Oxy (supposedly for pain). They were two hours away so we arranged to meet halfway at a restaurant where they handed the drugs to me in a parking lot – just like any other addict.

I had even had an embarrassing episode at my kids' school when I stopped by to drop off a backpack Victoria had forgotten. I was starting to drive even though I had OxyContin in my system (albeit a lower dose). I was oblivious to the effects it was having on me and believed I was "fine" to drive on the lower dose. An hour later, I got a call from a good friend and teacher to alert me I'd dropped my bottle of OxyContin on the way in. It had been discovered by an elementary student on the sidewalk who'd brought it to the office.

Immediately I was horrified. *What if this kid had taken a pill?* Here I was, a respected member of the community, walking and driving while on OxyContin, one of the most addicting pain meds around. I could almost hear God asking me, *"You're so much better than the drunk that hit you? Really?"*

Now, Mona and the kids needed me. I had been the patient on the receiving end of others' care long enough. In that moment, I decided I would no longer be an addict; I would not disrespect the community that had come to our aid, or disappoint my family after they'd struggled through so much. Mona and I had worked too long and hard building our veterinary practice and our relationship with this community to lose it all to drugs. I had let her down once and she had lost trust in me. She had seen the effects of the higher doses of OxyContin and knew I was taking way too much. I would not make her lose any more respect for me. If we had to deal with cancer, my mind needed to be clear.

I stopped cold turkey and did not take my nightly dose. Within two hours I was agitated and could not sit still. By the time three hours had passed, my legs began to kick uncontrollably. If you've ever wondered about the origin of the phrase, "kicking the habit," this is where it comes from – Heroin addicts. Since Heroin and Oxy are both in the opioid family, they are really no different. I told myself I could just stop the drug because I was mentally stronger than other addicts who were weak. Wrong again.

The kicking got worse as I became increasingly anxious. I craved my Oxy. My leg started to throb, though I wasn't sure if this was just me *wanting* to feel the pain so I could take my drugs. This was hell: I was finding out exactly why addicts can't stop. I wasn't stronger than them, I wasn't better than them, I needed my drugs just like they did. Another lesson in humility.

"Thanks God, I needed that."

Obviously I could not stop cold turkey; therefore I decided to start the weaning process, beginning with 60 milligrams that day. Soon the kicking stopped and I fell asleep. This would be a long journey. I learned I was not some superhero who could just get off this drug because I decided to. I wasn't Superman; I was human just like everyone else.

The next day I only took 50 milligrams though I needed another sixty at night. My hands shook some, I was a bit agitated, and I craved more, but I stuck to it. The craving further confirmed I was an addict. All my knowledge of drugs and my iron will to do whatever was needed in my life had not protected me. I was an addict just like the bum on the street corner needing a Heroin fix.

I'd needed a lesson in humility and I sure got one. God had stripped away all my pride, all the things that made me think I was better than everyone else. He had made me immobile for months, forced to urinate and defecate in my sheets like a baby and then call for a 20-something, pretty nurse to clean me up as I lay humiliated in my own mess. He had let my body become broken – wasted away to that of a prepubescent little boy. When I could eat anything I wanted, He would not allow me to consume more than half of a hamburger or a half a slice of pizza while I recovered. He had taken me out of my work, out of the business that Mona and I saw as ours, and showed me it could function fine without me. Just like Jacobs, I would not be able to hold down a job because I was an addict who had no business being around the types of drugs I stocked in my own office. I had lied to my wife and run away from it because I was too scared to face the truth about her cancer metastasizing, just as Jacobs had been too cowardly to face what he'd done and fled the scene of the crash.

He had taken me from my kids and wife and they had done fine also. He had made me an addict just like Jacobs so I could relate to the tragic events of his life that had led to his addiction. He had made sure I understood that my "plans" were of no use and only His plan counted. I had thought I was in control of everything until a Jeep careened across the highway and ripped that control away. Now I knew I was in control of almost nothing. I had strayed from where God wanted me to be, becoming more and more fixated on the "American Dream" of a bigger house, a faster car, bigger and better toys – all the while spending less and less time with those who needed me the most. Since I was being stupid He was not afraid to straighten me out. The crash was His method. It was the slap upside the head loving fathers are known to employ when their kid is screwing up. Although it hurts, it is done out of love and gets the message across. I'd received one heck of a slap and did not want to go through anything like that again.

He had humbled me in every way possible, breaking me down until I'd had no choice but to listen up. He, like any good father, had done it through love and given me exactly what I needed to become the man He wanted me to be. Only now was I ready for Him to build me up again.

## Chapter 39

## ∞ Finding Heaven ∞

I often hear people say they were "washed in the blood of Christ." In my case, I was washed literally and figuratively. As I lay there pinned in a smashed minivan my blood, my values, my goals, my priorities and life as I knew it began to slip away. As I rode in the helicopter and the doctors fought to save me at the hospital, my old life drained out of me. My angels replaced that blood with the blood of unknown people; countless angels who took the time to donate their blood to ultimately be given to me. They people performed a selfless act to save someone they would never know. I have no idea who these people were but have no doubt that they were believers in a greater good, that life was not about what they could get for themselves but what they could do for others. As their blood entered my body, Jesus entered also; it was the open door through which He had been waiting to pass. I was literally being washed in His blood and would be forever changed. He was now a part of me I could not remove. He would be their forever. I was transformed.

After completely breaking me down, He rebuilt me, bit by bit.

One on level, he was rebuilding me physically: I was already getting stronger and putting weight back on. My bones were healing and the pain was lessening significantly, enabling me to stop the pain meds. Even though my physical therapists had pushed me so hard I thought I'd break from the ensuing agony, I had persevered. For the first time in my life, I had proven to myself I was not the coward I had once been on the playground as a child; no longer would I shrink and run away when the going got tough. I'd tested and proven my mettle – just not to anyone else. Since none of my family or friends had seen my therapy sessions, I couldn't impress them with my toughness. From their perspective, I was still a thin, frail shell of a man who relied on crutches for mobility. They did not need to know about my remarkable progress and I made a point to avoid bragging about it (a lesson I'd learned when I wound up back in the hospital after having to be the center of attention at church when I'd first been released from the hospital). At this juncture, I knew I could now handle pain. I'd demonstrated to myself that I was a man – no longer the wimpy kid I remember growing up.

God was also teaching me about addiction and struggle after experiencing my "perfect" Midwestern childhood – far removed from the abuse, alcoholism, drugs, and dysfunction Jacobs had endured. I would no longer dismiss those struggling with their own addictions as weak and inferior people because I was no better. I had spent a lot of time hating Jacobs, a man whose childhood had been the polar opposite of mine, characterized by a broken home, emotional suffering, and sexual abuse. I thanked God again for another lesson. One more step in my rebuilding process.

Spiritually, I had grown immensely. I had heard His voice time and time again and now saw his works all around me. What I used to regard as fortunate coincidences, I now saw as "God moments," little events He set in motion out of His love for me. I began to notice them more and more, everywhere I went, and each time I did it made me smile: the parking spot left open at Walmart when I was on crutches; the X-ray revealing my bone had finally healed; and the sun pouring through my bedroom window, warming my face on a cold winter day. I saw God everywhere now.

Of course, it was also God who'd placed us in Jacobs' path that day so we could ultimately find Mona's tumor.

The third day after Mona's surgery while I was still at home with the kids, she called with a special request.

"They are letting me eat soup today but the soup they have here is awful. Could you bring me some when you get here? Nothing with any chunks; it has to be just soup."

This was the first step in getting her system to accept food again.

"Sure, I will be there as quick as I can."

Mona's dad and I immediately left for the hospital, stopping at the local grocery store on the way to honor my wife's request. I grabbed about 20 different varieties, along with a strainer in case of chunks. When we arrived, I got out while Joe parked the car. The nurses laughed as I made my way down the hall with the three bags of soup clanging and banging against my crutches.

"I could hear you coming all the way!" Mona exclaimed as I entered her room.

"I wasn't sure which kind you would like so I brought everything they had without chunks," I explained.

"Thank you, that was very nice."

I saw her smile for the first time in what seemed like forever.

She looked much better that day. The post-op pain had lessened and she'd developed an appetite. Although restricted to about one-and-a-half cans of soup a day, at least it was something. If all went well, she would be forbidden to eat anything "with chunks" for a week after surgery. In the end, she lost a total of about 20 pounds, living on watery soup. Most women would be absolutely thrilled to lose that much but Mona looked emaciated. She was gaunt and pale – almost skeletal – but if she dared to eat more, she'd become nauseated and want to vomit. Her system just wasn't ready for that yet.

Unlike me when I needed more calories and began eating again, Mona couldn't add ice-cream to her food. After any type of pancreatic surgery, a patient cannot ingest a lot of fats. Getting calories into her system would be difficult since she had to eat relatively bland food – nothing with fats. Mona would just have to slowly increase the amount and frequency of meals to provide her body with as many calories on a daily basis as possible. Ultimately, it would take her almost two months to regain the weight she had lost, though she would never again be able to eat many fatty foods without getting sick – another constant reminder of how her life had changed.

We were both still processing the fact that this was cancer. About a week out, as she was preparing to leave the hospital, we talked about it. To my surprise, she was starting to come to terms with the fact that we simply did not know how this was going to turn out.

She observed, "I thought about what you said with God wanting us to find the cancer. I think it may be best that we are not sure if it will come back. I have always been the planner and the worrier. Now I won't be able to plan for much. It will remind me of how precious life is and how easily it can be taken away. If the surgery had cured it, I would forget about living for today and just fall back into the daily grind of life. If it was more advanced, then I would just be counting the days until I die and not able to enjoy the ones I have left. I would have that constant thought of cancer in my head every minute. Maybe, for me, it is best to not be sure if it is coming back, not sure if it is cured or not. Maybe God just wants me to remember it, to never forget what He has done for me. I'm okay with that."

"I love you."

"I love you, too."

We were rebuilding the trust and love that had been waning after twelve years of marriage and the responsibilities of three kids and a business. Dealing first with our injuries and then with cancer had made us appreciate each other and our strength as a team: we could not have gotten through any of this alone. We had needed each other as well as our family and friends. We would never devalue each other or them again.

Another building block of our lives was in place.

Though neither of us knew it at the time, as Mona and I left the hospital that day we had found heaven – and we could only have found it after our journey through hell. It had started with pure fear and panic as a Jeep lurched straight at us at 70 miles per hour. At that point, I had realized life was not going to happen according to the plan I had carefully laid out. As strange as it was to give up control of our lives, it had removed most of the stress. Problems with work, family, money, bills, cancer, and fear of death were all still there but now we realized they were just little spiritual workouts put in front of us to make us better people. While they may not be fun, we could now deal with anything we faced because we knew it was mostly out of our hands. We had been made free of worry.

Family and friends were now a priority. We would attend more family functions and let the petty little arguments and perceived slights pass. We could now do this because we had learned to "forgive those who trespass against us."

Forgiving a brother or sister over something that was said or done, possibly decades earlier, was nothing compared to forgiving a man who'd nearly killed us all. Could we really hold a grudge against something that was *said* when we had forgiven Jacobs? Could we hold onto anger when we had found out about the years of terrible abuse he had endured? How it had put him on that path in front of our minivan? These petty little grudges that we all seem to carry now just seemed stupid.

Since the crash we'd been given much from our community, family, and friends. Now it was our turn to start giving back. Six months after receiving a check from the Boy Scouts for a little over one-hundred dollars from their pizza sales, we attended a festival in town where the scouts were selling brats and hamburgers for their own fundraiser. I order two brats and three burgers for us with sodas. The bill came to just under twenty dollars but I handed the kid $500 and told him to keep the change. He stood there stunned as we turned and walked away; no *thank-you's* needed or wanted. At about ten years-old, he didn't have a clue as to who we were, which was why we'd purposely approached him. We had learned it was best to help others anonymously. I had gone to church once before out of a desire to bask in everyone's attention and wound up back in the hospital for a week, nearly losing my arm. I would not make that mistake again. Humility was needed to find heaven. Anything I had was ultimately given by God, not me.

Two years later, I found out that Roger, my boss at my first job out of vet school, needed back surgery and would be unable to work for a while. I called his office and announced I would be there to help – just like my friend Mike had done for me. Although Roger's hospital was over two hours away, I was able to get there multiple times. Following Mike's example, I took no pay; I just wanted to help. Since Roger was the surgeon in his practice, he'd be forced to turn away cases requiring more advanced procedures. I told his staff to schedule as many of the tough surgeries as possible for when I was there because Roger's patients needed fixing and his practice needed the income. His vets and staff were tired and overworked, much like ours had been in the aftermath of our accident. Having an extra hand allowed them to just catch their breath. I knew this because I had been there too. I put in long days but felt great, convinced this was what God had intended: He wanted me to use the gifts He had given me to help. By paying it forward, I was finding heaven.

I also knew I needed to pay God back. While I was aware this was an impossible task, I needed to listen to Him more. Pastor Mary Anne, who had visited us so often in the hospital and had organized the meal drop off and prayer chains for us, asked me to lead a Bible study at church. I had never even read the Bible much and had never been to a Bible study before but now I would lead one. She thought that this one would fit me well since the study was titled "Dealing with Adversity." I had certainly done that. We formed a men's group that included five others and met regularly for the eight-week study. From that day on, we would continue to meet for two more years.

All of us in the group had been through our own private hell. One man, whom I will call Neal, was recently divorced with a child a year younger than Victoria. His wife had left him for another man and he was angry. He needed to forgive her for the sake of his daughter but did not know how. We talked about how forgiveness was the only way to get through this, just like I had to forgive Jacobs. He was carrying the baggage of hate but it was ultimately just weighing him down and preventing him from finding joy again. God would make him whole and rebuild him but he needed to forgive his wife and accept her new husband. This would allow him to live without the anger he now felt and teach his daughter to forgive also. Our little group would help him through.

Another man, whom I will call Ron, was a grandfather and had been in a terrible car crash on Christmas Eve of the previous year. He had been driving with his wife during a typical Wisconsin snowstorm when a 20 year-old woman coming the other way lost control, hitting a snowdrift and sliding sideways into his path. There was nothing he could do. He T-boned her car directly into the driver's side door, which instantly killed her. He later found out she was on her way from one job to another, having volunteered to work someone else's shift so that coworker could spend Christmas Eve with her kids. The guilt of her death had been crushing him.

We talked at length about God's plan and how Ron had not been in control of the events of that night: only God. I shared the story of finding Mona's cancer with him, which demonstrated how we only see just a small slice of God's plan. While I could not tell him precisely what good would emerge out of the tragedy, I did know it would make him stronger. Over the course of the two years we met, Ron lost his sales job, due to a downturn in the economy. This was very hard on a person nearing retirement; he was nowhere near ready to retire, mentally or financially. Consequently, he went back to work stocking shelves for close to minimum wage at Home Depot – a humbling job since he'd been a top salesman in his company just a month before.

However, Ron was doing what needed to be done to support himself and his wife. I saw him frequently since I shopped there often and would talk with him briefly. Within a few months he was put in charge of dealing with contractors and in a few more months, he was using his sales skills to set up remodeling projects for customers. Two years later he was offered a job selling water softeners by a company he'd worked with through his job at Home Depot. He was earning nearly the same pay as his previous sales job, but without the long days of travel he'd hated. By accepting God's plan, Ron had learned humility and found peace. He had gone through his hell, just like Mona and me, and like us, he had found his heaven.

Pete (again not his real name), was another man in our Bible study group, a sensitive, caring man who worked with mentally disabled teens and young adults. God had truly given him a gift, as his patience was endless, yet he was hurting also. One of his students, a boy named Brandon, came from a terribly abusive home, where he'd been beaten and neglected for years. His parents simply couldn't cope with his mental and physical disabilities. Eventually, he was removed from the home and wound up at Pete's school, where they developed a very close relationship. Given his traumatic background, Pete was especially protective of this 12 year-old.

But the boy had a heart defect that would ultimately claim his young life. He had died just over a year before our Bible group had started to meet. After participating for six months without ever mentioning his grief over Brandon, Pete finally broke down in tears as he recounted holding the boy's hand as he passed away in the hospital, his family nowhere around. He simply could not get past the injustice of this boy's life and kept Brandon's picture on his bathroom mirror, praying for him every day. Pete recounted how he'd tried to bring in some of the boy's drawings to show some of the other students in the class on the one-year anniversary of Brandon's death. However, as he turned into the school, his car slid on some ice and hit a light pole, requiring the fire department and an ambulance to extract him from his vehicle in front of all the parents and students. Peter was terribly hurt and embarrassed; for him it was just another kick in the gut.

After discussing it for a while, I asked him what had happened to Brandon's drawings. He replied that they were gone and that he suspected they fell out when they extracted him from the car and placed him into the ambulance. His careless driving had destroyed them and he had never seen them again. He had no idea where they went.

Once I'd given it a sufficient amount of thought I realized that there was a different explanation. I asked him, "What if Brandon had put you into that pole? Maybe Brandon was telling you that he was in a much better place, free from all his physical and mental disabilities and away from the abuse he had grown up with. Maybe it was Brandon who had destroyed all those drawings. Maybe he knew that these were holding you back and that you had to move on."

I told him about God putting us in a crash in a similar way. I had put the anger of the collision with a drunk driver behind me, much like turning a page in a book. I knew I needed to close that terrible chapter if I wanted to start a new one, and Pete had to do the same. His collision with a pole and loss of Brandon's artwork was a message it was time to do it. Pete was stuck in a rut and refusing to move on; therefore Brandon, now Pete's angel, had sent him a clear message with this accident. Pete needed this crash and the pain of his injury to force him to write the next chapter in his life, with the understanding that the tragedy was all part of a greater plan. Pete would never find his heaven if he kept obsessing over a chapter that God had already penned. After this breakthrough, he took Brandon's picture off his bathroom mirror and left it in the woods where they used to love to together: a final step in closing that chapter forever.

Helping Pete and Bob navigate successfully through their hardships was incredibly rewarding but I knew I was only in this Bible study because of the accident with Jacobs. Through my pastor, I'd been given the opportunity to share the lessons God had taught me and apply them in my efforts to help others. It was no coincidence the subject matter fit perfectly with my newfound strengths: "Dealing with Adversity." It was one of those "God Moments." Prior to the crash, the title of the Bible class would have just been another coincidence. By the time my pastor extended the invitation, I was perfectly positioned to get involved; another step toward heaven.

When I had fully recovered, Alexa, now fifteen, signed up to go on a mission trip to Kentucky and asked me to accompany her. We spent a week there repairing homes and helping the local population, providing yet another lesson how blessed I am. Both Alexa and I enjoyed it immensely and have since taken a mission trip each year. I even gave up a Canadian fishing trip to travel to an Indian reservation because Alexa wanted us to go together. How many teenage girls want to spend a week of summer vacation with their dad in New Mexico, laying shingles on roofs in the intense July heat, helping people they don't know and will never see again? I had to go with her.

Since then my second-oldest, Victoria, has joined us on a mission trip to repair hurricane damage, which she also enjoyed immensely. Their younger brother Chase is excited to join us when he is older. I am so proud of them all. *Would we be doing this if not for the crash?* Of course not: we were too busy with our own lives to bother with spending a week helping others. Another step toward heaven.

Mona gets her yearly reminder of God's will when she gets rechecked for cancer. Annually, she meets with Dr. Wilson to look for recurrence. Both of us are tense for a month prior to the appointment and the day of the test is filled with dread. If the cancer returns, we both know it will be terminal.

We went for the first recheck about six months after her surgery. After a CT scan of her liver, we met with Dr. Wilson to review the results. We both sat silently in the exam, holding hands and praying. We were absolutely terrified.

Dr. Wilson knocked and came in. He sat down at the computer screen to review the results and Mona and I watched over his shoulder. We were all looking for cancer.

As he approached one area of the liver, he slowed down. Both Mona and I could see why. There was a distinct, round, bright white area indicating something much denser than the surrounding liver.

Dr. Wilson pointed to it and said, "Look at that, that big round spot in the liver. Do you know what that is?"

Our hearts sank. We both knew that this round spot on the liver could only mean the cancer had returned. *It had only been six months.* This meant the tumor was much more aggressive and Mona only had a short time to live. My mind raced as I tried to figure out how to tell the kids that all this surgery had not stopped the spread of cancer and their mother was dying. I started to sweat and shake. As I looked at Mona, I could see she was as white as a ghost. Distinct tears began to form in her eyes.

Dr. Wilson continued, "That is an artifact (something that shows up on the image but isn't really there). It was caused by those metal coils they used when they thought this was an aneurism." He still hadn't forgotten about being doubted.

Mona and I looked at each other in disbelief. We had thought the cancer had come back and that "round thing in the liver" would mean that she would not have long to live. Instead, it was a piece of metal that cast a large, round shadow on the CT.

Dr. Wilson looked at us, realizing the sheer terror he had just caused.

"I thought they had told you the results were negative already. I didn't mean to scare you. I just wanted you to know it was there."

Now we could laugh a little. We had come a long way. We had traveled through hell and had come out the other side. We were now strong and content. We had been through the trauma of nearly dying and having to experience indescribable pain, multiple surgeries and cancer in a little over a year. Our relationship had not only survived but emerged from the experience even stronger. Mona knew I had learned my lesson and would not hide anything from her again. With that came complete trust.

By trusting now in God's plan and not our own, we left our worries behind, accepting that most of our lives are out of our control anyway. As a result of our ordeal, we'd realized that we were not, and never had been, in control of our lives. Instead of creating anxiety, this awareness had been a great relief: we accepted that God was in the driver's seat and we were just along for the ride. This provided us a great sense of peace; we could only worry about those things we could control, and we could control very little. Therefore, there was very little to worry about.

We had learned how to forgive, which gave us the ability to deal with all kinds of slights and annoyances that would once have aggravated us and ruined days or even weeks of our lives. We were humbled, having learned the lesson that we are no better than anyone else: we can get injured, contract cancer, and cope with an addiction. Obtaining college degrees, being "good people," and even sitting in church on Sundays did not shield us from tragedy, illness, and human imperfection.

But this journey had shaken us to the core. It had forced us to become stronger and reexamine our relationships with God and each other. We would never have done this had we not been forced to do so following the crash. Now we were confident we could handle anything. We had done the spiritual workout we needed just like the physical workouts they sell on TV. We had become lean and strong.

A friend once asked if all of the pain and agony I'd endured had really been necessary if it had been solely about finding Mona's tumor. To him, it didn't seem fair that I had to go through it because they would have found Mona's tumor anyway, given her injuries. Why did I have to get so beat up?

My response was simple. First, life isn't fair so why would I ever expect it to be? I know better than to want "fair." Second, I love my wife and God gave me the chance to save her. It required a terrible crash and life-threatening injuries but I, like most husbands, would gladly make this type of sacrifice if it meant saving the life of the woman I loved and the mother of my children. It was a gift from God that I could do this for them. The fact that He also allowed me to survive and remain relatively healthy when all was said and done was just another of His gifts. It showed how He acted with love, not vengeance. I thank Him every day for putting us in the path of Jacobs. Third, I needed to change and I wasn't going to do it on my own because I had no idea I needed to change anything. I thought I was doing pretty well. Fact was, I had to become a better person and this was my path to arriving at that destination; I had to go through the hell of my injuries and convalescence if I was ever to find my heaven.

Of course, what happened to us was not fun. We had received a practical lesson as to everything Hell entailed. We see such a small piece of God's picture in our daily lives we cannot possibly see the bigger plan. At the time of the crash, we could not see the good emerging out of what seemed to be a terrible tragedy. I had no idea when I woke up in a hospital bed with all four limbs immobilized; scars all over my body; multiple, looming surgeries; and months of rehab that I would one day thank God for what had happened. There was no way I could see anything good coming out of the crash. *Who would have predicted as Mona lay in another room with three spinal fractures and a major concussion that this would ultimately save her life and along with it, our family?*

We now stand and sing in church with all our hearts, rejoicing in Him. Nine times out of ten we cry during the service. It touches our souls.

Having experienced true pain, I became a better veterinarian. I'd developed my reputation by performing very complicated, major surgeries, using some basic pain control. After our experience, pain control became a passion for me. My favorite is the same mixture of drugs Mona had been given after her Whipple procedure, the one our angel, Jaime, had fought so hard to make sure she got. Now every animal that undergoes a major procedure or is suffering in pain for some other reason is automatically placed on the pain drip, even if I have to give it for free because the owner can't afford it. I am not going to let an animal lay there in pain like Mona did.

Since I returned to work, I go back in after hours and through the night to check on animals at the hospital. If they are uncomfortable, they get more pain meds. The thought of a dog or cat sitting there in agony for hours is guaranteed to keep me awake; I might as well drive in to check on them since I will not be able to sleep anyway. We even built a kennel inside our house so we can take animals home with us to monitor overnight. I would like to say we do this because we are such great people but I know better than to be that arrogant. Fact is, I know all about pain and how it saps your will to live. We call the owners with an update before bedtime so they can go to sleep without wondering if anyone is really checking on their beloved pet. This is all part of my mission to use the gifts God has given me to be the best I can be. Anything less would be an affront to Him.

Presently, money is the least of my worries and simply not why I do my job anymore. I know I could lose all the material things I own at any time so I no longer worry about it. It is true that I still have to make money to support my family and my employees, but money is not my motivation for working. I work because I love it and I know I am doing what God put me here to do. I am pleasing Him by using the gifts He gave me. The fact that I get paid for it just ensures I can keep doing it. I had it backwards before: I used God's gifts for me, now I use God's gifts for Him.

I am a better veterinarian, a better husband, a better father, and a better Christian. I was even asked to speak at a few legislative hearings about changing Wisconsin's ridiculously lax drunk driving laws. It will be a slow process but change is coming. I spoke in favor of a change in the law I had proposed; that those with a suspended or revoked license cannot purchase a vehicle. It would have prevented Jacobs from buying the Jeep that nearly killed our entire family.

Ultimately, the crash saved us in countless ways. It removed worry and hatred and made Mona and I better spouses, parents, and friends. The terrible violence of that day created great peace in our lives and with that peace, we found our heaven. Heaven is described as "a peaceful place free of earthly worries." We ask that those who have died "rest in peace" so doesn't it make sense that we will find our heaven when we find peace? Isn't that what the Buddhist monks are searching for, *Nirvana*? By learning to let go of hate and forgiving immediately and unconditionally – even those who don't ask for it or deserve it – we find peace. By choosing to see our struggles as a spiritual workout needed to gain strength, not an unfair burden of a vengeful God, we find peace. Haven't we then reached heaven?

We used the insurance settlement from the crash to buy a small farm. Now Mona and the kids have a place to raise her miniature horses, as well as chickens, turkeys, pigs and goats for the fair. For us, it is truly a little slice of heaven on Earth where we marvel daily at the beauty of God's creatures. My job on the farm is to manage the wildlife. My son and I spend the summers putting up duck nesting boxes and planting food plots for the deer. Chase has also developed a great love of the outdoors and the wildlife, with the ability to explain how and why to manage the woods and ponds to best serve the animals that call our piece of heaven their home. I see it as my way of thanking God for getting me to see His heaven here on earth; I will make sure his creatures are taken care of.

The crash and the cancer made me realize that heaven wasn't necessarily something that you had to attain *after* death. I am not a Biblical scholar so I can't quote any passages but I now believe heaven is something that is here on earth if we would just open our eyes. Jesus gave us detailed instructions on how to get there, along with angels all around us to help guide the way. We just have to do all those things he instructed us to do, like "turn the other cheek" and "trust in him."

Jesus also gave us the "Lord's Prayer" to guide us on the path toward heaven:

*"Our father, who art in Heaven, hallowed be thy name.*
*Thy kingdom come, thy will be done on earth as it is in heaven.*
*Give us this day our daily bread and forgive us our trespasses*
*As we forgive those who trespass against us.*
*And lead us not into temptation*
*But deliver us from evil.*
*Amen."*

I had repeated this prayer every week in church since I could talk but never really *got it*, never really thought about what it said. It took a trip through hell to make it clear to me. When I finally *did* understand and put it into practice, I found peace, and with peace I found heaven.

To get through it, we first had to reach out to God (hallowed be thy name).

We had to let "God's will be done on earth as it is in heaven" and accept that we did not control our fate. I had no control when a speeding Jeep crossed the median and hit us. I had no control over whether I lived or died; whether or not Dr. Lang would be there to save me; or whether I would be the one-in-one-hundred who responded to the Factor VIIII shot as I lay there bleeding to death.

Later on, when we'd discovered Mona's cancer, even the most state-of-the-art hospitals and medicines would've been powerless to stop its spread. Only God could. His "will" would be done.

Next, we had to forgive Jacobs. When I did that, I could be forgiven for lying to Mona and becoming addicted to drugs. God had "forgiven our trespasses" as we had "forgiven those who had trespassed against us." It didn't matter whose sins were worse, or who was a better person – all the sins were bad, requiring forgiveness. My addiction to pain meds was no different that Jacobs' addiction to alcohol. My driving with OxyContin in my system was no better than his driving with a dozen beers. Beating the addiction was God "leading me not into temptation" and "delivering me from evil."

By finally doing what we had repeated every week in church, I had found my slice of heaven on Earth. It had always been there; I just wanted to find my own path to it. I could have the career I wanted by studying hard; I could make good money and buy things to make me happy by making myself into a better vet. I had put my faith in ME. Now I knew that that was not enough. I had to put my faith in God to work *through* me.

With the crash I had been forced to stop relying on myself and become humble. Humility happens when you can't move enough to get out of your own crap and have to sit in it until the nurses have time to change your sheet and wipe your butt. In Mona's case, it comes when you can't eat for days because the thought of food makes you want to vomit. It happens when you have a major surgery and now have a scar the length of your abdomen as a reminder that you were saved by Him (scars that we now both have). It comes when you have no idea if the cancer is gone for good or will come roaring back at any time. These are the things that make you humble in a hurry.

I found that once we let go of our pride, we could see the path to the peace we'd always been seeking. The path was in the Lord's Prayer, not in my own ideas. I had been too arrogant to accept God's instruction before so He'd given me the slap upside the head I needed to wake up from my delusion – the delusion that I could find heaven on my own, that I could make my own path. I had tried taking a shortcut to heaven because *I* knew best; *I* could do it without undertaking God's spiritual workout.

God, of course, knew better. The crash and Mona's cancer had forced us to turn off of the road we'd been traveling on and forced us to contemplate what was truly important in life. Only by surviving the crash did we find the fortitude to successfully navigate through the Hell of her cancer and emerge on the other side stronger than ever mentally, emotionally, physically, and spiritually. *This* is where we found our Heaven. Traveling through hell first had been a prerequisite; there was just no easy path.

The angels who assisted us along the way had discovered this truth also. Robert, the flight nurse, had been through the hell of war and losing a soldier because of his mistake. That day in Afghanistan had transformed him into the flight nurse who would be skilled enough to save me.

Dr. Lang had been forced to learn about dedication to others through his autistic son and that experience had turned him into the surgeon who refused to let me die. He had also developed the necessary patience to calmly talk with upset family members and convince them of the right course.

The Amish, who had endured the hell of losing their children to a madman in Pennsylvania, had been strengthened in their faith in God and shown others, including me, the power of forgiveness.

All had discovered that there was no easy path.

Now, this all made perfect sense. Even Jesus, after He was crucified, descended into hell for three days before he ascended into heaven. I was in a coma for three days and woke to a new life; my own path to heaven. *Why would I think I could find heaven more easily than Jesus Himself?*

The one who hadn't taken the difficult path was Jacobs, the drunk driver who was now in prison for the next 47 years. Rather than confronting his demons of sexual abuse, he tried to take the easy path and drink it away. In the end, it destroyed him. It would not have been easy to admit to what had happened to him, especially as a young boy, and I can't say that I would have handled it any differently, but by not using the experience to become stronger, it had made him weaker. It had broken him to the point where he'd remained a victim instead of becoming a survivor. He had gone through hell but had not come out on the other side to find his heaven. Now he would spend the rest of his life in prison; he would stay in hell.

A few years after the trial, Jacobs sent me a letter outlining how unfair Mona and I had been to him at the trial. He complained about Mona calling him a "monster" for leaving us dying in the car and for having to spend so much time in prison for a "simple drunk-driving" charge. I felt bad for him because he had still not accepted what he had done and his motivation for doing it. He still hadn't dealt with the abuse and was still playing the victim. I knew he would never turn the page on that chapter in his life. He was stuck.

A few years later, we got a letter from the prison saying that Jacobs had died in prison. He was 45 years-old. He had never found heaven on earth – only hell. Maybe now he could find it, but only in death.

The growth and strength Mona and I developed is now forged within us permanently. This only happens when the changes come with great effort; when it is a trip through Hell. If the path to heaven were easy, the changes we had made in our lives would be only temporary and we would eventually go back to where we were before. We would lose our heaven. God had forced us to take the right path – the long and hard one. For us, like most people, there would be no easy way into heaven. God would make us earn it.

Mona and I recently attended a small Bible study group, something neither of us had ever even thought about doing before the crash, where the question was posed, "Who taught you the most about God in your life?"

As each participant took a turn, their answers were things you'd expect like "my dad" or "my mom" or "my pastor."

My response?

"Mike Jacobs, the drunk that hit us." While it may have shocked the other people in the room, it was the truth. By nearly killing my family and me, Jacobs had taught us and important lesson most of us rarely learn: how to forgive. He taught us how precious life was and how quickly it can be taken away. He taught us how to value those things that are truly important like family, community, purpose, and faith – not those material things we all work so hard every day to achieve. When I was in the hospital, for months all I wanted was to get back to my family – not my house or my cars – just my family.

Jacobs also taught me to listen for God's voice; the voice I heard in the cabin before the crash and countless times afterward, guiding me in the direction I needed to go. And he taught me to thank God for the goodness and hardship in my life. The goodness is not of my doing but His; the hardship is just another spiritual workout designed not to punish but to help me grow and become a better person. It is the next ramp I need to conquer. We all need to keep working out to stay strong. God just keeps letting us improve.

Through Jacobs, I learned that hate – like the hate he was holding onto for his brother – would destroy me just as surely as it had destroyed him. Only through forgiveness could we leave the hate behind. Dropping the rock, the baggage of hate, allows us to keep moving forward to better things. You can prevent even the greatest eagle from soaring by tying a weight to its leg. Similarly, we are prevented from reaching our own soaring heights by carrying the massive weight of hatred and anger. Yet we also have the power to choose to release it through forgiveness. It is our *choice*, yes, *choice* whether we drop it or not.

Forgiving Jacobs was not up to *him*, it was up to *me*. God gave us free will to enable us to let go of the things that are weighing us down. We just have to do it. Jesus changed the name of his disciple Simon to "Peter," meaning "The Rock" when Peter decided to follow him. Likewise, we have a choice as to whether we remain a "victim" or change our name to "survivor" when we accept His will and follow Him. Peter gave up his earthly things when he decided to follow Jesus. We can also choose to give up our earthly troubles and past hurts when we choose to follow His plan, and not our own

Most importantly, he taught me to give up the control I'd craved my entire life. My life was going to follow God's purpose for me and there was nothing I could do to change that. I needed to stop making plans since only His mattered. I had no idea what His plan even was; therefore, I just needed to shut up and listen.

Yes, it is just that simple. God had taught me to find heaven on earth but I was just so full of myself he had to send me through hell first.

As we got into the car after the Bible study, I turned on the radio. We were still contemplating what we had discussed in our group when a country song by Montgomery Gentry started playing. I always said you could find all the philosophical enlightenment you need from the lyrics of a country music song, and this one proved me right. The simple verse I heard streaming through the radio became my motto.

*"If you want to hear God laugh, just tell him your plan."*

Well said.

Scot Hodkiewicz

## The Ten Commandments of Patient Hospitalization and Recovery

1) Unless you are immediate family, do not visit the hospital for at least a week.

2) Cook meals and deliver them once they are home but do not come in the door. Hand them off, wish them well and leave. The person you are helping will undoubtedly be embarrassed that their house is a mess and they are wearing pajamas. Do not go in the door.

3) Do things without being asked. Do not say "call if you need anything." Instead text or email saying I will be over Sunday to mow the lawn.

4) Do not deliver anything you want back – disposable containers only.

5) Do not call – text, send cards or email so they can be read and reread when appropriate.

6) Do not say "you look great" unless the person actually does.

7) Do not question the use of pain meds unless there is a problem – a week after surgery or a broken bone, ibuprofen is not going to cut it so don't go on about how bad pain meds are. You are not the one in pain.

8) If you are the patient, allow people to help. Turning away help is a slap in the face; instead, plan on paying it forward.

9) Establish one person as a point-of-contact to keep everyone informed. One person will get the update for the day and relay it to family and friends. Do not have everyone call the nurse's station. They are busy enough.

10) As a patient, be nice. The medical staff will avoid you if you are a jerk.

# ABOUT THE AUTHOR

Dr. Scot Hodkiewicz was a successful veterinarian living the American Dream in Lake Geneva Wisconsin with his wife and three kids. He was King of *His* World with a thriving business, the respect of his community, and a beautiful young family. God had smiled on him.

That is, until the day they were all nearly killed by a drunk driver. So began his journey through the hell of near death, complete with a mangled body and broken spirit. God had humbled him in order to rebuild into the man He wanted him to be.

Today, Dr. Scot and his wife Mona are still practicing veterinarians who live on a 300-acre farm in Wisconsin — their piece of heaven — with their three children Alexa, Victoria, and Chase, where they raise horses and a menagerie of other animals. When not working, Dr. Scot devotes his time as a volunteer for youth mission trips and a local wildlife rehabilitation hospital. He also serves as a church leader. Mona volunteers every week at the local humane society, sterilizing animals free of charge and finding them homes.

His first book, *Getting to Heaven by Going through Hell* chronicles their journey from the top of the mountain to the depths of hell — one that ultimately led them to discover heaven here on earth.

Made in the USA
Middletown, DE
25 May 2015